SEO FITNESS WORKBOOK:

THE SEVEN STEPS TO SEARCH ENGINE OPTIMIZATION SUCCESS ON GOOGLE

2019 EDITION

BY JASON MCDONALD, PH.D.

© 2019, JM INTERNET GROUP

https://www.jm-seo.org/

Tel. 800-298-4065

TABLE OF CONTENTS

0

INTRODUCTION

Welcome to the *SEO Fitness Workbook*! Fully updated for 2019, this workbook explains how to succeed at *Search Engine Optimization (SEO)* in **seven steps**. SEO, of course, is the art and science of **getting your company, product,** or **service** to show at the **top** of relevant Google or Bing searches, for **free**. With most customers turning first to Google, Bing, or other search engines, SEO is your free gateway to more inquiries, more customers, and more sales.

SEO = FREE ADVERTISING ON GOOGLE

Free advertising on Google? Yippie! On Bing? Double Yippie! But, here's the rub: **SEO seems really complicated**.

Is it "too good to be true?"

Believe me, I understand your frustration with SEO and with the frauds, scoundrels, and dishonest robbers who plague my beloved SEO industry. I know the complaints, and I hear them often from students in my classes in the San Francisco Bay Area, including my popular "Marketing without Money" class at Stanford Continuing Studies as well as my online SEO course also taught via Stanford Continuing Studies (Learn more at **http://jmlinks.com/34y**). Here are some of the most **common complaints**:

- We need to get our company to the top of Google for relevant keywords; our competitors are there, but we're not!

- We redesigned our website and it looks fabulous. But now, we hardly show on Google at all, even for our own company name!
- We hired an SEO company, spent several thousands of dollars, and achieved nothing. So-called "SEO experts" are just thieves!
- I don't understand computers, can't write HTML, and I can't do SEO. Game over!
- I pay attention to Google, and SEO seems to change constantly. There's no way we can keep up with Penguin, Panda, Semantic Search, and Mobile-Friendly Website Design. *You've got to be kidding!*
- *Here's a new one for 2019.* Google has moved towards "artificial intelligence," so it doesn't matter anymore whether you know SEO. Google will just "figure out" what your website means. (*#NOTTrue*)
- We hired an obscure third world SEO firm, they built 50,000 blog links, and now we have been obliterated by Google's Penguin update.
- SEO is just too hard for anyone without a degree in Computer Science from Yale University to be able to do. We give up! (*They then start uncontrollably sobbing*).
- We'll just do AdWords (and spend thousands of dollars). *Google clearly needs more money from struggling small businesses just like ours, so they can invest in self-driving cars and gourmet meals for their pampered employees!*
- *And yet another new one for 2019.* It's all about Facebook, Twitter, Yelp, and Instagram. SEO is so "old school," no one does it anymore. (*Then they immediately search Google to find the closest pizza restaurant or best supplier of organic widgets for their business*).

I hear and feel your pain. I am just a regular guy, and I have been confronted with what I call **techtimidation** probably as much as you have.

TECHTIMIDATION = THE USE OF JARGON BY TECHIES TO INTIMIDATE MERE MORTALS

However, I firmly believe that a little education, a lot of hard work, and some common sense are all you really need to succeed in SEO. The computer nerds (and Googlers) would like us all to believe SEO is difficult – no impossible – without a computer science degree.

Poppycock. Hokum. Hooey. Malarkey, Rubbish, Baloney and even B.S.!

You can do SEO. You can succeed at it. It is easier than you think.

The purpose of this book is to, **first**, make you believe in yourself, **second**, empower you with the basic knowledge of how the SEO game is played, and **third**, help you make a detailed SEO plan for your business.

More on this later.

Let's return to SEO, *the art and science of getting your product, service or company to the top of the search engines.*

Google Algorithm Updates

Recent years have seen some terrifying Google search engine algorithm updates, such as *Penguin, Panda, Hummingbird,* and *Pigeon.* (*Google algorithm updates are named after scary animals in the zoo*). There's even been a so-called "Medical Update" and a public release of *Google Search Quality Raters General Guidelines* that talk about acronyms such as E-A-T (Expertise, Authoritativeness, and Trustworthiness) and YMYL (Your Money or Your Life) at **http://jmlinks.com/47v**.

Yikes! It's enough to make your head spin. Backwards. So hard you become an Internet meme.

Among the most important, *Penguin* has been an algorithm attack against "low quality" links, and *Panda* has been an algorithm attack against poor quality content. In addition, Google has recently penalized sites that are not "mobile friendly" and made major changes to local search results (*Pigeon*). The local "snack pack" box on local searches like "pizza" or "plumber," for example, has been reduced to three listings, or in some cases just two results, wreaking havoc on local small businesses that depend on Google for customer inquiries. In some markets, such as that for plumbers in the Bay Area, the Local Pack is being crowded with ever-more-annoying ads, and on the mobile phone, Google has done a good (*SIC!*) job of crowding out organic results with ads at the top and bottom of the page.

Google's other moves towards so-called "semantic search" via the *RankBrain algorithm update* have been moves to embed "artificial intelligence" into the Google search engine. Everything seems to be "going mobile," going "voice," and getting frightfully complex for your average small business owner or marketer. Is Artificial Intelligence a game-changer? Is Genesis Skynet? Will Arnold Schwarzenegger come back as the Terminator?

Google, in short, has been busy changing the rules of the SEO game. *Or has it?*

Here's an important tip: don't believe everything you read on the blogosphere, and don't believe every official statement by Google on SEO. There's a lot of disinformation and misinformation out there, and often changes apply to some industries but not to others.

Have you heard of "fake news?" Well, there's a lot of it in SEO, and one of the whoppers is that "SEO is constantly changing" and implicit to that "Just give up – write content for humans and spend money on Google AdWords."

I beg to differ. I beg to explain, and I beg you not to panic. Yes there have been changes, and yes Google is "going mobile" and moving to "voice search" and "Artificial Intelligence." But here's the good news: the **basics** haven't really changed, and if you stick to the **basics** according to "white hat" SEO – you'll be fine.

Let me repeat that:

the basics have not changed in SEO.

This workbook will explain what not to do, and what to do, to succeed at SEO in this post-*Penguin*, post-*Panda* world, RankBrain, AI, New World Order. And, it will also educate you on the unchanged basic rules of SEO success.

(If you don't know what *Panda, Penguin,* and *RankBrain* are… don't worry – I'll explain later).

Back to SEO.

What is SEO? SEO, of course, is the art and science of getting your company, product, or service to the top of Google's organic (free) results. If you're a seller of "industrial fans," it means that when customers search Google or Bing for "industrial fans," they will see your company's product at the top of the search results. If you're a local business like a pizza restaurant or a probate attorney, it means showing at the top of Google for searches such as "pizza delivery" or "probate lawyers in Houston."

Why is SEO so valuable? Simply put, SEO is valuable because nearly everyone turns first to Google to find products, services, or companies and because SEO costs nothing (other than knowledge, blood, sweat and tears). SEO, in short, is **free** advertising on Google! And there ain't nothing better than free, is there? (*Well, a few things, but please keep your mind on the subject at hand*).

How the Process Works

Let's step back and ponder how the marketing process works on Google. Customers turn to Google first to find new products and services, new companies and consultants. They tend to ignore ads, and they tend to read and click through on the organic listings that show on page one of Google, especially the top three positions. Looking at it from the perspective of a small business, Google is the beginning of a chain of very valuable marketing events.

Ranking on Google for *free* means you are getting *free* advertising,

free advertising means *free* clicks from Google,

free clicks from Google mean *free* web traffic, and

free web traffic means more sales inquiries and ultimately more sales.

SEO essentially turns "free advertising" into "paid sales," which if you think about it for a moment, is an incredible return on investment!

(Note that for most of the book I will refer to Google rather than search engines in general, or Google, Bing, and Yahoo specifically. (By the way, Bing powers Yahoo's search results, meaning there are really just two search engines in the USA, Canada, and Western Europe: Google and Bing). The good news is that the SEO methods to rank on Google will generally work just as well for Bing and Yahoo).

An SEO Checkup

Some questions for you:

1. Do your potential customers use Google or Bing to find companies, products or services like yours?
2. Taking a common search query relevant to your company (e.g., "industrial fans," or "best pizza in Tulsa"), do you see your company on Page 1 of Google, positions 1, 2, or 3? High on the page, or low on the page? Do you see yourself in the "local" results which occur for "local" searches such as personal injury attorney, CPA, or sushi?
3. Taking a whole bunch of relevant keyword search queries to your business (*the "universe" of search terms by which customers might search for your company, product or service*), do you generally show up on Page 1 of Google, positions 1-3? positions 1-10?, or not at all?

If you *generally* appear on Page 1 of Google, and especially in the top positions 1, 2, or 3, for *all* your relevant keywords, you can stop reading this book. You pass with an A+. If you generally do not appear, then keep reading. Or if you appear only on some search queries, but not others, or if you're not really sure what your search queries are, then you need help.

If you have no idea what search word "queries," "positions" on Google, or "high" vs. "low" on the page mean, don't worry. Don't feel stupid. You need help, and I am going to teach you.

Isn't SEO Hard?

Well, that's what Google would like you to think (*so spend money on AdWords…*) And that's what many in the SEO industry would like you to think (*so pay us big consulting fees, and don't ask any questions!*)

> *I don't agree. SEO isn't easy, but it isn't exactly hard either.*

I've taught thousands of people in my online classes, in classes at Stanford Continuing Studies and throughout the San Francisco Bay Area, and in corporate workshops, and I can confirm that there is a lot of confusion about SEO. People think it's hard, or impossible, or mysterious, and that's simply not correct.

SEO IS EASY; LIKE GETTING FIT IS EASY.

SEO, you see, is a lot like **physical fitness**. Although everyone can conceivably run a marathon, for example, few people make the effort to learn how and even fewer take the disciplined steps necessary to train for and ultimately finish a marathon.

> *Does that make running a marathon easy?*
>
> *No.*
>
> *But does that make running a marathon hard?*
>
> *Not really.*

Like running a marathon, SEO is **conceptually** simple (*exercise a lot, train with discipline, don't give up*) but **practically** hard (*you have to work at it nearly every day*).

And, of course, the Olympic champions don't just work *hard*, they work *smart*.

That's the beginning of the **good news**. If you just learn how to work smarter (not harder), you'll find that SEO isn't really that hard. And it gets better.

For one thing, you probably aren't really aiming to run an SEO marathon. You're probably aiming just to "get in shape," meaning to get to the top of relevant keywords that narrowly fit your industry and/or your geographic area. Your more modest goal of helping your business to get free advertising on Google via SEO means only basic knowledge is required, and only modest effort.

Indeed, once a small business website is in decent SEO-friendly shape, my guess is about five hours a week on "Internet marketing" will suffice to keep you at the top of Google. Results vary, of course, as every situation is unique. But SEO is much, much easier than you'd think.

You're Smarter than Your Competitors!

Even better, in most industries, you'll find that your competitors are not that smart. Most industries are not as competitive in SEO as you would think, and metaphorically speaking, you don't have to run faster than the bear; you just have to run faster than your buddy.

> *Let me rephrase that. You are not competing against Google. You are competing against your competitors, and they aren't that much smarter than you. In fact, I bet they might even be dumber.*

Indeed, I'd wager that 90% or more of your competitors are doing little to nothing in terms of SEO. If you just make a modest effort, and if that effort is channeled with the effective knowledge I will teach you in this book, I'll wager that there's a very strong possibility that you'll be on page one of Google, if not in the very top positions.

The Seven Steps to SEO Success

This workbook guides you through the **seven steps** to successful SEO. Along the way, we'll set goals, understand technical details, and have fun. Along the way, I will be your "fitness coach" to explain how it all works and to motivate you to keep trying.

You can do this!

Throughout this workbook, I will share with you other examples of businesses that understand SEO and succeed using the **seven steps**.

The **seven steps to SEO fitness** are built on a philosophy of empowerment. Can you understand SEO? *Yes you can!* Can you implement SEO? *Yes you can!* It takes some knowledge, it takes some effort, but yes you can do it.

Get motivated! Imagine me as your personal fitness coach, dressed in hot pants and with a hot pink megaphone exclaiming, "Work harder! Work smarter! You Can Do This!" while you sweat to the oldies on the treadmill with just a few "miles" to go…

OK, stop imagining me in hot pants with a hot pink megaphone. It's getting weird. But the point is that with a little knowledge, a lot of hard work, and a "never give up" attitude, you can succeed at SEO. You can get your company, product, or service to page 1 of Google. *Certain restrictions and limitations apply, see store for details.* (We'll discuss many technical issues, going forward, but yes, you really can do SEO).

Before we dive in, allow me to share just a few more points of background.

» MEET THE AUTHOR

Well, first of all, who am I and what makes me an expert? My name is Jason McDonald, and I have been active on the Internet since 1994 (*having invented the Internet along with Al Gore*). I have been teaching SEO, AdWords, and Social Media since 2009 - online, in San Francisco, at Stanford University Continuing Studies, at workshops, and in corporate trainings. Over 4000 people have taken my paid trainings; over 25,000 my free webinars, and over 10,000 subscribe to my YouTube channel. I love figuring out how things work, and I love teaching others! SEO is an endeavor that I understand, and I want to empower you to understand it as well.

Learn more about me at **https://www.jasonmcdonald.org/**, at my corporate website **https://www.jm-seo.org/**, or be brave and email me a question or comment to **j.mcdonald@jm-seo.net**. Just Google "Jason McDonald," and you'll find me there at the top, beating out several much better-looking guys who have six pack abs and careers in sports as well as a New Age Guru who does spiritual trainings in Australia. *#RevengeOfTheNerds*

Don't believe I'm good at SEO, Google "SEO Expert San Francisco" (*you'll see me there*), Google "AdWords Expert Witness" or "SEO Expert Witness" (*Yes, I do legal work – there's good money in it, and I have kids to support*), or Google "SEO Classes Chicago" (*You'll see the JM Internet Group," my training and consulting company which isn't even in Chicago*). Try going to Amazon and entering, "SEO" or "Social Media Marketing." You'll find my books. Amazon is a search engine, and yes I do Amazon SEO as well. But I digress.

Here's a screenshot of *Bay Area SEO Consultant*:

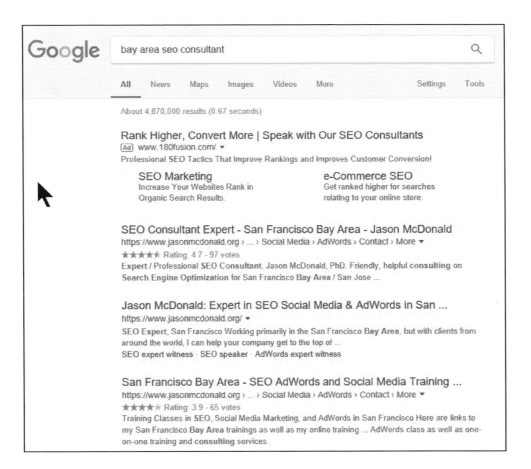

And here's one for AdWords Expert Witness:

I rank at or near the top for San Francisco and Bay Area searches for "SEO expert," "SEO consultant," and "SEO agency;" for expert witness searches for my legal work in SEO, AdWords, and Social Media Marketing; and for niche searches such as "AdWords Coupons," "Best Books on SEO 2019," and "Best SEO Conferences."

Uncle? Give up? Still don't believe me? Call me up, or email me before you buy this book, and I'll give you reference examples of my SEO clients (*who don't want their competitors to know about me*).

» WHY THIS BOOK IS DIFFERENT

There are quite a few books on SEO out there! There are zillions of blog posts! There are thousands of SEO consultants! There are hundreds of crazy harebrained schemes…

But there is only one **workbook**: the *SEO Fitness Workbook*.

How is a *workbook* different from a *book*? Here's how.

First of all, this workbook speaks in **practical, no-nonsense English**. Whereas most of the SEO books out there are *by* experts *for* experts, this workbook explains SEO in plain English and does not get lost in the details. Most businesspeople don't need to know every gory detail about SEO; rather they need practical, hands-on advice about what to do first, second, third and so forth. The *SEO Fitness Workbook* is as much about "doing SEO" as it is about "understanding SEO."

Secondly, the *SEO Fitness Workbook* is **hands-on**. Most SEO books are meant to be passively read. *SEO Fitness Workbook*, by contrast, gives you "hands on" worksheets and deliverables. In fact, each Chapter ends with a **DELIVERABLE** marked in **bold**. Each Chapter also has **TO-DOS** (marked in **bold**) because a workbook is not just about reading, it's about **doing** and **succeeding**. Each Chapter has a list of "action items" and a quiz to test your knowledge.

Third, while most books are outdated on the day they are published, the SEO Fitness Workbook connects to up-to-date **Internet resources** such as free SEO tools via the companion *SEO Toolbook*, and hands-on YouTube videos that show you how to succeed. After all, in the 21st century, a "how to" book should be more than a book, shouldn't it? It should be a gateway to up-to-date knowledge.

Fourth, I encourage you to reach out to me with your **questions**. Simply email **j.mcdonald@jm-seo.net** or visit **http://jmlinks.com/contact**. I truly enjoy the teaching of SEO, and I truly encourage my readers to ask questions. In fact, I learn as much from my students as they do from me because either I quickly know the answer to the question, or it's something weird and puzzling, and we'll learn the answer together. Don't be shy! Obviously I can't give you hours of expensive consulting time for free, but – within reason – I answer each and every short question that comes in.

» WHO THIS BOOK IS FOR

I have written *SEO Fitness Workbook* for the following groups of practical business folk:

Small Business Owners. If you own a small business that gets (or could get) significant customer traffic from the Web, this book is for you.

Small Business Marketers. If you are in charge of marketing for a small business that gets (or could get) significant customer traffic from the Web, this book is for you.

Marketing Managers. If you lead a Web team of inside or outside bloggers, SEO content writers, or other Internet marketing technicians including external SEO companies, this book is for you.

Web Designers. If you design websites but want to design sites that not only look good but actually rank high on Google search, this book is for you.

Non-profit Marketers. If you work at a non-profit or governmental agency that depends on Web search traffic, then this book is also for you.

Anyone whose organization (and its products, services, or other offerings) would benefit from being at the top of Google, for free, can benefit from the *SEO Fitness Workbook*.

» THE SEVEN STEPS TO SEO FITNESS

Here are the seven steps to SEO fitness:

1. **Goals**: Define Your Goals
2. **Keywords**: Identify Keywords
3. **On Page SEO:** Get Your Website to "Speak Google"
4. **Content Marketing**: Create Quality Content for Google and for Humans
5. **Off Page SEO**: Build Links, Leverage Social Media, and Go Local
6. **Metrics**: Measure and Learn from Your Results
7. **Learn**: Never Stop Learning!

And here are the seven steps to SEO fitness in more detail –

Step #1: GOALS. SEO, like physical fitness, is purpose-driven! You can't achieve your goals if you don't define what they are.

1.1 Attitude – attitude is everything, and SEO requires a commitment to learning how SEO works as well as a desire to implement positive SEO-friendly changes. Goal 1.1 is to have the right attitude.

1.2 Goals – define what you sell, who your customers are, and how best to reach them. Define website goals such as to get online sales or acquire customer names, phone numbers, and email addresses as sales leads.

Step #2 KEYWORDS – identify your keywords. Keywords drive nearly every aspect of SEO, so you need a well-structured, clearly defined "keyword worksheet."

2.1 Keywords – identify high-volume, high-value keywords.

2.2 Keyword Worksheet – build a keyword worksheet and measure your rank on Google and Bing.

Step #3 ON PAGE SEO for your website. Once you know your keywords, where do you put them? It begins with page tags, proceeds through website organization, and ends with an "SEO audit" that outlines your SEO strategy. The nerd word for this is "On Page" SEO.

3.1 Page Tags – understand basic HTML tags, and weave your target keywords into strategic tags such as the TITLE, META DESCRIPTION, and IMG ALT tags.

3.2 Website Structure – build landing pages, restructure your homepage, and optimize website layout through keyword-heavy link sculpting.

Step #4 CONTENT MARKETING. They say that "content is king" in terms of SEO, and they are right. In this section, you'll create a long-term content strategy that moves beyond the "quick fix" of your site to a day-by-day, week-by-week system of SEO-friendly content.

4.1 Content SEO – devise a content strategy, specifically who will do what, when, where, how, and how often – that is, a short and long-term SEO content marketing strategy including an inventory of the content you need to succeed.

4.2 Blogging – set up a blog that follows best SEO practices, including all-important connections to social media platforms like Google+ and Twitter.

4.3 Press Release SEO - leverage press release syndication services for SEO, because press releases are an easy technique to get links and build buzz on social media.

Step #5 OFF PAGE SEO – links and social media. "Off Page" SEO leverages external web links and social media to boost your website's authority on Google. Use the traditional tactic of getting relevant inbound links. Then, leverage social media platforms like Twitter, Facebook, LinkedIn and YouTube to enhance your SEO efforts via "social authority!"

5.1 Link Building – conduct a link building audit and create a long-term link building strategy.

5.2 Social Media SEO – look for social media mention opportunities, and enable relevant social profiles to enhance Google's trust in your website as an authoritative resource.

5.3 Local SEO – local SEO stands at the juncture of SEO, local, and review based marketing, and so we dive into how to optimize a website for local searches.

Step #6 METRICS – measure and learn from your results. Like physical fitness, SEO is a process that starts with a defined set of goals and employs specific measurements about goal achievement.

6.1 Metrics - measure your progress towards the top of Google, inbound keywords, and paths taken by customers once they land on your website.

Step #7 LEARN - never stop learning. SEO starts with self-discovery, proceeds through technical knowledge, and ends with the hard work of implementation.

7.1 Learning – use Chapter 7 to get access to companion **worksheets** and the very important *SEO Toolbook* and my *secret dashboard*, which provide hundreds of free SEO tools, tools to help you in all aspects of SEO, from identifying keywords through page tags to links and social mentions.

» REGISTER YOUR WORKBOOK FOR FREE ONLINE RESOURCES

Please **register** your *Workbook*. You'll not only get a full-color PDF copy of this *Workbook* to download with active, clickable links to the resources (very handy to read at your computer). You'll also get my updated *SEO Toolbook*, my secret *SEO Dashboard*, and all the Workbook's companion worksheets to help you step-by-step. You'll even get a free pony! (OK, you won't get a free pony, but you'll get loads of hands-on materials to help you start "doing" SEO).

To register, follow these easy steps:

1. Go to the **JM Internet Group** Website, click on "Register Your Workbook," or just go directly to **http://jmlinks.com/seo19tz**.
2. Reenter your passcode: **seo19tz**
3. If you have any problems, contact me via **http://jmlinks.com/contact** or call 800-298-4065 for help.

Sign up for email alerts at **http://jmlinks.com/free**, and - last but not least- watch a few of my YouTube videos at **https://www.youtube.com/jmgrp**; you'll find I am as crazy and enthusiastic on video as I am in this book!

Access Jump Code Links

Note: throughout this book I use the website **http://jmlinks.com/** to point to resources. You can either click on the resource directly in the book (if you're reading in digital format). Or, simply go to **http://jmlinks.com/** and enter the **JUMP code**. For example, to visit **http://jmlinks.com/7a** simply go to **http://jmlinks.com/** and enter "**7a**". That will take you to the referenced Internet resource.

> **VIDEO.** Watch a video tutorial of how to use the jump codes at **http://jmlinks.com/jump** or just visit **http://jmlinks.com/** directly and enter *jump*.

» SPREAD THE WORD: TAKE A SURVEY & GET $5!

If you like the book, please take a moment to provide honest feedback. Here's my special offer for those eager enough to take a short survey –

1. **Visit http://jmlinks.com/survey**.
2. **Compete** the survey on the book, as indicated.
3. Include your **email address** and **any feedback** (good, bad, positive, negative) about the book).
4. I will gift you $5 via Amazon gift eCard.

This offer is subject to change without notice.

» COPYRIGHT AND DISCLAIMER

This is a completely **unofficial** guide to SEO. Neither Google nor Bing / Yahoo have endorsed this guide, nor has Google, Bing, or Yahoo nor anyone affiliated with Google, Bing, or Yahoo been involved in the production of this guide.

That's a *good thing*. This guide is **independent**. My aim is to "tell it as I see it," giving you no-nonsense information on how to succeed at SEO.

In addition, please note the following:

- All trademarks are the property of their respective owners. I have no relationship with nor endorsement from the mark holders. Any use of their marks is so I can provide information to you.

- Any reference to or citation of third party products or services whether for Google, Yahoo, Bing, or otherwise, should not be construed as an endorsement of those products or services tools, nor as a warranty as to their effectiveness or compliance with the terms of service of Google, Yahoo, or Bing.

The information used in this guide has been reviewed and updated as of December, 2018. However, SEO changes rapidly, so please be aware that scenarios, facts, and conclusions are subject to change without notice.

Additional Disclaimer. Internet marketing is an art, and not a science. Any changes to your Internet marketing strategy, including SEO, Social Media Marketing, and AdWords, is at your own risk. Neither Jason McDonald nor the JM Internet Group nor Excerpti Communications, Inc. assumes any responsibility for the effect of any changes you may, or may not, make to your website or AdWords advertising based on the information in this guide.

» ACKNOWLEDGEMENTS

No man is an island. I would like to thank my beloved wife, Noelle Decambra, as my personal cheerleader in the book industry. Gloria McNabb has done her usual tireless job as first assistant, including updating this edition as well the *SEO Toolbook*. My daughter, Ava, inspired me on YouTube, and my daughter, Hannah, has inspired me with her grit and determination as the best audio editor ever. Last but not least, my black Lab Buddy, kept my physically active and pondering the mysteries of Google on many jaunts through the San Francisco Bay Area.

And a huge thank you to my students – online, in San Francisco, and at Stanford Continuing Studies. You challenge me, you inspire me, and you motivate me!

II

BASICS

I love **analogies** because, as a teacher, I find that they help my students quickly understand new things. Thinking of SEO like fitness, for example, helps people realize that they need to set "fitness goals," learn some tips and tricks about how to "get fit," and then create a systematic plan (and stick with it) to achieve their goals. As opposed to having your head swimming with technical mumbo-jumbo, the *fitness analogy* helps you see that SEO is something you can do. It's empowering.

Before we get into the technical details, I want to give you another analogy that will help you in your quest to get to the top of Google. **SEO is like getting a job**. It has its **job desired** (your *keywords*), its **resume** (your *website*), its **references** (your inbound *links*), and its job **interview** (your website *landing*).

In this Chapter, I will give you a *conceptual framework* to understand search engine optimization. Once you have a conceptual framework, you can then refer back to it, as you dive into very specific tasks such as optimizing a landing page or soliciting inbound links. It's a map that will keep you oriented in the right direction.

Let's get started!

TO-DO LIST:

» Understand that SEO Parallels Getting a Job

» Keyword Research

» Understand "On Page" SEO

» Understand "Off Page" SEO

» Set Landing Page Goals

» Understand That SEO Parallels Getting a Job

Let's consider the search for a job. How does the job market work? People want to "be found" as the "ideal" candidate for a position. So what do they do? Four important things:

Job Desired – Identify a Desired Job. Job seekers take a look inside their souls and identify the job they want. If they're smart, they took a look outside at the job market as well, and look for **connection points** between the job of their dreams, and the jobs that are in demand in the labor market. For example, my dream job is sipping margaritas in Puerta Vallarta, Mexico, writing science fiction novels, but the demand for that isn't so high. So I've taken a passion for language and turned that into a job as an SEO writer and consultant. Notice how the "job desired" matches "keywords" as in (*SEO consultant*).

Resume - Create a resume. Job seekers create a keyword-heavy **resume** that explains the job that they want to get, and their qualifications for that job. If, for example, they want a job as a *BMW auto mechanic*, they create a resume that emphasizes keywords like "auto mechanic," "auto repair," and even "BMW repair" by prominently displaying them in the right places, including the subject line of emails they send out to prospective employers. And employers "scan" resumes looking for those resumes that "match" their keywords. Notice how "keywords" are embedded in the written resume.

References - Cultivate References. Beyond a great resume, the next aspect of job search is cultivating great **references**. Knowing the boss's spouse, having the head of the BMW auto mechanic school, or someone else important or influential put in a good word can elevate your resume to the top of the heap. In short, strong references get your resume looked at, substantiate that your resume is factually accurate, and possibly get you a job interview. Notice how "references" are external validations that you are as great as your resume claims you to be.

Job Interview – Wow Them Face-to-Face. Once you get their attention, what's next? The job **interview** is the next step towards landing the job, it's the "free glimpse" of what you have to offer that "sells" the employer on making a financial commitment by hiring you. Notice how a "job interview" is a "free" taste of you as an employee. The use of something **free** is obvious, *once you notice it*, and notice how strong websites usually offer customers something **free** as well.

The **marketing equation** is: **job desired** > **resume** > **references** > **job interview** > **job**.

Hopefully you can already see that SEO is a lot like getting a job. How so?

Identifying the job you want equals identifying keywords that are in demand. Before you put virtual pen to virtual paper to build out your website, you have to understand your Business Value Proposition, and who wants what you have to sell. "Keywords" connect what you have, with what customers want. This is called "**keyword research.**"

Creating a resume equals creating a strong, keyword heavy website. Your website, in a sense, is your business resume, and it needs to have keywords placed on it in strategic places to "talk to" Google as well as human searchers, and just as with a job search, you have to research the hot-button keywords that people are searching for and place those in strategic positions. This is called "**On Page**" SEO.

Cultivating references equals getting links and going social. Just as you cultivate references to get your resume elevated to the top of the heap, so you cultivate inbound links, fresh buzz, and social authority to elevate your website to the top of Google search. Getting other websites to link to you, positive reviews of your business on Google, and mentions on social media sites like Google+ or Twitter is called "Off Page" SEO.

The job interview equals the website landing. Once you get noticed, your next step is a fantastic job interview. The equivalent of the job interview is the **landing behavior** on your website. Once they land from Google, you want them to "take the next step," usually a registration or a sale just as at a job interview, which leads to the final step, getting hired or making a sale.

The **SEO equation** is **keyword research** > **On Page SEO** > **Off Page SEO** > **website landing** > **sales inquiry** or **sale**.

Keep this conceptual framework that SEO is like a job search in the back of your head as you read through this Workbook. Here's a simple model of the parallels:

Job desired = *keywords* = identify keywords that customers search for.

Resume = *On Page SEO* = create a keyword-heavy, easy-to-understand website.

References = *Off Page SEO* = solicit many inbound links, social authority / mentions, and freshness via blogging.

Job Interview = optimize the *landing page experience* to lead to a registration or a sale.

Metrics = is it working? Am I getting relevant job interviews ("inquiries") and job offers ("sales")?

Build a Better Resume (or Website)

Once you realize that the process of SEO parallels the process of getting a job, you'll realize something else. Just because the process is easy-to-understand does not mean that most people do it correctly. If you've ever had the *(mis)*fortune of having to look through job applications and resumes, for example, you can vouch for me that many (if not most) resumes are terrible. They're hard to read, they're ambiguous about the job desired, and they don't systematically substantiate their claim that they are the "perfect" candidate for the job.

Most resumes, in short, stink.

Looking over to the Web, you'll realize that just because SEO is conceptually easy to understand does not mean that most Web sites are SEO-friendly. In fact, most websites are ambiguous at best vis-à-vis their keyword targets, have terrible landing experiences, and don't have any systematic link-building in place.

Most websites, in short, stink.

But just because most people have terrible resumes, or terrible websites, does not mean that yours has to stink, too. In fact, this is the first *hugely optimistic observation*. With a little knowledge and a little hard work, you can elevate your website above your competition. You can "build a better website" via SEO and vastly improve your performance on Google.

Of course it depends on how competitive your industry is, and how skilled your competition is. It varies industry by industry. But in my experience, most small business websites can see a vast improvement by following a few simple SEO guidelines.

Your website, just like your resume, does **NOT** have to be **perfect**. It just has to be **BETTER** than that of your competition. And your competition is not made of Albert Einsteins and Madame Curies, but just regular guys and gals most of whom probably know less about SEO than you do.

» KEYWORD RESEARCH

Let's drill down into the first element, "keyword research," the equivalent of identifying a job that you want that's also in demand in the marketplace. We'll get into some cool tactics and tools in Chapter Two, but for now, here are the steps:

1. Write down your Business Value Proposition, with an eye to the "words" that "describe" what you have that people want.
2. Look for "words" that connect "what you sell" with what "customers want."
3. Brainstorm how customers might search Google to find your company, product or service.

4. Write down a "keyword list" with special attention to those keywords that are really, really hot matches connecting a customer who's "ready to buy" with "what you have to sell."

At the end of this process, you'll have a list of keywords that your customers type into Google. (If you need help on the marketing ideas that exist "before" SEO, consult my *The Marketing Book* at **http://jmlinks.com/twaggle**).

❯ "ON PAGE" SEO

Let's drill down into the second element, "On Page" SEO, the equivalent of a great resume. What are the steps? We'll assume that you have your keyword list in hand; that is, you know "which job" you want, or in SEO terms, which keywords you want to optimize for. Once you know your keywords, where do you put them?

In terms of "On Page" SEO, the main places you put your keywords are as follows:

Page Tags. Place your keywords strategically in the right page tags, beginning with the TITLE tag on each page, followed by the header tag family, image alt attribute, and HTML cross-links from one page to another on your site.

Keyword Density. Write keyword-heavy copy for your web pages, and pay attention to writing quality. Complying to Google's *Panda* update means placing your keywords into grammatically correct sentences, and making sure that your writing contains similar and associated words vs. your keyword targets.

Home Page SEO. Use your homepage wisely, by placing keywords in relatively high density on your homepage and, again, in natural syntax, as well as creating "one-click" links from your homepage to your subordinate pages.

Website structure. Organize your website to be Google friendly, starting with keyword-heavy URLs, cross-linking with keyword text, and using sitemaps and other Google-friendly tactics. I also recommend writing a short, keyword-heavy **footer** on your website with links to your main **landing pages**.

"On Page" SEO is all about knowing your keywords and building keyword-heavy content that communicates your priorities to Google just as a good resume communicates your job search priorities to prospective employers. We'll investigate "On Page" SEO more deeply in Chapters Three and Four.

Write for Google, and for Humans

Among the trends of recent years and one getting stronger in 2019 is the trend towards "natural syntax," "semantic search," and "artificial intelligence." Google is getting smarter and smarter, which means that your prose needs to be more "natural" than ever. Answering customer questions via your website as if you were talking to a customer is a key writing strategy for the "new" On Page SEO in an environment of voice search and artificial intelligence. Yet you want to write keyword-heavy content that is Google-friendly but also easy-to-read, relevant content that is good for humans. It's not Google OR humans; it's Google AND humans.

» "OFF PAGE" SEO

Let's drill down into the third element, "Off Page" SEO, the equivalent of great references. Here, you do not fully control the factors that help you with Google, so the game is played out in how well you can convince others to talk favorably about you and your website. Paralleling job references, the main strategic factors of "Off Page" SEO are as follows:

Link Building. As we shall see, links are the votes of the Web. Getting as many qualified websites to link back to your website, especially high authority websites as ranked (secretly) by Google, using keyword-heavy syntax, is what link building is all about. It's that simple, and that complicated.

Social Authority / Mentions. Social media is the new buzz of the Internet, and Google looks for mentions of your website on social sites like LinkedIn, Twitter, and Facebook as well as how robust your own social media profiles are.

Online Reviews. If you are a local business, customer reviews especially on Google and, to a lesser extent, on Yelp and industry-specific websites like Avvo.com for lawyers and Healthgrades.com for doctors, etc., greatly influence your SEO performance. Accordingly, you want to solicit reviews from real, happy customers so that they write online reviews about your business on Google, Yelp, and other major review sites.

Freshness. Like a prospective employer, Google rewards sites that show fresh activity. "What have you done lately?" is a common job interview question, and in SEO you need to communicate to Google that you are active via frequent content updates such as blog posts and press releases.

"Off Page" SEO is all about building external links to your site just as getting good references is all about cultivating positive buzz about you as a potential employee. We'll investigate "Off Page" SEO more deeply in Chapter Five. Oh, and due to the recent Google algorithm change called *Penguin*, we'll emphasize that you want to cultivate *natural* inbound links as opposed to *artificial* links that scream "manipulation" at Google! It's good *believable* references that help you in a job search, and, post-*Penguin*, it's good *believable* links that help you with SEO.

» Set Landing Page Goals

Let's drill down into the fourth element, "Landing Page Goals," the equivalent of great job interview skills. The point of a great website isn't just to get traffic from Google, after all. It's to move that potential customer up your sales ladder – from website landing to a registration for something free (a "sales lead") or perhaps even a sale.

So in evaluating your website, you want to evaluate each and every page and each and every page element for one variable: do they move customers up the **sales ladder**? Is the **desired action** (*registration* or *sale*) clearly visible on each page, and if so, is it enticing to the customer usually with something free like a free download, free consult, free webinar and the like?

Just as after a job interview, your family and friends ask whether you "got the job," after a Web landing you are asking yourself whether it "got the action" such as a registration or a sale. Web traffic just like sending out resumes is not an end in itself, but a means to an end!

> **VIDEO.** Watch a video tutorial on the basics of SEO explained in "plain English" at **http://jmlinks.com/17k**.

We shall now explore each of these topics in-depth.

1.1

ATTITUDE

Most books on SEO start with the technical details. What's a TITLE tag? How do you understand your Google PageRank? Which factors in the Google algorithm have changed recently? We'll get to all that, but I want to start this book with a pep talk about **attitude**.

Attitude, they say, is everything.

And nowhere is that more true than in SEO. This is an industry full of information overload, pretty rude intimidators of a technical geeky type, and an 800 lb Gorilla (Google), that would really rather you just spend money on AdWords advertising than understand how you can get to the top of Google without paying it a penny.

To succeed, you'll need a positive, "can do" attitude.

Let's get started!

TO-DO LIST:

» Learn from Francie Baltazar-Schwartz that "Attitude is Everything."

» Identify "Can Do" vs. "Can't Do" People.

» Learn to Measure.

»» Deliverable: Inventory Your Team & Get Ready.

» FRANCIE BALTAZAR-SCHWARTZ AND ATTITUDE IS EVERYTHING

The Internet is a wonderful place, and Google sits pretty much at the center of it. Got a question? "Just *Google* it!" We certainly know the reality of "Just *Google* it" in terms of customers looking for companies, products and services. But it also goes for more important questions like the *meaning of life* (*42*), and *what is a LOL cat*, anyway?

For example, Google "Who said 'Attitude is Everything?'" and you'll find out that this quote is attributed to one Francie Baltazar-Schwartz. You can read it at **http://jmlinks.com/5i**. The point of "attitude is everything" is that you have two choices every day: either to have a **positive**, **can-do** attitude or to have a **negative**, **can't do** attitude. (**Remember**: if you are reading this book in print format, visit **http://jmlinks.com/** and enter the JUMP code, in this case "**5i**").

This relates very dramatically to success at SEO, just as it does to success in pretty much everything else in life from physical fitness to your job to your marriage.

How does it apply to SEO? Well, let's look at the facts and let's look at the ecosystem of people and companies in the SEO industry.

Fact No. 1. SEO is technical, and at least on the surface, seems pretty complicated and hard. So, if you start out with the attitude that you "can't do it," you're already on the path to defeat. If, in contrast, you start with the attitude that you can do it, that other people are clearly doing it (*people no smarter than you*), you're on the path to success. **Attitude is everything.**

Fact No. 2. Google does not want anyone to believe that SEO is easy. In fact, because Google makes its money from *advertising* (nearly 90% of nearly $20 billion per quarter - see **http://jmlinks.com/13k**), it wants you, too, to believe that *advertising* is the way to go. Google has no incentive to explain how SEO works, and in fact, has every incentive to do the opposite. *If you are intimidated by Google, you're already on the path to defeat.* If, in contrast, you pay attention to the facts and realize that SEO is free, while ads cost money, that you can do SEO, and that you can get to the top of Google for free… you won't worry about the propaganda from a multibillion dollar corporation. **Attitude is everything.**

Fact No. 3. The SEO industry is full of so-called experts, gurus, tools providers and others who pretty much make their money by intimidating normal folk into believing that SEO is incredibly complicated and only nerds with Ph.D.'s in computer science can do it. They want you to stay in a state of dependency and keep paying them the big bucks... So if you allow technical nerds to intimidate you, you're already on the path to defeat. If, in contrast, you realize that they aren't really any smarter than you and that SEO isn't just about technology, it's about words and concepts and marketing messages, you're on the path to success. **Attitude is everything.**

Oh, and as SEO becomes more and more social, you'll want to have an open mind about social media as well. You can really get yourself motivated by watching a video by "Kid President" (Robby Novak), who is twelve years old, has several million views on YouTube, and was actually invited to the White House by then-President Obama.

VIDEO. Watch a "Can Do" attitude video by "Kid President" at **http://jmlinks.com/5j**.

For your first **To-DO**, therefore, concentrate your mind and create a **positive attitude**: this is going to be fun, this is going to be educational, this is going to be a journey! Your **attitude is everything** as to whether you'll succeed or fail at SEO!

In fact, since the video screenshot was taken, this video now tops 43 million views as of December, 2018! If a *twelve-year-old* can get 43 million views and meet the President, don't you think you can at least get to page one of Google?

» IDENTIFY "CAN DO" VS. "CAN'T DO" PEOPLE

In most situations, you'll need to depend on other people. In fact, the attitude of the people on your team (your webmaster, your content writers, your product marketing managers, your executives…) is also incredibly important. Are they "can do" or "can't do" sort of folks?

Henry Ford, the great industrialist, once made this clear observation:

"Whether you think you can, or you think you can't--you're right."
— Henry Ford

In terms of SEO, there are those people who think that a) they can't learn it, or b) it can't be done. And, guess what: they're **right**. And there are those who think that a) they can learn it, and b) it can be done. And, guess what: they're **right**, too.

Which camp are you in? Your team members? Can, or can't?

So for your second **To-DO**, look around your organization and make a list of those people who need to be involved with your SEO project. For example:

Management and Marketers. These people are involved in the sense of understanding who your customers are, what you sell, and what the sales objectives are for your website. Your website, after all, isn't an end in itself but a means to an end: more sales.

Content Writers. Who writes (or will write) content for the website? These people need at least a basic understanding of your keywords and, even better, an understanding of how "On Page" SEO works so that they know where to strategically place keywords on web content.

Web Designers. News flash: your website isn't just for humans! It's also for Google. You'll have to educate your web design team that your website needs to "talk" to Google just as much as it "talks" to humans. As we will learn, what Google likes (*text*) isn't generally what people like (*pictures*).

Web Programmers. The folks who program the backend, like your URL structure, your XML sitemaps and all that technical stuff. Who are these people and how will you get them on board for the SEO project?

Link Builders. Google heavily rewards websites that have many inbound links to them, and so you'll need "link builders" to ask directories, trade associations or trade shows, bloggers, journalists, and other websites to link back to your website. What people in your company interface with outside websites, and are in a position to solicit inbound links?

Social Media and Outreach Experts. Social media is the new wave in SEO, so you'll need those folks who are (or will be) active on Twitter, YouTube, Facebook and the like to be "SEO aware," in the sense of how social media impacts SEO performance. You'll need folks who participate in social media and can encourage social influencers to share your website URLs. (For an in-depth discussion on social media marketing, see my *Social Media Marketing Workbook* at **http://jmlinks.com/smm**).

Indeed, if you have some really obstructionist "Can't Do" people, you'll need to strategize either how to a) **persuade** them to participate, b) **get them out of the way**, or c) **work around** them.

» LEARN TO MEASURE

As you assemble your team, you'll want to get their buy-in on learning SEO. It isn't rocket science, but it's also not something you'll learn in a day. First, they'll need to learn the basics (as we discussed in the previous Chapter). Second, they'll need to learn many of the more esoteric topics as needed. Content writers, for example, will need to be keenly aware of keywords and how to write semantically friendly SEO text. Web programmers will need to understand XML sitemaps and so on. Third, they'll need to be committed to lifelong learning, as SEO changes over time. A good strategy is to schedule monthly meetings or corporate email exchanges about your SEO progress.

Let's also talk a little about **measurement** and **metrics**. One of the biggest stumbling blocks to successful SEO is the idea that it can't be measured. It can. How so?

Know your keywords. Once you know your keywords, as you'll learn in Chapter 2.1, then you can start to measure your **rank** on target Google searches.

Inbound search traffic. Once you set up Google Analytics properly as you'll learn in Chapter 6.1, you can measure your inbound "organic" traffic from Google, including some data on inbound keywords. You'll learn how people get to your website, and what they do once they get there.

Goals. Every good website should have defined goals, usually registrations and/or sales. Once you define goals in Google Analytics, you can track what traffic converts to a sale, and what doesn't. (Then you can brainstorm ways to improve it).

When you first start, you'll often have little idea of your target keywords, little idea of your rank on Google, and little idea of your traffic patterns from landings to conversions. But that doesn't mean SEO isn't a measurable activity! It just means you are not yet measuring.

Why is this important? As you set up your team, and establish the right attitude, you want to establish the idea that SEO is measurable. If someone has crazy ideas (*such as*

Google doesn't pay attention to URL structure, or keywords don't matter), you can measure these ideas vs. correct ideas (*that keywords in TITLE tags do matter a great deal, keyword-heavy URL's help a lot*). Establishing a culture of measurability will help you get everyone on your team, even the most recalcitrant "Can't Do" people to realize that SEO works, and SEO can get your website to actually generate sales or sales leads.

Measurability is a critical part of Step No. 1: **Setting (Measurable) Goals.**

»» DELIVERABLE: INVENTORY YOUR TEAM AND GET READY

Now we've come to the end of Step 1.1, your first **DELIVERABLE** has arrived. Open up a Word document and create a list of all the people who are involved with your website, from the marketing folks who identify the goals (sales or registrations?), to the content writers (those who create product descriptions, blog posts, or press releases), to the Web design people (graphic designers), to the Web programmers, and to your outreach team for social media and links. Make an inventory of who needs to be involved in what aspects of SEO, and if possible, set up weekly or monthly meetings about your SEO strategy.

At a "top secret" level, you might also want to indicate who has a "Can Do" and who has a "Can't Do" attitude. You'll want to work to bring everyone over into the "Can Do" column!

Consider having an "attitude is everything" meeting about SEO, and get everyone to stand up on the tabletops and shout: "We can do this!"

1.2

GOALS

SEO, like physical fitness, can't be accomplished without **goals**. Are you training for a marathon, or a sprint? Want to look better naked, or just be healthier? Want to dominate Google for "industrial fans," for "organic baby food," or for "probate attorney St. Louis?" Is the purpose of your website to get sales leads, or to sell products via eCommerce? SEO can tell you *how* to get to the top of Google, but it can't tell you *what* your company's *goals* are vis-à-vis potential customers. To succeed at SEO, you need to have a clear vision of your *sales ladder* starting at the customer *need* and then proceeding as follows: keyword search *query* → *landing* on your website → sales *inquiry* → *back* and *forth* → actual *sale*. For an eCommerce site, the goals and sales ladder would be the same, except that rather than a "sales inquiry" the goal would be an actual website purchase.

Let's get started!

TO-DO LIST:

> » Define Your Business Value Proposition

> » Identify Your Target Customers by Segment or Personas

> » Establish Marketing Goals

> »» Checklist: Goals Action Items

> »» Deliverable: A Business Value Proposition Worksheet

» DEFINE YOUR BUSINESS VALUE PROPOSITION

What does your business sell? Who wants it, and why? In this Chapter, you'll sit down and fill out the "business value proposition worksheet." A **BVP**, or "business value proposition" is a statement that succinctly defines what your business does and the value that it provides to customers. For example, a cupcake bakery bakes yummy cupcakes that people want to eat; a dry cleaner cleans people's dirty clothes; and an automobile insurer provides insurance for people's cars. You produce something that other people want, so what is it?

Define Your Business Value Proposition

One way to define your business value proposition is to look at other companies on the Web, and "reverse engineer" their BVPs.

Here are some more examples, with links to sample websites.

For a Chicago retailer of Rolex watches such as **Howard Frum Jewelers** (**http://www.howardfrum.com/**), the business value proposition is selling both new and used Rolex watches, plus servicing and repairing Rolex watches.

For an industrial fan company like **Industrial Fans Direct** (**http://www.industrialfansdirect.com/**), the business value proposition is to provide quality industrial fans for harsh environments such as factories or farms.

For a San Francisco mortgage broker, such as **Natasha Lovas**, the business value proposition is to help people get cheap mortgages easily. Her website is **http://www.san-francisco-mortgage-broker.com/**.

For any business, a *business value proposition* is your "elevator pitch" to a potential customer - what do you offer, that they want?

> For your first **TO-DO**, write a sentence or short paragraph that succinctly defines what your business does and how it provides value for customers. For the **worksheet**, go to **http://jmlinks.com/seo19tz** (reenter the passcode "seo19tz" to register if you have not already done so), and click on the link to the "business value proposition worksheet."

» IDENTIFY YOUR TARGET CUSTOMERS BY SEGMENT OR PERSONAS

Your *business value proposition* explicitly describes the relationship between what you sell and what they want. Now dig deeper: *segment* your customers into definable groups or what are called "customer personas." Literally imagine a potential customer. What does she look like? What does she want? What are her pain points? Imagine her unique characteristics and needs, and how they point to how her "needs" can be addressed by your product or service.

For instance, **Howard Frum Jewelers** might segment its customers into the following personas:

- Chicago office workers seeking quick and convenient watch repairs for their Rolex watches on their lunch hours (*Time-conscious and location-sensitive*).
- Folks looking to buy "used" Rolex watches as collectibles (*Watch collectors*).
- Chicago residents looking to purchase Rolex watches (*Luxury and/or Rolex watch lovers*).
- USA residents who own Rolex watches but live in smaller cities and towns yet need repair (*Mail-in Rolex repairs nationwide*).

Similarly, a Las Vegas real estate broker might segment his customers by space need – office, warehouse, retail. Moreover, there might be a segmentation based on those looking to rent vs. buy. And a Miami divorce attorney might segment her customers or clients into men vs. women, those with substantial property vs. those without, those who have children vs. those who do not.

In summary, a "segment" or "buyer persona" is a group of like-minded customers.

For your second **TO-DO**, open up the "business value proposition worksheet" and identify your **customer segments** or **buyer personas** – customers who differ by type (income level, geographic location), by need (high end, low end, rent vs. buy), or even geographic location. Try to see your customers as specific groups with specific needs, rather than one amorphous mega group. Begin to think about how each might search Google differently, using different keywords.

For a fun tool to help you visualize your buyer personas, visit **http://jmlinks.com/29s**. And if you're new to marketing, let me suggest my new book, *The Marketing Book* at **http://jmlinks.com/twaggle**, which is a "prequel" to this book on SEO. It will help you overview your entire marketing strategy in a quick and easy read.

» ESTABLISH MARKETING GOALS

Moving from business value proposition and customer personas, it's time to think about definable **goals** or **actions** for your website. For most businesses, a good goal is to get a registration / email address / inquiry in exchange for something free such as a free consult, eBook, or webinar. A Las Vegas real estate company, for instance, might want visitors to the website to "send a message" about their property needs, or register for a free consult with a leasing specialist. Similarly, a divorce attorney might want a potential client to reach out for a free phone consult, and a watch repair shop might just want people to call or email to discuss their watch repair needs, and get directions to the shop.

For most businesses, marketing **goals** on the Web usually boil down to –

- A Website **registration**, **contact form**, or **email via the website** – for a free consult, a software download, a free e-book, a newsletter sign up, etc.
  - o Note: a **phone call** generated via the website should count the same as the above.
- A **sale** – an e-commerce transaction such as the purchase of a candy gift tin on an e-store, or an iPhone skin via PayPal.

A well-constructed website will lead customers to an easy-to-see first step. Here's a screenshot from **http://www.reversemortgage.org/**, one of the top websites for the Google search "reverse mortgage," with the goal marked by a red arrow:

Reversemortgage.org knows what it wants: first, to **rank** at the top of Google search for "reverse mortgage," second, to **get the click**; and third, for a potential customer to start towards the **goal**, i.e. the process of *finding a lender* (and giving the Website his name, email address, and phone number for a sales follow up!).

Abstractly, your process and goals are probably as follows:

1. **Rank high** on a Google search query ("reverse mortgage" in this case).
2. **Get the click** from Google to your website.
3. Once they land, get them to take the "first step" or "**goal**" (usually fill out a feedback form, send an email via the website, or for an eCommerce site to make a first purchase.).
4. **Follow up** with them by email or phone, if necessary, to complete the sales process.

Your Sales Ladder

Defining your next steps or goals of your website is inseparable from defining your **sales ladder**. Web searchers are actively looking for an answer to their query, and they are anything but passive: if they don't see what they want, *click*, *bounce*, *bye*, and they're gone.

*(Some marketers talk of a "sales funnel," a concept I do not like because it implies that customers are **passive**, like little marbles that fall into your website and into your registration or sale. I do not think people on the Web (or in life) are passive at all. I think of people as **active** searchers, searching Google, clicking to websites, finding what they want (or not), and being quite skeptical about whether they should take the next action.)*

Customers Are Like Salmon

Let me explain why thinking of customers as jumping "up" a "sales ladder" is a better way to think than "down" a "sales funnel."

I think of *customers* like *salmon* jumping up from sea level in frigid Alaskan rivers, jumping higher and higher up fish ladders (put there by the Alaskan Department of Fish and Game) to get to their goal: the spawning ground. The fish are motivated (*after all, there's mating to be done*), and they are **active** participants in the process. You can't "bait" them with junk either: they need something good at the end of the process.

A good Alaskan fishery expert doesn't engineer one **huge**, **high** jump for the salmon but rather a series of **smaller**, **easier-to-jump** hurdles that can move the fish from goal one to goal two, etc. Why? Because if the first jump is too high, and too scary, the fish won't make it.

Similarly, make your own "first step" non-threatening, and easy! Don't attempt to go from a website landing to a major purchase; rather break the process into smaller, easier, and less threatening "baby steps." One of the best early steps in your goals is to give away something **free** like a free consultation, free eBook, or free Webinar.

GIVE AWAY SOMETHING FREE IN EXCHANGE FOR CONTACT INFORMATION

Having something **free** (a free webinar, a free consultation, a free e-book) is a tried and true way to make the first step of your ladder easy and non-threatening. People love free, and will give away their email and phone contact information for something free that is also useful. (*From your perspective, this then gives you their email and/or phone number for you and your sales staff to follow up on*). If you are selling something, think of a free sample or money back offer; anything that reduces the risk of making that first buying decision.

A good example of this is in the hair loss / hair restoration industry. Take a look at Oxford Biolabs, a purveyor of hair restoration products at **https://us.oxfordbiolabs.com/**. Notice how they have links to a "frcc cBook" and "Buy Now" in the header on every page. Here's a screenshot:

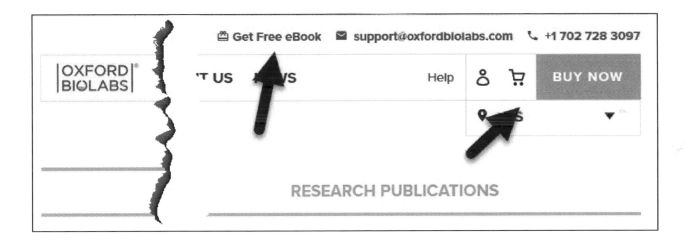

In other words, they have a way for you to "nibble" on a free eBook if you're not quite ready, and a garish "Buy Now" button if you are. This is a website that knows the goals it wants users to perform.

Using this strategy of free and/or clear goals, make the first step of your sales ladder exciting, enticing, and ideally free!

VIDEO. Watch a video tutorial of the importance of giving away something free on your website at **http://jmlinks.com/17p**.

Don't Make Customers Think!

Your customers are busy, harried people. The phone is ringing, the baby is crying, the boss is there waiting outside the office as they search Google for products or services. They're busy, multi-tasking people. The design of your website needs to be easy and non-threatening from the perspective of a customer. If you ponder this "as if" you were "inside" the head of the customer, for example, he would be thinking something like the following (using the example of a person who has *international tax problems* and is looking for a CPA or accountant with knowledge of international tax issues):

1. **Customer identifies a need**. "I have income tax issues with respect to international taxes. I need help doing my bookkeeping and preparing my taxes for state, federal, and international tax compliance."
2. **Customer turns to Google**. "I think I'll search Google for 'international tax accountants' in Oklahoma City, OK" (which is where he lives).
3. **Customer refines his keywords**. "I will type into Google searches such as 'international tax CPA,' 'Accountant for International Tax problems OKC', and 'accounting firm overseas taxation in Oklahoma City.'"
4. **Customer browses Google results**. I will browse the first three or four listings on Google (*ignoring the ads*), and click over to the first website at the top of Google.
5. **Customer clicks FROM Google TO each website**. He thinks to himself, "Hm. This looks interesting! They seem to do international taxes, but I don't know…what else is on this website?"
6. **Customer sees a free offer, or first easy step on the sales ladder**. "Oh look, they have a YouTube video that explains their firm, let me watch that."
7. **Customer takes the next easy, non-threatening step on the sales ladder**. "That was pretty good, but oh look, they have a 'free consultation by phone'

offer. Let me fill out their feedback form with my name, email address, telephone number, and good time to call."

8. **Customer transitions from the Web to human to human interaction**. Ring, ring. "Who is it?" "Jason McDonald Accountants, we see you are interested in our free 20-minute consult." "Yes, I am... I have these international tax problems... blah, blah, blah." (Conversation with the customer begins).

9. **Customer consummates the sale.** Enough trust has been established, and the customer signs up for the service.

At the end of this process from customer *need* to keyword *search query* to *landing* to *browsing* the website to taking the *easy free actions* such as watching a YouTube video and signing up for a free consultation, hopefully the lead turns into a sale. What you want to do for your own company is take out a piece of paper, and outline steps similar to the ones above. Work backward from #9 to #1, and customize the process for your own company, product, and/or service.

You will then see that keywords start the process on Google, but the process (hopefully) ends on your website with a sale or sales lead.

Set up a Focus Group

Don't make them think! Don't make your website hard to navigate! Take a moment and look at your web pages from the perspective of a Google searcher. Does it answer a search question? Is the "next step" or "goal" easy to see? Does it look easy or free to take that "next step"" **Don't make customers think!** Don't make customers hunt for goals, or they'll bounce back to Google and be gone.

Indeed, it's a good idea to get friends, family, or others outside your company to come in as a "focus group" and have them look at your website, and attempt to find your goals. If they struggle, you need to revise your website to make it easy. **KISS:** *keep it simple, stupid* is a good motto for effective website design!

If average people can understand your website, and can clearly see the "next step" that they should take like a free consultation, free webinar, or free eBook download, then your website works. If not, you need to redesign it.

Put it All Together

For your fourth **TO-DO**, open up your "business value proposition worksheet" and brainstorm your desired web landing next steps or goals (registrations and/or sales) as well as your sales ladder, including the possible use of something "free" to make that first step easy for customers.

For extra credit, begin to think about how you will **measure** these goals. As we will learn in Chapter 6.1, you can use Google Analytics to measure goals such as registrations or sales. But you can also use tactics like call tracking software (for a sample call tracking vendor, check out *CallRail* at **http://jmlinks.com/34z**), special toll-free 800 numbers, vanity phone extensions, and offer codes to track whether someone is coming from a Web search to a phone call into your call center.

Goals and measurability go hand-in-hand.

»» CHECKLIST: GOALS ACTION ITEMS

Test your knowledge of goals! Take the *Goals and BVP quiz* at **http://jmlinks.com/qzbv**. Next, here are your goals **Action Items**:

❑ **Define** your business value proposition and write a short, one paragraph summary of it. What do you sell?

❑ Brainstorm and identify your **customer segments** or **personas**. Who wants, what you sell?

❑ Identify **marketing goals** for your website, namely –

❑ **Early stage goals** such as ranking on Google or web traffic.

❑ **Intermediate stage goals** such as registrations for a free giveaway like an eBook or eLetter

❑ **Late stage goals** such as sales leads and/or eCommerce sales

❑ As part of the above, brainstorm what you can give away for "**free**" in exchange for capturing customer names, email addresses, and contact information.

»» DELIVERABLE: A COMPLETED BUSINESS VALUE PROPOSITION WORKSHEET

Now that we've come to the end of Step 1.2, you should have your **DELIVERABLE** ready: a completed **business value proposition worksheet**. This worksheet should define your business value proposition, customer segments, search paths, desired next steps (goals) and your sales ladder, and even how you plan to measure customer progress along the sales ladder. In Chapter 2.1, we will turn to defining your keywords (which builds upon this knowledge), but first let's turn to the "big picture" of how SEO works.

2.1

KEYWORDS

If Step #1 is "Set the Right Expectations," Step #2 is to define your **keywords**. Customers start their quest to "find you" by typing in **keywords** or **key phrases** into Google, Yahoo, or Bing. (For simplicity's sake, I'll use the word *keyword* to mean either a *single* or *multi-word* phrase as a search engine query). Identifying **customer-centric keywords** is the foundation of effective SEO. Your best keywords match your **business value proposition** with **high volume, high-value keywords** used by your customers.

- In **Step 2.1**, we'll brainstorm our list of keywords, focusing on "getting all the words" on paper as a **keyword brainstorm** document.
- In **Step 2.2**, we'll turn to organizing these keywords into a structured **keyword worksheet**.

For now, don't worry about how to *organize* your keywords. Your goal in this Chapter is to *identify* **all** your possible keyword targets on paper; this Chapter is about brainstorming your keyword universe.

Let's get started!

TO-DO LIST:

» Brainstorm Your Keywords

» Use Google Tricks to Identify Possible Keywords

» Reverse Engineer Competitors' Keywords

» Use Free Keyword Discovery Tools

» Understand Some Keyword Theory

»» Checklist: Keyword Action Items

»» Deliverable: Keyword Brainstorm Worksheet

» BRAINSTORM YOUR KEYWORDS

Sit down in a quiet place with a good cup of coffee or tea, or if you prefer, a martini, i.e. *anything to get your ideas flowing!* Your first **TO-DO** is to brainstorm the **keywords** that a customer might type into Google that are relevant to your company, your product, and/or your service. Ask yourself and your team:

When a potential customer sits down at Google, what words do they type in?

Which keywords are DEFINITELY those of your customers?

Which keywords are CLOSE to a decision to buy? Which are farther away, earlier in the customer journey?

Which customer segments or buyer personas use which keywords, and how might keywords differ among your customer segments?

Which keywords match which product or service lines as produced by your company?

Conduct a Keyword Brainstorming Session

Set up a formal **keyword brainstorming session** with your marketing team (it might be just you by yourself, or it might be your CEO, your marketing manager, and a few folks from the sales staff). Devote at least ONE HOUR to brainstorming keywords; close the door, turn off the cell phone, tell your secretary to "hold all calls" and start drinking (either coffee or martinis).

Brainstorm, brainstorm, brainstorm the keywords that customers are typing into Google. Try not to miss any possible keyword combinations!

Do this, first, individually – take out a piece of paper, and write keyword ideas down WITHOUT talking to the others in your group.

Don't be shy. Don't leave anything out. The goal is to get EVERYTHING on paper, no matter how ridiculous it might be.

After folks have written down their ideas one-by-one, have a group session and go over all the keywords each person has identified.

Drink some more coffee, or more martinis, and keep brainstorming – write all possible keywords on a whiteboard, a piece of paper, or a Word / Google document.

Don't censor yourself because there are no wrong answers! The goal of this exercise is to get the complete "universe" of all possible keywords that customers might type into Google.

"Think like a customer" sitting at his or her computer screen at Google:

- **Assume you are a completely new, novice customer.** Assume you know next to nothing. What single words or multi-word phrases (keywords) would you type into Google?
- **Segment your customers into different "buyer personas."** What keywords might each group use, and how would they differ from other groups?
- **Are there are any specific "helper" words that a potential customer might use?** Common helper words specify geographic locality (e.g., "San Francisco," "Berkeley," "San Jose"), for example. Others specify things like "free," "cheap," "trial," or "information."
- **Don't miss your synonyms and adjacent terms!** If you are a "lawyer," don't miss "attorney." If you are a "dry cleaner," don't miss "wash and fold" or "laundry service." If you are an "SEO expert," don't miss "SEO

consultant" or "digital marketing expert." If you are an orthopedic surgeon, don't miss "knee doctor" or "hip specialist."

If you're working with a team in multiple locations or your team members can't all meet at the same time, there's a online tool called "Seed Keywords" at **http://jmlinks.com/29f**. Take each buyer persona or buyer scenario and type it into this tool. Then distribute the URLs to your team to collect their individual ideas as to how a customer might search Google.

To conclude this first **TO-DO**, open up the "keyword brainstorm worksheet" in either Word or PDF, and begin to fill it out as completely as possible. For the worksheet, go to **http://jmlinks.com/seo19tz** (enter the password code "seo19tz' to register if you have not already done so), and click on the link to the "keyword brainstorm worksheet."

For right now, don't worry about the *organization* of your keywords. Don't police your thoughts. Write down every word that comes to mind - synonyms, competitor names, misspellings, alternative word orders. Let your mind wander. This is the keyword discovery phase, so don't exclude anything!

» USE GOOGLE TRICKS TO IDENTIFY POSSIBLE KEYWORDS

With a list of just a few keywords from your brainstorm session, it's time to turn to some Google tricks and tools to beef up your keyword list from these "seed" or "starter" keywords. You can find a complete list of keyword discovery tools in the companion *SEO Toolbook* (*Keywords Chapter*) or on my SEO dashboard (available at **http://jmlinks.com/seodash**), but here are my favorite strategies starting with Google's own free tools.

First, simply go to Google and start typing a keyword. Pay attention to the pull-down menu that automatically appears. This is called **Google Suggest** or **Autocomplete** and is based on actual user queries. It's a quick and easy way to find "helper" words for any given search phrase. You can also place a space (hit your space bar) after your target keyword, and then go through the alphabet typing "a", "b", etc.

Here's a screenshot of **Google Suggest** using the key phrase "motorcycle insurance:"

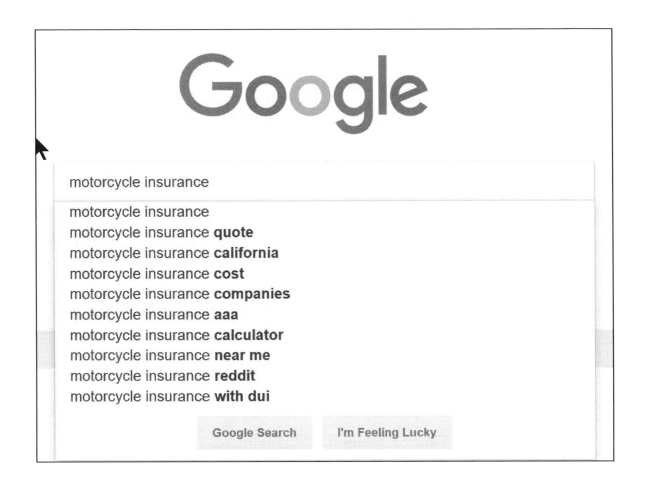

Hit your space key after the last letter of the last keyword (e.g., after *motorcycle insurance*) and more keyword suggestions appear. You can also type the letters of the alphabet – a, b, c, etc. and Google will give you suggestions. Here's a screenshot for the letter "b":

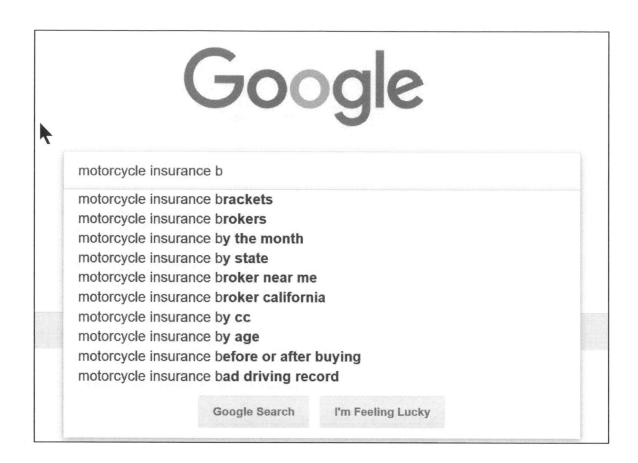

Second, type in one of your target keyword phrases and scroll to the bottom of the Google search page. Google will often give you **related searches** based on what people often search on after their original search. Here's a screenshot of Google's related keywords for "motorcycle insurance" -

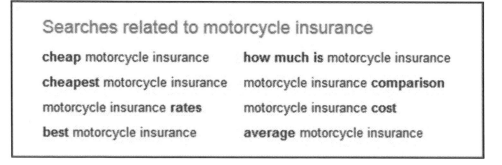

Note the **helper words** it tells you people use to search: *cheap, rates, best, "how much," comparison, cost,* and *average.* These are wonderful clues as to how customers search Google? You can also click on a "related keyword," then hit the space key to see more autocompletes, type in "a," "b," or "c," etc., as well as scroll to the bottom and look at related searches.

In this way, you can use Google autocomplete and related searches to quickly and efficiently brainstorm your keyword list.

Ubersuggest

A fantastic third-party keyword tool is **Ubersuggest** at **http://jmlinks.com/35a**. It basically types through the alphabet for you, and gives you closely related keyword phrases. Here are your steps:

1. Visit Ubersuggest via **http://jmlinks.com/35a**.
2. Type in a "seed" or "starter keyword" such as "motorcycle insurance" in the box.
3. Click on "keyword ideas" on the left.
4. Add relevant keywords to your list.

Ubersuggest also provides volume and CPC (cost per click) data, but for now, just use the tool to formulate keyword ideas. It is especially good at identifying helper words. In the case of "motorcycle insurance" we get "quote," "cost," and "online" for example.

> **VIDEO.** Watch a quick video tutorial on how to use Google autocomplete and related searches to generate keyword ideas at **http://jmlinks.com/18n**.

Keyword Patterns

As you work on your keyword brainstorming session, remember that you're looking for these types of keywords:

- **Core keywords** (often also called starter or seed keywords). These are the minimum necessary to make a relevant search query. Examples would be "knee doctor," "knee surgeon," or "orthopedic surgeon."
- **Synonyms.** These are words that mean essentially the same thing. "Lawyer" vs. "attorney," "doctor" vs. "surgeon" vs. "specialist," "car" vs. "auto" vs. "automobile." It is critical to identify all synonyms as a search for "knee doctors" is not the same as search for "knee surgeons."
- **Helper words.** These are words that are added on to the core keyword or key phrase such as "quote," "online," or "free" in the case of "motorcycle insurance."

You should already begin to see patterns, realizing that helpers can cross many keyword types and that synonyms such as lawyer vs. attorney exist. You should also note that people generally use about 6th-grade level English to type into Google. Almost always, the 6th-grade level word like "knee doctors" will have more volume than the Ph.D. level word like "orthopedic surgeons."

Don't let reality confuse you! A search for "NYC knee doctors" is not the same as a search for "NYC knee surgeons" or "New York City knee specialists" even though "in reality" they are the same thing. We're playing a word game with Google, not a game about reality, and it's a rookie mistake to think that Google will figure out that a website that only mentions "orthopedic surgeon" is also the same thing as one that mentions "knee doctors."

> *Google is a machine, not a mind reader, so you need to capture every relevant word pattern at this phase. Don't miss synonyms or adjacent keywords!*

For your third **TO-DO**, open up your "keyword brainstorm worksheet" and write down the keywords garnered from these free tools. You want a messy, broad and complete list of the "universe" of possible customer keywords via your own brainstorming process, via reverse engineering your competitors, via Google tools such as autocomplete and related searches, and via third-party tools like Ubersuggest.

≫ REVERSE ENGINEER COMPETITORS

After you've completed this first wave of brainstorming, you and your group members should then do some searches on Google for target keywords to identify high-ranking websites. Take a few of the keywords you've already identified, and type them into Google. As you search Google, identify your "Google competitors," that is, companies that are on page one of the Google results and therefore doing well in terms of SEO. You'll want to **reverse engineer** their keywords.

Here are your steps:

1. Type a keyword into Google from your list.
2. Identify the top three or four websites that show up, especially ones that are companies / competitors.
3. Click over to their website, whichever page ranks for the Google query you entered in step one.

Next, you're going to view the HTML source code of their ranking page. Here's how.

First, click over to their homepage or whatever page is showing up on page one of Google for a search that matters to you. Next, view the HTML source code of this page. To do this, in Firefox and Chrome, take your mouse and *right click*, then **View**, **P**age Source. In Internet Explorer, use **View**, **S**ource on the file menu. **CTRL+U** will also pull up the source code for any web page. Finally, find the following tags in the HTML source code:

```
<Title>
<Meta Name="Description" Content="...">
<Meta Name="Keywords" Content="...">
```

If you have trouble finding these HTML tags, use CTRL+F (on a PC) or Command+F (on a Mac) on your keyboard, and in the dialog box type

<title *(to find the TITLE tag) (Note: you need that "<" character!)*

description *(to find the META DESCRIPTION tag)*

or

keywords *(to find the META KEYWORDS tag)*

Note that there are some vagaries in the rules of HTML. So while it's always <Title> for the TITLE tag, the DESCRIPTION or KEYWORDS word can be close to or far away from the word META. So you may have to play around with CTRL+F / find to locate these tags. Also, while every page must have a TITLE tag, not every page will have a META DESCRIPTION or META KEYWORDS tag. Don't worry if you don't find each of these three tags on every page, as not every page follows correct HTML or uses all tags.

And, for now, don't worry about what this tags do. We're just using them as a tool to brainstorm keyword ideas.

Here's a screenshot of **http://www.globalindustrial.com/c/hvac/fans**, one of the top Google performers for the search "industrial fans" with the three critical tags highlighted -

```
<title>Industrial &amp; Pedestal Fans | Global Industrial</title>

    <meta name="category" content="Fans" />

    <meta name="keywords" content="Fans, Industrial Fans, Pedestal Fans,

    <meta name="description" content="Shop for high-quality commercial &
```

In this way, you can take a starter keyword like "industrial fans," find competitors that rank high, look at their HTML source code for TITLE, META DESCRIPTION, and KEYWORD and then identify synonyms and helpers. In this case, we'd go from "industrial fans" to "pedestal fans" with helpers like "quality" and "commercial."

SEOCentro offers a nifty, free tool to analyze META TAGS at **http://jmlinks.com/37w**. Again, do a search, identify a competitor that ranks high on Google, and then take the URL and paste it into this tool. For example, for "motorcycle insurance," this URL ranks in position #3:

https://www.csurance.com/insurance/motorcycle

Then, paste this URL into the tool. Scroll down the results and you get a summary of all the keywords starting with the TITLE and DESCRIPTION and ending with density. Here's a screenshot of the keyword densities for the eSurance page:

Keywords found on page.		
These are keywords found on the web ...s).		
Keywords (one word)	**Freq**	**Density**
insurance	36	3.33%
motorcycle	28	2.59%
coverage	16	1.48%
get	12	1.11%
esurance	11	1.02%
claims	11	1.02%
save	9	0.83%
states	8	0.74%
state	7	0.65%
home	7	0.65%
discounts	7	0.65%
car	7	0.65%
auto	7	0.65%
safety	6	0.55%
homeowners	6	0.55%
policy	6	0.55%
quote	5	0.46%
us	5	0.46%
bike	5	0.46%
renters	5	0.46%

Using this tool, you can quickly "reverse engineer" any competitor on the Web and browse their keywords.

Read Out Loud

As you look at competitor source code and the SEOCentro tool analysis, read the results out loud to your group members. That is, read the <TITLE> tag of your competitor's ranking page, the META DESCRIPTION tag, and the KEYWORDS tag out loud. Read some of the data output from the SEO Centro tool as well.

As you read tags and content out loud, listen for keywords, and keep in mind the question, "Would a customer likely type this into Google?" The goal of viewing the source of your competitors' pages is to "steal" their keyword ideas, and write down any relevant keywords onto your "keyword brainstorm" document.

VIDEO. Watch a quick video tutorial on how to use "view source" to reverse engineer competitors at **http://jmlinks.com/5k**.

A Note about the Keywords Meta Tag

Note that at this point you are just using "View Source" to "reverse engineer" your competitors and their keywords. The TITLE and META DESCRIPTION tag are very important for On Page communication, as they communicate keywords to Google. The META KEYWORDS tag, however, is ignored. That said, many people still use the META KEYWORDS tag and it's a useful window into your competitor's thought process. (*It isn't always in use, so you may not always find it in the HTML source code*). So, at this point, you're just peeking behind the curtain at their keyword targets to double check your own keyword list and identify any keyword patterns you may have missed in our own brainstorming session. Don't worry (yet) about what the HTML tags do, including the fact that the META KEYWORDS tag does nothing.

For your second **TO-DO**, open up your "keyword brainstorm worksheet," and jot down the top five competitors who appear at the top of Google for your target keywords, use the tactics above to view their source, and then write down keyword ideas taken from their TITLE, META DESCRIPTION, and META KEYWORDS tags as well as the SEOCentro tool.

Did you discover any keywords you left out in your first brainstorming session? If so, be sure to write those on your list.

» USE FREE KEYWORD DISCOVERY TOOLS

Now it's time to use some more sophisticated tools. We'll start with the most powerful tool, Google's **Keyword Planner**. Recent changes have meant that you can use only use Google's official Keyword Planner tool, effectively, if you have a **paid** Google Ads (AdWords) account and are actually spending money. So, although we'll first investigate how to use this tool, I will also point you to two alternative keyword tools: the Twinword Ideas keyword tool and Bing's Keyword Planner, which are more open to "free" users.

VIDEO. Watch two quick video tutorials on how to use the Google AdWords Keyword Planner *in general* at **http://jmlinks.com/17j** and *to brainstorm keywords* at **http://jmlinks.com/18m**.

Sign up for AdWords

To use the Keyword Planner you'll need to sign up for Google Ads (formerly known as AdWords) at **https://ads.google.com/**. You'll need a credit card to set up an account. I recommend doing your best to identify relevant keywords, create some ads, and allocate no more than $300 / month for your ads. You just want to fund it with enough money so that *after a few months it will fully share data with you*; then you can de-activate your campaigns.

(You can even call Google Ads at 866-246-6453 and ask them for help on how to set up your advertising campaigns; just set a low budget such as $100 / month). If you're worried about credit card fraud, just go to your local grocery store and get a "gift card" with the VISA logo to set up your Google Ads account. I know it's a bit of a pain, but once you have an operational Google Ads account, you can use the Google Ads Keyword Planner to research SEO keywords. It's a worthwhile investment!

Now, let's return to the Keyword Planner. Here are the steps to access the tool:

1. Log in to your Google Ads account at **https://ads.google.com/**.
2. Find the "wrench" icon at the top right of the screen and click on it.
3. Click on "Keyword Planner" on the left.
4. Click on "Find new keywords"
5. Enter a "core" or "starter" keyword such as "knee doctor".

Once you have entered a "core keyword," the tool gives you a nice list of suggestions including the "average monthly searches." As it is a far from perfect tool and we are only brainstorming keywords, you can ignore everything except the far right column. Scan it to look for:

Synonyms. For example, "knee doctor" vs. "orthopedic surgeon" vs. "knee specialist".

Helper words. For example, "best," "top," and "near me."

Here's a screenshot for "knee doctors."

You can filter by "closely related keywords" as well to zero in on helper words by clicking the "add filter" button and you can sort by "Average monthly searches" to look at volumes. Do not get fixated at volume at this point, however. Look for synonyms first and foremost, and then for helper words.

As you brainstorm, keep in mind the distinctions among keyword types as well:

> **Educational or early stage keywords.** These are words like "knee replacement" or Knee surgery" in which the searcher is just beginning to learn about the topic and is not necessarily close to a buy decision or engagement.

> **Transactional keywords.** These are words like "knee specialists" or "knee doctors Boston" that indicate they're close to a buy decision or engagement.

> **Branded or reputational searches.** These are searches for individual companies or, in this case, doctors, and indicate searches just before an engagement. "Reviews" is a very common helper word.

I'll return to these distinctions in a moment, but for now, just start to wrap your head around how a search for "knee pain" is an early stage search query while a search for "best knee doctors in St. Louis" is a late stage search query, close to a buy or engagement decision. It is the latter that are most valuable for SEO.

Don't Miss Your Synonyms and Adjacent Terms!

Notice how the tool gives you both *helper* words and *synonyms*. For example, you get *best* knee replacement, telling you that *best* is a helper word, and you get *doctor* as well as *surgeon*, *orthopedic* as well as *knee*. The tool is telling you how people search: some people search for *knee doctors*, and others for *orthopedic surgeons*. Many people search for *best* knee surgeons (and to the contrary, few search for *worst* knee surgeons). Because to Google *a word is just a word*, you want to be sure to capture ALL your key synonyms. A search for "best knee doctor in San Francisco" is different from a search for "best orthopedic surgeon in San Francisco," even though the latter may include the former, i.e. many people searching for orthopedic surgeons who do knees. This is true across all domains;

a *lawyer*, to Google, is not the same as an *attorney*. In summary be sure to identify all your helpers and synonyms, and write these down on your Keyword Brainstorm Worksheet.

Revert to the Old Tool

Google has a knack for taking out really useful features as it "upgrades" its tools. It's very frustrating and is a constant reminder to me to never set foot in a Google self-driving vehicle nor get in front or in back of one. Despite Google's brand identity as an all-knowing tech company, its tools are sloppy and disorganized. *Go figure.*

So click back up wrench icon, and then "Keyword planner" on the left. Then find the link to "Open previous Keyword Planner" which at the time of this writing was still available. The old interface was better and had some nifty features which are not yet in the new tool and which I hope that Google, in its infinite wisdom, does not abolish. Once there, click on "Search for new keywords using a phrase, website, or category" and enter in your "core keyword" such as "knee doctors" and then the blue "get ideas" button. This gets you into the old interface.

Here, you can do some neat tricks to learn more about your keyword universe. Since we're focusing on discovery, click on the "Ad group ideas" tab. Here's a screenshot:

Find keywords	Review plan		
Ad group ideas	**Keyword ideas**		
Ad group (by relevance)			**Avg. monthly searches** [?]
Knee Specialist (45) knee specialist, knee specialist near me, kne…		〰	8,700
Total Knee (12) total knee replacement, total knee replacem…		〰	16,700
Orthopedic Surgeons (15) orthopedic surgeon, orthopedic hand surgeo…		〰	121,360
Orthopedic Doctors (20) orthopedic doctor, orthopedic surgeon doctor…		〰	54,860
Replacement Surgery (34) knee replacement surgery, knee replacemen…		〰	31,280

Google's "Ad group ideas" are a quick and easy way to identify synonyms and adjacent terms. So, starting with "knee doctors," it gives us "knee specialist" as well as "orthopedic surgeons," which are both wonderful synonyms for this pattern. Note how "knee specialist" is a synonym, while "orthopedic surgeons" which means someone who might do hips, knees, and shoulders is an adjacent term.

Your job is to first identify these terms and then ask whether they represent what you sell or not. Some terms will be "hot," that is dead on for what you sell, while others will be "cold," meaning an adjacent terms that is just so-so. Some will be micro searches – very specific, and some will be macro searches, groups "up" the hierarchy that include what you do but also other thing. A knee surgeon is an orthopedic surgeon, but so is a hip surgeon, and so on and so forth. It's a word game, so pay attention to the patterns of words.

Even better, you can click into a group and see helpers for that group. If you click on "Knee specialist," for example, here's a screenshot:

Ad group: **Knee Specialist**		
←		
Keyword (by relevance)		**Avg. monthly searches** [?]
knee specialist ▼	∿	3,600
knee specialist near me	∿	1,900
knee pain specialist	∿	170
orthopedic knee specialist	∿	260
knee doctor specialist	∿	260

You can easily see that "near me" is a helper word indicating geography and then with a little brainstorming you'll realize people search for "San Francisco," "Oakland," and "Bay Area" when searching for a knee specialist. Note that my account is receiving exact data for "Average monthly searches," while if you have a brand new account, you might just be receiving data ranges. This is why it pays to advertise on Google ads; you get more complete data in the tool.

Refocusing the Keyword Planner

You may notice that the tool gives you very broad and often irrelevant keyword suggestions, so I often recommend that you refocus it to just your target phrase and related phrases. To do this, on the left-hand column where it says "Keyword Options," click there, and then select "Only show ideas closely related to my search terms" by moving the blue button to "on" and clicking on the blue "save" button. Here's a screenshot:

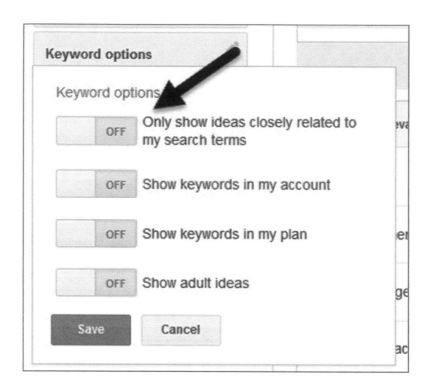

Once you click "off" to "on" for "Only show ideas closely related to my search terms," you've reset the Keyword Planner to zero in on more specific keywords. The old interface tool will also give you data comparing keywords to each other by volume and value. To do so, type a string of keywords into the tool such as:

knee pain, knee surgery, knee surgeons

Here's a screenshot of the data returned:

Ad group ideas	Keyword ideas			Co
Search terms		Avg. monthly searches [?]	Competition [?]	Suggested bid [?]
knee pain	〰	165,000	Medium	$1.50
knee surgery	〰	12,100	Medium	$5.36
knee surgeon	〰	1,600	Medium	$5.46

You can see that there are 165,000 searches per month for "knee pain" vs. 12,100 for "knee surgery" and just 1,600 for "knee surgeon." (**Note that these search volumes refer to exact match only: they take into account only when a searcher enters that phrase and nothing more.**)

Other tools such as the Bing Webmaster Tools keyword tool, the Twinword Ideas tool, or robust paid tools such as those offered by MOZ.com or AHREFS.com keyword tools also give us keyword ideas, volumes, and bids or "values."

What does this data tell us?

⏩ UNDERSTAND SOME KEYWORD THEORY

As you're drinking martinis or coffee, brainstorming with your teammates, using Google and other keyword tools, and doing search after search on Google, you want to wrap your head around the fact that you're playing a word game with Google. First and foremost, it's all about what are the search queries typed in by customers (or spoken by customers to their phones or Google devices). Visualize a buyer persona, grasp his pain point or desire, and research those search queries he'll type into Google.

> **That's the key point of keyword research: getting a comprehensive yet laser-focused understanding of the keywords used by customers.**

Next, however, with all your keywords jotted down on a whiteboard, Google doc, or Word doc, it's time to begin to understand some keyword theory. Just as if you were playing Scrabble or Words with Friends, you'd want to know that the "x" is worth more than the "e" and that the word "xylophone" is worth more than the word "everyman," you need to understand that in SEO, not all keywords have the same value.

To understand what this all means, let's use an analogy: **fishing** and **fish**. As the SEO technician, you're the **fisherman** of course.

First, you want to "fish where the fish are." Let's review the previous screenshot from the Google Keyword Planner:

Ad group ideas	Keyword ideas			Co
Search terms		Avg. monthly searches [?]	Competition [?]	Suggested bid [?]
knee pain		165,000	Medium	$1.50
knee surgery		12,100	Medium	$5.36
knee surgeon		1,600	Medium	$5.46

Note that it says the "Average monthly searches" is 165,000 for "knee pain" vs. 12,100 for "knee surgery." This is called **volume**, and it corresponds to "where the fish are." Generally speaking, you want to optimize on keywords that have a fair amount of volume, just as if you are a fisherman, you want to "fish where the fish are."

But it's not just about **volume**, it's also about **value**. Take a look at the "Suggested bid" column and you'll see that while advertisers are willing to pay just $1.50 for a click from Google to their website for "knee pain," they'll pay four times more or $5.36 for "knee surgery" and $5.46 for "knee surgeon." All of the paid tools, and not just the Google tool, will give you some type of column called CPC or "Cost per click." Remember that Google makes its money off of advertising through an auction system. Advertisers compete in the Google Ads auction to get clicks FROM Google TO their website. They're spending money via advertising to make money; and the crowd isn't stupid. It will bid **UP** the value or cost-per-click of keywords that are likely to end in a sale and likely to end in a profitable sale and bid **DOWN** the value or cost-per-click of keywords that are just tire-kickers or not likely to end in a sale.

It's easy to see this in a fish market. Go into Whole Foods or your local fish market, and you'll notice that the price per pound of Tilapia (sort of a garbage, farmed fish) isn't very expensive, while the price of wild Salmon is quite expensive. Farmed Tilapia might be $2.99 a pound, farmed Salmon might be $9.99 a pound, and wild Salmon might be $19.99 a pound. Consumers are bidding "up" the price per pound of yummy, healthy fish and bidding "down" the price of not-so-yummy and not-so-healthy fish. In addition, in terms of quantity or volume, there's a lot of farmed Tilapia and farmed Salmon to be had and (unfortunately) not a lot of wild Salmon due to overfishing. Scarcity also plays a role in the supply and demand of the fish market.

So it goes with keywords. Advertisers are bidding up keywords like "knee surgery" or "knee surgeon" because these are likely to end in a very expensive sale or engagement (a knee surgery can cost upwards of $75,000), while bidding down keywords like "knee pain" because these are likely to end in, at most, the purchase of an aspirin or ibuprofen which costs less than $1. The CPC column, in other words, is a clue as to the **value** of keywords. This is why advertisers are willing to pay just $1.50 for a click from Google to their website for "knee pain," but they'll pay four times more or $5.36 for "knee surgery" and $5.46 for "knee surgeon."

As you look at your keywords, therefore, you can start to identify those keywords that are high value vs. those that are high volume. You'll also see there's a trade-off, just as in the fish market. Generally, the higher the volume, the lower the value and vice-versa. But you're looking for keywords that have sufficient value and sufficient volume for your keyword plan.

Secret Fishing Holes are Best

Indeed, you're looking for "secret fishing holes." If you find keywords that have good volume and are high value TO YOU, meaning they are likely to convert to sales or sales leads FOR YOU but have not been "discovered," these are very good keywords! This means a keyword that is "nichey," that gets at exactly what you have to offer and yet isn't so discovered by the crowd that the price (and competition in SEO) hasn't yet been bid up.

For example, there are many hypnotherapists. Most focus on weight loss, anxiety, and smoking cessation. But suppose you use Ericksonian hypnosis, which is a special kind of hypnosis based on indirect and metaphoric suggestions. People who know something about hypnosis may be drawn to this methodology and might search for:

Boston Ericksonian hypnotherapists

This "nichey" keyword isn't completely discovered. It's a "secret fishing hole" that very tightly matches what you have, that they want. It will be easier to rank for, and you'll more easily convert people who click from Google to your website.

Riches are in the niches.

Be on the lookout for "secret fishing holes."

To use a different example, a knee surgeon who specializes in knee surgery for athletes or arthroscopic knee surgery, for instance, may have found a highly specialized and lucrative niche. It's not all about volume, after all. It's about value. And it's not all about value to the crowd, it's about value to you as a business, meaning which searches really indicate a person who is very hot for your product or service and very likely to buy.

Back to our fishing examples:

The worst thing to do is to fish where there aren't any fish.

The next worst thing to do is to fish for low-quality fish that aren't good to eat.

The next worst thing to do is to fish where all the other fisherfolk are competing against you.

The smartest and most wonderful thing to do is to discover a "secret fishing hole" and keep it secret.

More on Educational vs. Transactional Keywords

Another way to look at this issue is to focus on keywords that are *early* in the sales ladder occur usually when a person is just learning, just educating himself about an issue and not likely to buy something. These are called **educational keywords** and generally have low cost-per-click in AdWords. Keywords that occur *late* in the sales ladder are when they are looking to buy something, or make an engagement. These are called **transactional keywords** and generally have high cost-per-click in AdWords. In general, you want to optimize for transactional keywords as they are "where the money is."

> **VIDEO.** Watch a quick video tutorial on distinguishing educational vs. transactional keywords, volume vs. value at **http://jmlinks.com/18k**. .

You're **best SEO** occurs at focused, transactional keywords, not educational keywords. You're looking for the "sweet spot" between volume and value, education and transaction.

Let me emphasize this:

Identify and optimize for transactional, late stage, high-value keywords.

I, Jason McDonald, do not want to be at the top of Google for "SEO." But I do want to be at the top of Google for "SEO Expert San Francisco." Why? Because the former is an early stage, low-value educational search, while the latter is a late stage, high-value transactional search: someone who wants to hire me as a high-paid consultant.

A knee surgeon wants to be at the top of Google for "San Francisco Knee Surgeons" and not for "knee pain," because the former are potential patients looking for knee surgery and the latter could be practically anyone with a sore knee and just needing an aspirin.

That said, you still need to rely on your instinct to determine your best keywords and then bolster that with real data from your Google Analytics, which we discuss in the last Chapter. The Keyword Planner is only a tool, and the art of SEO still means a lot of head-scratching to identify those keywords that are not just high volume but also high value.

Micro Search Queries

"Niche" keywords aren't just long tail (multiword), either. A Los Angeles watch repair shop focusing on high-end watch repair, might optimize for "Watch Repair Los Angeles" (lots of *volume*, but low in *value* as it may be people who just need a battery or have a Timex they want repaired). But a little research will identify brand-oriented searches such as "Rolex Repair LA," "Breitling Repair Los Angeles," or "Tag Heuer Repair LA." People who know their brand and are looking for an expert in repairing that brand are likely to convert; watch repair "riches" are in the "niches" of brand-oriented search queries.

Alternatives to the Keyword Planner

As I've indicated, Google now requires that you spend money to get accurate data out of the Keyword Planner. Accordingly, my recommendation is to allocate a hundred dollars per month to Google AdWords and run some actual ads for your keywords for three months. For less than $300 or so, you'll then be able to use the Keyword Planner for keyword discovery, and Google Ads gives you the absolute best data about actual search queries. (Once you've done your research, you can turn off your Google Ads campaigns).

If you don't have a few hundred dollars to pay to Google for AdWords, then I recommend you use one (or all) of the following free keyword tools: Bing Webmaster

Tools' Keyword Tool (**http://jmlinks.com/19g**) or the Twinword Ideas tool (**http://jmlinks.com/47a**). Here's a screenshot from the Twinword Ideas tool for "knee doctors":

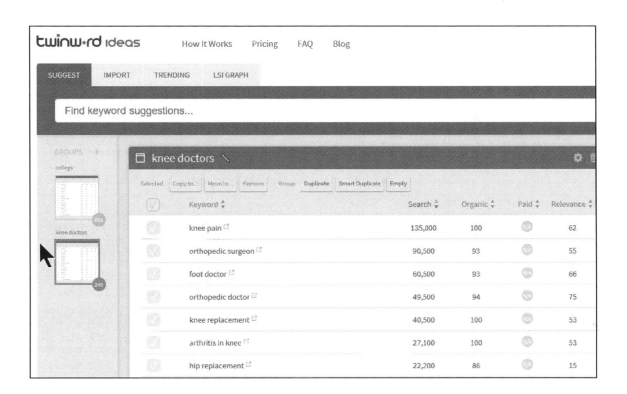

Like the Keyword Planner, this tool gives you keyword ideas, helpers, volumes, and value. Paid tools such as AHREFS.com or the MOZ.com tools also have robust functionality. For a little money, whether spent on Google Ads or on a paid tool, you can get access to keyword synonyms, helpers, volumes, and value as measured by the CPC (Cost per click) advertiser are willing to pay.

> **VIDEO.** Watch a video tutorial on alternatives to the Google AdWords Keyword Planner at **http://jmlinks.com/19d**.

Get ALL Your Keyword Ideas Down on Paper

For your final **TO-DO**, open up your "keyword brainstorm worksheet," and jot down keyword volumes and the CPC values of relevant keywords. Again, don't worry about being organized. Just indicate – in general – which keywords are higher volume vs. higher value, which ones are educational vs. transactional. It won't be a perfect map, but you will start to see patterns as to volume and value.

»» CHECKLIST: KEYWORD ACTION ITEMS

Test your knowledge of keywords! Take the *keyword quiz* at **http://jmlinks.com/qzkb**. Next, here are your keyword **Action Items**:

❑ Hold a **keyword brainstorming session** with your team, and write down your "starter keywords" based on your knowledge of what potential customers type into Google.

❑ Use **Google autocomplete, UberSuggest.io**, and Google's **related searches** to build out your keyword list based on your "starter keywords."

❑ Identify **competitors** who rank for Google on your keywords, visit their websites, view their HTML source code and use their TITLE, META DESCRIPTION, and KEYWORDS tags to help you identify the complete universe of keyword relevant to your business.

❑ Use the **Keyword Planner** or **alternative free or paid Keyword Tools** to look for ideas, volumes, and values as you build out your keyword list.

❑ Begin to **organize keywords into logical groups** with core keywords and helper keywords, with an eye to their **volume** vs. **value** data.

❑ Be on the lookout for "**niche**" or "**micro**" keywords that indicate high-value search queries by customers who are late in the sales ladder and likely to make a purchase. "Riches are in the niches."

Check out the **free tools**! Go to my *SEO Dashboard > Keywords* for my favorite free tools for keyword discovery. Just visit **http://jmlinks.com/seodash**.

▶▶ DELIVERABLE: A COMPLETED KEYWORD BRAINSTORM WORKSHEET

Now we've come to the end of Step 2.1, and you should have the Chapter **DELIVERABLE** ready: your completed **keyword brainstorm worksheet**.

Remember the "Keyword Brainstorm" document will be messy. Its purpose is to get all relevant keywords, helper words, and keyword ideas about volume and value down on paper. In Step 2.2, we will turn to **organizing** our keywords into a structured **keyword worksheet**.

YOUR SAMPLE TEXT

YOUR SAMPLE TEXT YOUR SAMPLE TEXT YOUR SAMPLE TEXT

2.2

KEYWORD WORKSHEET

Now that you have a keyword **brainstorm document**, it's time to get organized! Step #2.2 is all about taking your *disorganized* list of keywords and turning them into an *organized*, structured **keyword worksheet** that reflects your **keyword groups** as well as keyword **volume** and **value**. You'll use your keyword worksheet as your "SEO blueprint" for many tasks, such as measuring your rank on Google, structuring your website to tell Google which keywords matter to you, writing better blog posts and so on. In my method of doing SEO, I emphasize that it is <u>absolutely essential</u> that your company create and use a keyword worksheet to guide your SEO efforts.

Do not skip this step!

The **DELIVERABLES** for Step 2.2 are your **keyword worksheet** as well as a **rank measurement / baseline** of where your website ranks for target keywords searches on Google.

Let's get started!

TO-DO LIST:

» Identify Your Main Keyword Groups

» Create Your Keyword Worksheet

»» Deliverable: Your Keyword Worksheet

» Measure Your Google Rank vs. Keywords

»» Deliverable: Rank Measurement and a Baseline Score

»» Checklist: Keyword Worksheet Action Items

» IDENTIFY YOUR MAIN KEYWORD GROUPS

After you complete your keyword brainstorm worksheet, your head may be spinning (*especially if you and your team were drinking martinis rather than coffee as the elixir of choice during the brainstorm exercise*). Now it's time to shift gears and to organize those keywords into **"keyword groups"** with an eye to both keyword volume and value.

Here's where we're going:

> **Brainstorm** *your keywords* > **organize** *them by* **keyword group** *into a keyword worksheet* > **measure** *your* **rank** *on Google / Bing for sample keywords* > **restructure** *your website to better "talk to Google" vis-à-vis your keyword patterns.*

Let's look at some example websites.

Most businesses have a few different product or service lines, and often a few different customer segments. Take a look at Progressive Insurance (**https://www.progressive.com/**), for example, and you'll quickly realize that they have different types of insurance offered such as auto insurance, motorcycle insurance, RV insurance, and even Segway insurance. Take a look at **https://www.progressive.com/insurance/** as well as **https://www.progressive.com/sitemap/** to see the organizational structure of their website, and you'll quickly realize that the "structure" of the website reflects the "structure" of how people search for insurance. Those who are on a Harley-Davidson motorcycle are searching in one way, and those looking to ensure their Segway are searching in another.

So in terms of **keyword groups** and **matching landing pages**, we have:

> *motorcycle insurance* = a group of keywords around *motorcycle insurance* like *cheap motorcycle insurance, motorcycle insurance quote*, etc. = a landing page on the website.

Car insurance = a group of keywords around *car insurance* like *cheap car insurance, automobile insurance, car insurance quote*, etc. = a landing page on the website.

Segway insurance = a group of keywords around *Segway insurance* like *cheap Segway insurance, people mover insurance*, etc. = a landing page on the website.

etc.

Outline a Hierarchy of Your Keywords

If you think of keywords as living in "keyword groups" inside a **hierarchy**, you can actually sketch out a **structural hierarchy** to your website. If you worked at Progressive Insurance, for example, you'd have a hierarchy like this:

Home Page: introduce the major keyword themes of the website around "insurance," and then:

> **Landing Page**: "Motorcycle Insurance"

> Informational / blog posts: additional pages on "motorcycle insurance" such as "unique motorcycle coverages," etc.

> **Landing Page**: "Car Insurance"

> Informational / blog posts:" additional pages on "Car insurance" such as "comparing types of auto insurance coverage," etc.

> **Landing Page**: "Segway Insurance"

> Informational / blog posts:" additional pages on "Segway insurance" such as "types of Segway coverage," etc.

If you pay attention to the URL structure of the website, you can also see how the organization of the URLs follows the keyword groups:

https://www.progressive.com/ - "homepage"

https://www.progressive.com/auto/ - "auto insurance group"

https://www.progressive.com/auto/discounts/snapshot/ - "subordinate page"

https://www.progressive.com/auto/discounts/compare-car-insurance-rates/ - "subordinate page"

etc.

In other words, Progressive has conceptualized their keywords into a structured keyword worksheet that reflects "core" keywords and related "helper" keywords and phrases, and then implemented a highly organized website hierarchy that literally reflects this.

Your key to-do is to take your keywords and organize them into a **hierarchy** *because Google (run by engineers) prefers websites that have a clear organization.*

Here's a diagram of a very common and effective SEO-friendly, hierarchical **website structure** that reflects how people search:

Homepage

Landing Page #1 (Core keyword #1)

Sub landing page #1a (Core keyword plus helper #1a)

Sub landing page #1b (Core keyword plus helper #1b)

Landing Page #2 (Core keyword #2)

Sub landing page #2a (Core keyword plus helper #2a)

Sub landing page #2b (Core keyword plus helper #2b)

Blog

Blog post #1a (on a micro topic)

Blog post #1b (on a micro topic)

Of course, there will be other pages on your website that are "for humans," but in terms of SEO optimization, you can't really do better than a simple category- and subcategory-based hierarchy. In Chapter 3.2, we'll return to this topic and discuss the need for a keyword footer, sitemap, and "link-sculpting" to connect all your pages together around your keyword themes. But for now, start to look at your keywords and organize them into categories and subcategories as you might for *animals > mammals > rodents* and *animals > mammals > canines*, etc.

SEO Silos

Bruce Clay, one of the gurus of the SEO industry, has coined the term "SEO Silos" to explain how keyword structure should determine website architecture. You can read an excellent article by Clay entitled, "SEO Siloing: How to build a website silo architecture," at **http://jmlinks.com/37u**.

KEYWORD HIERARCHY = WEBSITE ORGANIZATION

Another example of a well-designed hierarchy is Industrial Fans Direct (**http://www.industrialfansdirect.com/**). Take a look at their website, and you'll see that they have product categories such as blowers, man coolers, ceiling, bathroom fans, etc., and that these reflect the "needs" of consumers who "search Google" using words that reflect those needs.

blowers = a group of keywords around *blowers* = a landing page on the website.

roof exhaust = a group of keywords around *roof exhaust* = a landing page on the website.

etc.

As on Progressive.com, you see coherent URLs that reflect the keyword hierarchy:

https://www.industrialfansdirect.com/

> **https://www.industrialfansdirect.com/collections/blowers-and-blower-fans**
>
>> **https://www.industrialfansdirect.com/collections/blowers-and-blower-fans/low-pressure-volume-blowers**
>>
>> **https://www.industrialfansdirect.com/collections/blowers-and-blower-fans/inflation-blowers**
>
> etc.

If you look carefully at the top left quadrant of each web page, you'll also see that the subordinate pages have a **"breadcrumb trail"** which is a hierarchical set of links up and down the categories. Here's a screenshot:

HOME ▶ BLOWERS & BLOWER FANS ▶ LOW PRESSURE VOLUME BLOWERS

Again, if you were privy to their internal documentation, I am sure that we'd find a Keyword Worksheet that is guiding the structure of the website from homepage to landing pages ("core keyword groups") to sub-landing pages (subordinate keyword phrases).

If you're using WordPress, there are easy plugins that will create a hierarchical breadcrumb trail for your website (see **http://jmlinks.com/47b**).

Organize Your Keywords into a Keyword Worksheet

With these examples in mind, it's time to revisit your own keyword patterns, and transform your *disorganized keyword brainstorm document* into an *organized* **keyword worksheet**. First, circle the "core keywords" that reflect your basic product or service categories. Usually you'll see a one-to-one correspondence of a "product group" that matches a "core keyword," as you see in the examples above. These "core keywords" become your "keyword groups." Second, you'll also see a bunch of helper words like *cheap, best, San Francisco, quote, rate,* etc., that are often entered alongside the core keyword. Third, look for phrases that combine a "core keyword" with a "helper keyword" to make a phrase. These become the "subordinate keyword groups" in a child-to-parent relationship to the "keyword groups" above them.

Taking as our example, Commuter Cleaners (**http://www.commutercleaners.com/**), you'll see

Core Keyword	Dependent Phrases
Dry Cleaning	dry cleaning Stamford, dry cleaning Greenwich, specialty dry cleaning, same day dry cleaning, etc., as well as helper words like "best" or "top-rated."
Home Pickup & Delivery Dry Cleaning	home pickup and delivery dry cleaning Stamford, Greenwich home pick up dry cleaning, etc., as well as helper words like "best" or "top-rated."

Wash and Fold	wash and fold Stamford, wash and fold New Canaan, etc., as well as helper words like "best" or "top-rated."
Specialty Cleaning	purse cleaning, leather cleaning, wedding dress cleaning, fur cleaning, etc., plus city names like Stamford or New Canaan as well as helper words like "best" or "top-rated."

Remember: a "core keyword" is the minimum necessary to make a logical search, and it is often more than one word. So it's:

dry cleaning (not *dry* or *cleaning* alone) (and *dry cleaner* as a close synonym)

wash and fold (not *wash* or *fold* alone)

and even

home pick up dry cleaning, home pickup and delivery dry cleaning to represent the very high-value service of when Commuter Cleaners literally picks up, cleans, and then redelivers your dry cleaning and wash straight to your home. (It's OK to combine very closely related words into one keyword group).

Throughout, there would be helpers such as *best, top, top-rated, Stamford, Greenwich, local, same-day*, etc. Notice how some of these are qualifiers (like best, top, top-rated) and others are geographics (like Stamford, Greenwich, local, or near me). Many companies have this sort of pattern, and end up with what I call "service line" landing pages (e.g., "wash and fold"), and geographic landing pages (e.g., "Stamford CT").

Remember: "don't let reality confuse you!"

How so?

Well, though Commuter Cleaners doesn't actually do "wash and fold," consumers still search for that service. In their brain is the idea that they want to get someone else to do their laundry, and they know the word pattern, "wash and fold." They might not know the word pattern, "home pickup and delivery laundry," so the Commuter Cleaners website reaches out to them on the keywords that they actually search. The searcher is never wrong, and in Google's universe "lawyer" is different from "attorney," and "laundry service" is different from "wash and fold service." Even "SF" is different from "San Francisco" and "NYC" from "New York."

Words matter because you're playing a word game, not a reality game.

Similarly, "specialty cleaning" doesn't correspond one-to-one with keyword searches like "purse cleaning" or "leather cleaning" but it's close enough to be the "parent" of that "family." The point is that the core keywords are like the "parent" in a keyword "family," so that "specialty cleaning" is the "parent" to the "children," i.e., "purse cleaning," "wedding dress cleaning," and "fur cleaning." And, because this is a local business, we realize we need to "pepper and salt" the city names Stamford, Greenwich, New Canaan, Port Chester, etc., throughout the content of the website. Why? Because people often search for "specialty dry cleaners" plus a city, as for example, "specialty dry cleaners Norwalk."

Indeed, because **city searches** are incredibly important to this website, the website sports city-specific landing pages such as **http://www.commutercleaners.com/lp-norwalk_ct/** in order to rank for searches such as "Norwalk specialty dry cleaners" on Google and Bing. (Note: do not overdo these "city" search pages, as technically speaking, they can be considered "doorway pages" (**http://jmlinks.com/37v**) by Google!)

In short, a keyword group isn't entirely driven by reality. It's driven by a group of interrelated keywords that you want to rank for, some of which exist in reality and some of which do not. It's about linguistic patterns, not reality, so put your linguistic thinking cap on as you outline your keyword worksheet.

How Many Core Keywords do You Have?

People often mistakenly think that they have "hundreds" of keywords, when in fact they usually have only about five to ten **core keyword groups** or **structural patterns**, and these then form hundreds of possible keyword queries. As on *Progressive.com*, *IndustrialFans.com,* and *CommuterCleaners.com,* as listed above, you'll see that a core keyword should become one, and only one, landing page on the website.

Let me repeat that:

> **One *core keyword* will (ultimately) become one *landing page* on your website.**

Looking at keywords for SEO in terms of core keywords makes it easy to see that a company will usually have about five to ten *core keywords*, and about five to ten corresponding *landing pages* on the website. (I explain landing pages in more detail in Chapters 3.1 and 3.2).

Keyword Volume and Value

As for keyword *volume* and *value*, you'll then see that you take a core keyword and you can look at the volume of the entire "cluster" of keywords around it, as well as the value as measured in Google's Keyword Planner or other keyword tools that reflects the "value" of these keywords in the sense that they are likely, or not, to end in a sale.

> **Volume** = are there a lot, or just a few, searches on Google that reflect the core keyword and its dependent phrases?

> **Value** = if a searcher enters any one of the search queries in the cluster, is it of high, or low value, to your company, as measured in the likelihood that it can become a sale, and if it becomes a sale that that sale makes you a lot (vs. a little) of money?

Essentially, any keyword that has sufficient volume AND sufficient value as to be a likely customer should become a landing page. You should create landing pages for:

Core keywords. These are keywords with sufficient volume and value.

Micro / high value. These are very nichey keywords that are of such high value as to be a likely sale and/or a high-value sale even if they do not have very high value.

Long tail / high value. These are very nichey keywords that are of such high value as to be a likely sale and/or a high-value sale even if they do not have very high value.

Your blog posts will become long tail keywords and other long tail patterns (or micro patterns) that are odds and ends, but not keywords that rise to the level of evergreen, high-value keywords. At this point in your SEO project, keep one eye looking forward to your website organization but realize that, for now, you're lumping together your keywords into core keywords, micro keywords, and long tail keywords and placing them in a hierarchy on your keyword worksheet.

For your first **TO-DO**, download the **keyword worksheet**. For the worksheet, go to **http://jmlinks.com/seo19tz** (then re-enter the passcode "seo19tz"), and click on the link to the "keyword worksheet." Note this is a Microsoft Excel document but can be converted to a Google spreadsheet.

VIDEO. Watch a video tutorial on how to create a Keyword Worksheet at **http://jmlinks.com/17m**.

Inside the document, list each major pattern of your keywords (which reflect a product or service grouping of your company) on a line all by itself in the first column. Return to the Google AdWords Keyword Planner (or other keyword tool) and note both the keyword volume and keyword value (suggested bid) that correspond to each core keyword.

» CREATE YOUR KEYWORD WORKSHEET

Now it's time to fill out your keyword worksheet in more detail. In your spreadsheet, you'll be filling out columns for the following:

Core Keywords. These are the minimum words necessary to create a relevant search. If you are a watch repair shop servicing high-end watches, for example, your core keywords would be phrases such as "watch repair," "Tag Heuer Repair," "Rolex Repair," etc. This is the first column, and reflects the core, structural keyword patterns and indicates volume and value.

> **Note.** If, to your business, a phrase is important enough (e.g., *Rolex watch repair* vs. *Tag Heuer watch repair* vs. just *watch repair*), then break it out into its own core keyword group / line item on your keyword worksheet. Do this even if these words are closely related (e.g., Rolex repair vs. Hamilton repair vs. Tag Heuer repair for watches).

Helper Keywords. Common helpers are geographics like San Francisco, Berkeley, and Oakland. In the watch examples above, other helpers would be "best," "authorized," "NYC" etc. that combine with the core keywords to make the actual search query (e.g., "Best watch repair NYC" or "authorized Rolex repair NYC").

Sample Search Query Phrases. Take your core keywords plus your helpers and build out some "real" search queries that potential customers might use. Group these by keyword family. For example, you'd have a keyword group called "Rolex Repair" and underneath, related keyword phrases such as "Rolex Repair NYC," "Authorized Rolex Repair Midtown," or "Best Rolex Repair Shop New York," etc.

Search Volumes. Indicate the volume of searches (where available) as obtained from the Google AdWords Keyword Planner.

Search Value. Indicate whether a given keyword family is of high, low, or negative value to you and your business. Does it indicate a searcher who is probably a target customer? If your answer is strongly yes, then this is a "high value" search term! Does it clearly indicate a non-customer? If so, this is a "low value" or even a "negative" search term. I often mark "hot," "warm," or "cold" next to a keyword group.

Competitors. As you do your searches, write down the URL's of competitors that you see come up in your Google searches. These will be useful as mentors that you can emulate as you build out your SEO strategy.

Negative Keywords. Are there any keywords that indicate someone is definitely not your customer? Common examples are *cheap* or *free*, as these are often indicative of people with little or no money, or little or no intention to buy something. *(These negative keywords are not so important for SEO, but if you engage in AdWords, they will become very useful.)*

Priority Order

Not all keywords are created equally. Some are **high volume** (*lots of searches*), and some are **high value** (*they are customers ready to buy something, or take an important action like filling out a feedback form, or calling with an inquiry*). With respect to your business, take a look at your keyword worksheet and think about which queries are a) the *most likely* to be a potential sale, b) the *most likely* to be a high-value sale, and c) the *least likely* to be ambiguous. (An ambiguous or problematic keyword is one that has several meanings, that might cross business products or services, and is, therefore, more difficult to optimize on than an unambiguous keyword. Compare *fan* for example, which could be a *hand fan*, an enthusiast for a *sports team*, or an *electrical appliance* to *blow air* with *insurance* which refers to one, and only one, type of product.)

VIDEO. Watch a video tutorial on educational vs. transactional, volume vs. value keyword theory at **http://jmlinks.com/17n**.

Prioritize Your Keywords: Hot, Warm, or Cold?

Prioritize your keyword families on the spreadsheet from TOP to BOTTOM with the highest priority keywords at the top, and the lowest at the bottom.

Remember the *volume* vs. *value* trade-off. "Transactional" keywords (those close to a sale) tend to have higher *value*, but lower *volume*; whereas "educational" keywords (those early in the research process) tend to have lower *value*, but higher *volume*.

However, here's the rub: because of the see-saw between value and volume, there is no hard and fast rule as to what should be your top priority. It can't be just *volume*, and it can't just be *value*.

In fact, I recommend you use a column on the far left and call it "hot / warm / cold." Sit down with the CEO or sales staff, and play a "hot / warm / cold" game by asking IF a customer entered such-and-such into Google, would it be hot (*definitely our customer*), warm (*probably our customer*), or cold (*not our customer*)?

Prioritize the "hot" keywords at the top of the Keyword Worksheet, and the "warm" keywords towards the bottom. I often throw out the "cold" keywords entirely. This will help you see the complexity of keyword patterns as some keywords will be "easy" to categorize as hot / warm / cold and others might be more challenging – perhaps they have a lot of volume, but are ambiguous, or perhaps they are high value but just so little volume, or the customers don't know to search for them.

> *The art of SEO is targeting the keywords most likely to generate high ROI, which is a function of BOTH volume and value.*

Competitive Level

Another tricky attribute is **competition**. As you research your keywords, pay attention to the competitive level. You can guess that a keyword is competitive (many vendors want to "get the click") based on:

- The **suggested bid** in the Keyword Planner: the *higher* the suggested bid, the *more competitive* a keyword.
- The **number of ads** shown for related search queries: the *more* ads you see, the *more competitive* a keyword.
- The *more* you see the **keyword phrase in the ads**: the *more* competitors have "discovered" a high-value keyword phrase, the more likely they are to include it in their ad headlines, and the *more competitive* is the keyword.

Remember, you can use the Google AdWords Keyword Planner or another Keyword Tool to gauge the competitive level as measured by volume and cost-per-click. If you are using the Keyword Planner, be sure to click on the *Columns Chevron* and enable "suggested bid" and "competition." Note: use the "old" Keyword Planner as Google has stupidly taken away some of the data in the "new" Keyword Planner.

Here's an example screenshot for *knee pain, knee surgery,* and *knee surgeon* for location of United States:

Note that *knee pain* has 110,000 average monthly searches, competitive level is "medium" and suggested bid is $3.69. Contrast that with *knee surgeon*, which has only 720 searches per month, competition is also seen as "medium," but the bid is substantially more at $4.96. *(Remember that this tool only gives you exact match: in those 720 searches are ONLY the exact phrase "knee surgeon." If the searcher typed in "best knee surgeons," that does not count in the total of twenty. Therefore, the tool grossly underestimates volume.)*

If you were a New York City knee surgeon building out his keyword worksheet, you'd want to prioritize "knee surgeon" and "knee surgery" over "knee pain," yet realize that the competitive level is higher for these terms.

VIDEO. Watch a video tutorial about how to gauge competitive level at **http://jmlinks.com/17q**.

Search Patterns

For now, let's return to the structural patterns or keyword groups. It is very important to conceptualize the way that people search, i.e., the mindsets by which they approach your business. Let's take the example of the **Walkup Law Firm**, a personal injury law firm in San Francisco at **https://www.walkuplawoffice.com/**.

Notice how the organization of the website follows the logical keyword hierarchy for a personal injury law firm in San Francisco:

Personal Injury. This, in combination with terms such as "lawyer," "attorney," or "law firm" and geographics like "SF" or "San Francisco" is the umbrella term for what they do. Note the landing page at **https://www.walkuplawoffice.com/areas-of-specialty/**.

Specific Injury Searches. These are searches by people who have a specific legal need such as they've been in a car accident or have suffered from medical malpractice. Note the landing page for "car accident lawyer" at **https://www.walkuplawoffice.com/auto-accidents/**. Take a look at that page and pay special attention to the content, how it has both "lawyer" and "attorney," both "Northern California" and "San Francisco," and so on and so forth. Someone thought through the synonyms and helper terms and placed these into the content on the page. It's no accident (pardon the pun)!

Micro or Long Tail Searches. These are searches for super specific types of legal needs such as "wildfire litigation attorney" at **https://www.walkuplawoffice.com/ca-wildfire-loss/**. These are not flagship, high *volume* searches but are micro or long tail searches which are high *value*. Someone who's fighting an insurance company over a wildfire loss will be overjoyed to find a lawyer that specializes in this, and hence the conversion rate will be high.

Trending, Micro, or Long Tail Searches. Take a look at the law firm's lively blog at **https://www.walkuplawoffice.com/blog/**. The lawyers blog on topics that are trending or fit within their matrix of keywords. For example, there's a blog post entitled, "San Francisco Skateboarders: Know Your Legal Rights," which obviously targets folks who have been in a skateboard accident. How's that for a laser-focused search?

Branded or Reputational Searches. Your brand image is very important to the success of your marketing. You want to monitor your online reputation by ranking highly for your branded or reputational searches, populating the Internet with positive information, and crowding out any negative information about your company. These are important for your keyword worksheet. A branded search, for example, is *Walkup Law Firm or Walkup Law Firm reviews,* which you can check out at **http://jmlinks.com/47c**. Obviously, the law firm is working hard on its online reviews and reputation!

We'll get into website organization in Chapter 3.2, but for now you can use Walkup Law Firm's website as a good mental map against your own keyword patterns. It's a well-organized hierarchy of keywords and it reflects a keyword worksheet or blueprint that was used behind the scenes in the SEO optimization of the site.

In sum, the **keyword worksheet** for your company should reflect keyword *volume, value* (as measured by the "fit" between the keyword search and what your company has to offer), and the *structural search patterns* that reflect the "mindset" by which people search.

VIDEO. Watch a quick video tutorial on building a keyword worksheet at **http://jmlinks.com/17m**.

» DELIVERABLE: YOUR KEYWORD WORKSHEET

After some brainstorming, hard work, and organization, and perhaps a hangover after all the martinis you drank, you should have your first **DELIVERABLE** ready: a completed **keyword worksheet** in an Excel or Google spreadsheet. The first "dashboard" tab should be a high-level overview to relevant keywords, reflecting the structural search patterns that generate the **keyword groups**, next the keyword volumes as measured by the Google Keyword Planner or other keyword tool, and finally the values measured by the Google cost-per-click data and your own judgment as to which search queries are most likely to lead to a sale or sales lead. Other tabs (which you will fill out over time) include a tab for reporting, a tab to measure your rank on Google vs. keywords, a tab for local search rank, and a tab for landing pages.

Your keyword worksheet is your blueprint for successful SEO, but don't think of it as a static document! Rather, think of your keyword worksheet as an evolving "work in progress." There is as much art as science in SEO, and in many cases, the formal tools like the Keyword Planner only get you so far.

The Art of SEO: SEO and Cooking

Gut instinct as to how your customers search, especially which searches are likely to be close to a sale, is just as valuable as quantitative research! In fact, rather than think of SEO as a science, I strongly recommend you use other analogies. For example, I like to think of **SEO like the art of cooking**: it has *technical elements* for sure, but it also has *inspiration* and a *je ne sais quoi* of tricks and techniques that you just have to "do" rather than "learn."

In fact, at my Stanford Continuing Studies class, I often have students watch a very fun video on Julia Child and then compare the art of SEO to the art of French cooking.

VIDEO. Watch a quick video tutorial on how SEO is more like cooking than science at **http://www.jmlinks.com/5q**. Get motivated!

You cannot learn to cook by just reading cookbooks and philosophizing about cooking; you have to actually break some eggs, and make an omelet. And truly good cooks aren't just technical robots; they have a passion for their patrons, and an instinct about what makes something truly great.

> *SEO – like cooking – is an endeavor that has both technical and artistic elements.*

The point here is that although you should spend time researching the volume, value, and competitive levels of your target keywords, ultimately you'll see somewhere between five and ten keyword structural patterns. At that point it's "good enough" and you're ready to start optimizing your website. *Good cooks, cook, and good SEO's, do SEO.*

» MEASURE YOUR GOOGLE RANK VS. KEYWORDS

I'm sure you're eager to start optimizing your website, now that you've built out your keyword worksheet. We'll start that process in the next Chapter. Let me advise you, however, to take a moment and begin to measure some **baseline metrics** for your website. Why? Because you want to establish a baseline of your rank on Google at the beginning, before you optimize. This will help you chart your progress, stay motivated, and have a record to show to your pesky boss when she barges in six months from now and says that "SEO is stupid" and you haven't made any progress.

Install Google Analytics

I highly recommend that, if you haven't already done so, you install Google Analytics (**https://analytics.google.com/**) on your website, if possible via Google Tag Manager (**https://www.google.com/analytics/tag-manager/**). Just make sure that the tracking code is on your website and pulling data. We'll discuss Google Analytics in detail in Chapter 6.1. But for now just get it installed on your website, so that it's recording user behavior.

Measure Your Rank vs. Your Target Keywords

Returning to your rank measurements, Google rank refers to whether your website is on the first page Google returns for a search queries. In the industry it's called *SERP rank* for "search engine results page rank." Counting the organic results only, there are positions 1, 2, and 3 (the "Olympic" positions) and then positions four through ten ("page one" positions). Anything beyond position ten is not good. *(Note that because of localization there is also your rank on the local "snack pack" of three local results originating as Google reviews - more on this below.)*

You want to measure your website rank vis-à-vis your target keyword phrases, whether you are on page one (< 11) or in the "golden" positions of 1, 2, or 3.

Why Rank Matters

Why do we care about our Google rank? First of all, the Olympic positions (1, 2, and 3) capture the lion's share of clicks; by many estimates, over 60%! Second, being on page one (top ten results) means you are at least "in the game." But third, as good SEO experts, we want to measure our rank before, during and after our SEO efforts to measure our progress and return on investment (ROI). We can also feed this data back into our strategy so that we can then focus our content and link efforts (e.g. blog posts, product pages, press releases, link building) on searches where we are *beyond* page one vs. creating new content for searches for which we are *already* in top positions. Indeed, if you are spending money on Google AdWords advertising, you can use your rank for the organic results to optimize your spending; minimizing your spend on words for which you show "for free," and increasing your spend on keywords for which you do not rank well.

In short, measuring Google rank makes us work **smarter**, not **harder**!

Measure Your Rank Manually

With your keyword queries in hand, as built out from your **keyword worksheet**, you can measure your rank manually by simply entering your target search queries, and counting your position on the first page. Be sure to be "signed out" of your Google account or use "incognito mode" (**http://jmlinks.com/18p**) as Google customizes search results. You want to see your true rank on Google searches, not your personalized rank. Here are your steps:

1. Open up a web browser such as Google Chrome or Firefox in "incognito" or "private window" mode.
2. Go to Google.com.
3. Input a keyword phrase from your keyword worksheet.
4. Find your website, counting down from the top of the organic results.
    a. If you appear on page one, note your rank as in 1, 2, 3, 4, 5 up to 10. Be sure to count only the organic results, ignoring a) the ads on Google, and b) the local "snack pack" results which can be visible in a box of three on local searches such as "Sushi" or "probate lawyer," etc.
        i. If applicable, record the local "Snack Pack" rank separately as A (#1), B (#2) or C (#3).
    b. If you do NOT appear on page one, note your rank as NP (not present) as it doesn't really matter if you are position 11 or position 110 as few people go beyond page one.
5. Record your rank on your keyword worksheet, on the rank tab.
6. Repeat for other keywords on your keyword list.

Usually, a company will have between five and ten core keyword patterns, and between fifty and one hundred variations of keyword phrases built by combining the core keywords and helper words. Don't get discouraged if your rank is poor when you begin an SEO project. Be positive: the only way you have to go is up!

Measure Your Rank Using Tools

While it's getting harder and harder to use free tools to measure your rank on Google because Google doesn't like to share this data with external companies, there remain a few free tools that allow you to input keywords and check your rank on Google. One of the best is the FATRANK plugin for Chrome (**http://jmlinks.com/25w**). After you've installed the plugin, here are your steps:

1. Visit the website you want to check rank for (i.e., your own website or that of a competitor).
2. Click on the FATRANK icon at the top right of Chrome, which looks like an orange Pokemon.
3. Enter a keyword and click the blue "check" icon. Here's a screenshot:

You can do this for multiple keywords. Then click on "Session Report" and it will give you a nice list of your keywords and rank which you can export into a CSV file. Another good free tool is SerpSurf.com at **http://jmlinks.com/38w**.

> **VIDEO.** Watch a video on how to measure your rank using FAT Rank as well as the Google AdWords Preview tool at **http://jmlinks.com/18h**.

Because rank checking is an important metric, I recommend you graduate to a paid tool such as Whitespark.ca, AHrefs.com, or MOZ.com. These tools allow you to upload a list of tens or even hundreds of keywords and check your rank on Google and Bing as well as the "local pack" if you are a local business.

Record Your Keyword Rank Data

I recommend recording your keyword rank on at least a monthly basis, and inputting this into your keyword worksheet on the rank tab. This will give you a baseline before, during, and after you start your SEO project.

On an on-going basis, use the resulting rank data to identify "strengths" (places where you appear in the top three or top ten) and "weaknesses" (keywords for which you appear beyond page one, or not at all). Having identified your keyword rank weaknesses, you now know where to target your SEO efforts!

Measure Local Search Results Manually

As you check rank, be sensitive to the fact that the free tools generally measure only your organic rank on a non-localized basis. Google "localizes" search results, especially short tail phrases: searchers in different cities, see different results. For example, a search for "probate attorney" in Dallas will return *Dallas probate attorneys*, whereas the same search in San Francisco will return *San Francisco probate attorneys* even though the searcher does NOT enter the city.

This happens with many "short tail" searches that have a local character such as: *attorney, CPA, accountant, pizza, sushi, massage therapist, marriage counselor*, etc. – any search terms that generally indicate someone is looking for a local small business.

The free Rank Checker tools listed above, unfortunately, do **NOT** calculate your rank in a localized fashion. Therefore, if **local search rankings** are important to you, you need to **manually** check your rank on Google+ local as shown in the "snack pack" usually consisting of three results on Google.

To check your local rank (varying your position city-by-city), use the Google AdWords Preview Tool at **http://jmlinks.com/18r** or the free SERPS local rank checking tool at **http://jmlinks.com/18s**.

VIDEO. Watch a video on how to measure your local rank using the Google AdWords Preview tool at **http://jmlinks.com/17s**.

Here's a screenshot showing the search for "Pizza" and the "snack pack" of three local results with location of Fremont, California:

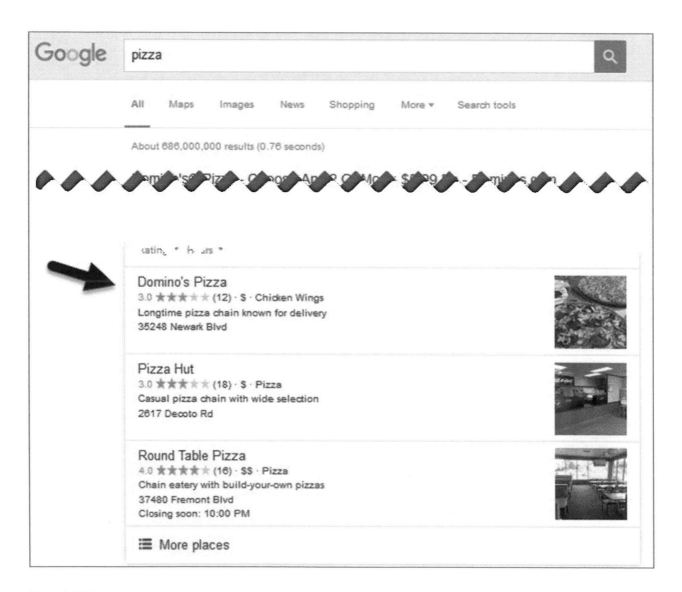

In this example, therefore, you'd record position #1 (A) for Domino's, #2 (B) for Pizza Hut, and #3 (C) for Round Table Pizza. Positions greater than #3 appear on the "second page" of local results (on both the phone and the desktop) and are worth considerably less than positions, #1, #2, and #3. (Note: it has become industry-standard practice to record local rank in the "snack pack" as A / B / C not 1 /2 / 3).

For your own company, identify short tail local searches and record these on your keyword worksheet, on the "local rank" tab.

Measuring Your Rank in Different Cities

Let's say you want to look at your locations in multiple cities such as San Francisco, San Jose, and Oakland. You cannot do this directly in Google, you have to use the AdWords preview tool which you can get to directly in AdWords by logging in, and on the top menu, selecting the "Wrench icon" and then "Ad Preview and Diagnosis." Alternatively, you can access the preview tool directly at this URL **http://jmlinks.com/13m**.

Here's a screenshot of the tool with location set to Tulsa, Oklahoma, device set to "mobile," and search term set to *accountants*:

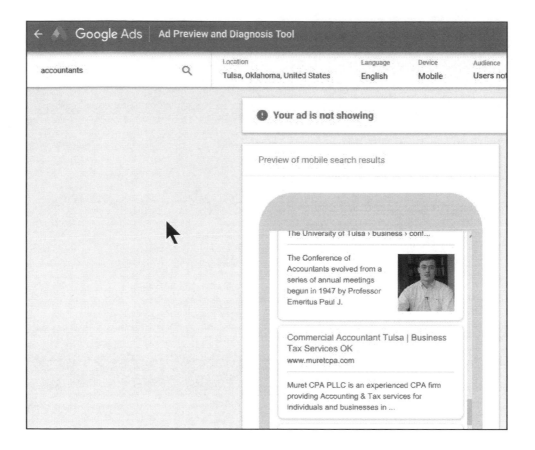

(You can ignore the warning that says "Your ad is not showing" as that refers to advertising).

If you want to measure your local rank, you'll need to manually change the tool city by city. In addition to the "snack pack," notice that the organic ranks themselves will also change for localized keywords. So, in this case, you'll have to manually rank check both your rank in the snack pack and in the organic results. You can do this for the mobile phone, desktop, or tablet plus vary the city. To do this, change the "Device" on the far right. Mobile rank does not yet vary as dramatically as rank based on localization but it does vary.

VIDEO. Watch a quick video tutorial on using Google and/or the AdWords Preview Tool to measure your local rank at **http://jmlinks.com/17s**.

Because of localization and differences on rank for mobile, tablet, and desktop, it can be very time-consuming to measure your rank for fifty to a hundred keywords and many tens of target cities. For this reason, if local SEO matters a lot to you, I highly recommend paying for a *paid* rank-checking tool such as Whitespark.ca, as this tool can measure your rank in different cities for many different keywords in a systematic and automated fashion.

Time is money, and a paid rank-checking tool will save you a lot of time.

»» DELIVERABLE: RANK MEASUREMENT AND A BASELINE SCORE

The final **DELIVERABLE** for this Chapter is to measure your rank across a statistical sample of between twenty and one hundred keywords, depending on how complex your company is. Using either free or paid tools, input these data on a monthly basis into your keyword worksheet rank tab(s).

»» CHECKLIST: KEYWORD WORKSHEET ACTION ITEMS

Here are your keyword worksheet **Action Items**:

❑ Build out your **Keyword Worksheet** with columns for "core keywords," "helper keywords," "sample search queries" as well as volume and value.

  ❑ **Identify** your core keyword groups, led by one keyword "parent" with various keyword "children" or phrases. Also identify your helper keywords which, in combination with the core keywords, build out the universe of target keywords and key phrases you want to rank for.

  ❑ **Prioritize** your keyword groups as *hot, warm,* or *cold,* placing the hot keyword groups at the top. Look for specific micro or long tail searches that are high value to your company.

  ❑ Identify **competitors** and place them on your Keyword Worksheet.

❑ Use FATRANK or one of the paid rank-checking tools to do your first **rank analysis** of your website vs. your keywords targets.

❑ If necessary, chart your rank for "short tail" searches that vary by city location.

Check out the **free tools**! Go to my *SEO Dashboard > Keywords* for my favorite free tools for keyword discovery. Just visit **http://jmlinks.com/seodash**.

SURVEY OFFER

CLAIM YOUR $5 SURVEY REBATE! HERE'S HOW –

- Visit **http://jmlinks.com/survey**.
- Take a short, simple survey about the book.
- Claim your rebate.

WE WILL THEN –

- Rebate you the $5 via Amazon eGift.

~ $5 REBATE OFFER ~

~ LIMITED TO ONE PER CUSTOMER ~

SUBJECT TO CHANGE WITHOUT NOTICE

RESTRICTIONS APPLY

GOT QUESTIONS? CALL 800-298-4065

3.1

PAGE TAGS

Once you know your keywords, where do you put them? "Page Tag" SEO is the quick and easy answer to that question, and it is the most important to-do in **Step #3**. In **Step #3**, you take your keywords from your keyword worksheet, place them in strategic locations on individual web pages via **page tags** and also **restructure** your website to send clear signals to Google about your keyword targets. In other words, you work at two levels: first, the level of individual page content, and second, the level of your website as a whole. If you don't know HTML, don't worry; modern CMS systems like WordPress, Squarespace, or Drupal do the hard work for you.

Let's get started!

TO-DO LIST:

» Understand Page Tags, HTML, and Talking to Google

» Page Tags and Poker

» Weave Keywords into Page Tags

» Use WordPress for Key SEO Tags

» A Visual Test for Keyword Density

» The Answer Box

»» Deliverable: A Completed Page Tag Worksheet

» Set Up Your Homepage

»» Deliverable: A Completed Homepage Page Tag Worksheet

»» Checklist: Page Tag Action Items

» Understand Page Tags, HTML, and Talking to Google

HTML is the language of the Web, and it is based on what are called "tags" in HTML. At a very simple level, if you want a word to appear bold on a web page, you put the "tag" **<strong>** around the word such as *"We sell **<strong>**running shoes**</strong>**"* in the HTML text of the web page. This will display in browsers with the phrase "running shoes" in **bold** as for example:

We sell **running shoes**.

If you are using a WYSIWYG editor like WordPress or Dreamweaver, the editor will "hide" this code from you, but behind the scenes the true foundation of the Web is HTML, and the foundation of HTML is **page tags**. For a super simple introduction to HTML, visit **http://jmlinks.com/13n**.

HTML: the Browser, the Website, & Google

Here's what most people do, and don't, understand about page tags and the Web:

- **The Browser.** Page Tags such as <strong>, <a href>, <img alt>, etc., structure how the browser displays information to the user – bold, a link, an image, etc. (*Most web designers and marketers understand this*).
- **The Website.** Page Tags structure the interrelationship between pages on a website, especially through <a href>, the "anchor" or "link" tag but also through CSS style sheets. (*Most web designers understand this in terms of navigation for humans, but not communication to Google*).
- **Google and other Search Engines.** Page Tags send signals to Google about which keywords are important with respect to an individual website, and even the website as a whole (*Few people outside the SEO community understand this*).

Indeed, a very unfortunate fact in web design is that most web designers are visual people who only look at how a website looks "to humans" and fail to understand how it communicates "to Google." Not surprisingly, many beautiful websites fail to "speak Google" and thus fail to rank on search engines.

Viewing the HTML Source / Page Tags

To see the true HTML behind the visible Web, go to any webpage with your browser, right click on your mouse (or CTRL+U on the PC/ COMMAND+U on the Mac), select "View Source" in Firefox, Microsoft Edge, Safari, or Chrome. The HTML code you see is the true language of the Web, and this code is what Google or Bing actually uses to index a web page. For example, here is a screenshot of the HTML source code for Geico's page on "Motorcycle Insurance" (**https://www.geico.com/motorcycle-insurance/**) showing the all-important TITLE tag:

```
27      <title>Free Motorcycle Insurance Quotes Online | GEICO&reg;</title>
28
29          <link rel="stylesheet" href="/public/design-kit/4.0/css/geico-design-kit-light
30          <link href="/feo-cdn/i/y/Ren-UTF-8~iy6BkLMPImogh-XbDGDWZTwjUQniKYfbhgC-b6mGBQc
    rel="stylesheet" type="text/css"/><script blzsys="1" type="text/javascript">aFeoOverri
31              <link href="/feo-cdn/5/C/Ren-UTF-8~5CKkT9Bnx4TLmopa3tLeQZix-MXnuUt8XHT
    rel="stylesheet" type="text/css"/><script blzsys="1" type="text/javascript">aFeoOverri
32          <style type="text/css">@font-face {font-family:'geico';src:url("https://www.ge
    xlxh80");src:url("https://www.geico.com/public/design-kit/4.0/fonts/geico.eot?#iefix-x
    kit/4.0/fonts/geico.woff?-xlxh80") format('woff'),url("https://www.geico.com/public/de
    format('truetype'),url("https://www.geico.com/public/design-kit/4.0/fonts/geico.svg?-x
33
34
35                      @media all and (min-width: 768px) {
36                  #headline-wrapper {background-image:url("https://www.geico.com/pub
37                  }
38          }</style>
39
40      <link href="https://plus.google.com/104558085076978197022" rel="publisher" />
41
```

Here's their TITLE tag:

```
<title>Free Motorcycle Insurance Quotes Online |
GEICO</title>
```

The TITLE tag controls the top of the browser, the text you see if you bookmark this page, and the headline of the page on Google. And here's their H1 (Header) tag:

```
<h1 class="h1">Motorcycle Insurance</h1>
```

The H1 makes this sentence appear in a big bold font. Here's a screenshot of what it looks like "to humans:"

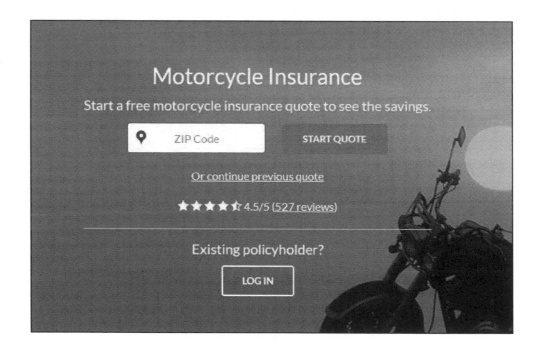

Most web designers understand that this HTML code structures how the browser displays the information about Geico's landing page around the phrase *Motorcycle Insurance*, putting it in a big font at the center of the page. But what they miss is that this HTML code is also sending **powerful signals to Google about keyword targets**.

In a very simple way, if your page has ****running shoes**** on it, you are not just bolding the word **running shoes** in the browser; you are also signaling Google that the keyword phrase **running shoes** is important to you. In our Geico example, their page is sending a powerful signal with both the TITLE and H1 tag by including the phrase "Motorcycle Insurance" in them. Guess what? Geico ranks #2 on Google for the search query "motorcycle insurance."

PAGE TAGS SIGNAL KEYWORD PRIORITIES TO GOOGLE

If, for example, you write an HTML page like this:

```
<h1>Learn about our Car Insurance</h1>
```

We sell the best car insurance in Houston

Which will render in a browser like Chrome, Firefox, or Safari as:

Learn About Car Insurance

We sell the best **car insurance** in Houston

This is doing two things:

1. Telling the **Web browser** to render the first sentence in big, bold letters, and to render the phrase "car insurance" in bold text.
2. **Signaling** to **Google** that the words: *Learn, About, Our, Car, Insurance* are important to you – these are words that you would like to rank for on Google.

(Google ignores common words like *learn* or *about*, which are called "stop words" and instead will focus on *car* and *insurance* as the important words).

It's an unambiguous communication to Google that when someone searches for "motorcycle insurance," Geico would like to rank this specific page for that query.

Your Website is Your Google Resume

Remember the "Job Search" analogy? Your *website* is like a *resume*. If you are looking for a job as a ***BMW auto mechanic***, for example, you would **bold** the words ***auto***, ***mechanic***, and ***BMW*** on your resume, wouldn't you? That bolding would not only make the words appear blacker on the page, it would also "signal" to the person reading your resume that you want to "rank" (i.e., be considered for a job for) those terms.

Your Website = a Resume

Manipulating Page Tags = Bolding / Making Bigger Keywords on the Resume = signals to Google

Now that I've drilled this concept into your head through repetition (*it's that important!*), you should realize that you must design for two audiences: humans and Google. Fortunately, you do not have to be an HTML expert. You need to understand just the basics of HTML because modern WYSIWYG editors like WordPress do the HTML coding for you. Using WordPress, for example, here's a screenshot of my webpage on *AdWords Expert Witness* services as seen inside the editor:

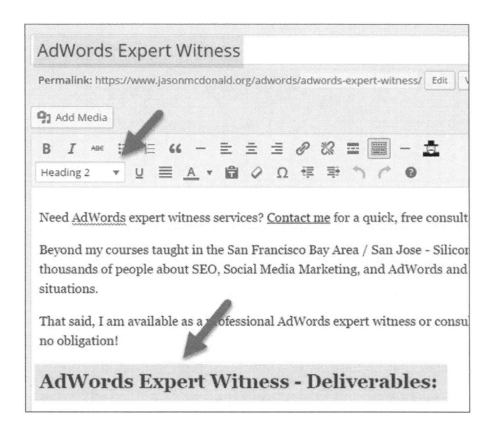

I have highlighted the Page Title (which becomes the TITLE tag), and the H2 (which becomes the Header 2 Tag) in yellow. The red arrows show where you can change the header tag in WordPress, as well as where the actual header text is located. You can view the actual page on the Web at **http://jmlinks.com/5r**. (Right click, and view source to see the HTML code that underlies the browser-visible web page).

In this way, WordPress makes it easy to "speak HTML" and "talk to Google." You just have to know which tags are important for SEO, and how to get those tags implemented in WordPress. (If you are using another editor, such as Squarespace or Dreamweaver, accordingly, you have to figure out what items in the editor yield what items in HTML).

The Yoast Plugin

Even better, if you are using WordPress, I highly recommend the Yoast WordPress Plugin at **http://jmlinks.com/5s**. It enables you to "split" the WordPress HEADLINE from the SEO-friendly TITLE tag, as well as easily add a META

DESCRIPTION tag to your pages. Yoast creates a little box at the bottom of each page where you simply enter your TITLE and META DESCRIPTION information for Google (with an eye to your keyword targets). Here's a screenshot:

» PAGE TAGS AND POKER

By inserting keywords into your HTML Page Tags, you are "talking to Google." You want, however, to do more than talk to Google: you want to win.

But which tags send the strongest signals?

To understand which tags are the most important, let's use a new analogy: **page tags are like the cards in poker.**

PAGE TAGS = POKER CARDS

Now any good poker player knows that the *Ace* is more powerful than the *King*, and the *King* more powerful than the *Deuce*, and that *Full House* beats *two of a kind*. These are the "rules of poker." (*The fact that many people don't understand the rules or strategies of poker is akin to the fact that many people do not understand the rules or strategies of Page Tags in SEO. Accordingly, most people play poker poorly, and most people play SEO poorly, too. You, my friend, are going to learn some basic rules, however, and begin to "crush your competition."*)

Your first step is to learn the values of the key HTML tags. To begin, examine the following table showing the most important page tags "as if" you were playing a game of poker with Google and your competitors:

TAG	POKER	COMMENT
<TITLE>	Ace	Most important tag on any page, place your target keyword in the <TITLE> tag of each page. <TITLE> of the homepage is the most powerful tag

		on any website. (59 visible characters; about 80 indexed).
\<A HREF\>	King	Keyword-heavy links cross-reference pages to each other, and communicate keywords to Google.
\<IMG ALT\>	Queen	Have at least one image per page, and put your target keyword into the ALT attribute of the image.
\<H1\>	Jack	Google loves the header family, so use at least one \<H1\> per page. Use \<H2\>, \<H3\> sparingly.
\<META DESCRIPTION\>	10	If you include the target keyword in the \<META DESCRIPTION\> tag, Google will use it 90% 0f the time. (300 character limit).
\<BODY\> or keyword density	9	Write keyword-heavy prose on each and every page of the website. Aim for natural syntax and about 5% keyword density.
\<STRONG\>, \<B\>, \<EM\>	3, 4, 5	Use bold and italicize keywords on the page, strategically.
\<META KEYWORDS\>	Joker	Ignored by Google. Use it as a "note to self" about the keyword targets for a particular page.

The above table is very important. It tells you that once you know the target keyword for a given page, then place that keyword inside of the \<TITLE\>, \<A HREF\>, \<IMG ALT\>, \<H1\>, \<META DESCRIPTION\> and \<BODY\> (visible content). Don't overdo this, but don't underdo it, either. (*More on writing Google-friendly content in a moment*)

Get and Read Google's Official SEO Starter Guide

Google produces an official guide to SEO that emphasizes just how important tag structure is to Google and SEO. I strongly recommend that you download the guide and read it thoroughly at **http://jmlinks.com/googleseo**. It doesn't tell you everything, but it's a good, basic guide to On Page SEO, the art and science of structuring your content to "talk" to Google in terms of your target keywords.

Besides explaining the basics of On Page SEO, the guide also has two other usages:

Sleep Aid. It is an excellent sleep aid, so when you just can't get drowsy, simply start reading. You'll be dreaming ZZZZZs in no time. (*I keep a copy under my pillow for this very reason*).

Attack Weapon. If you're working with a recalcitrant web designer, team member, or CEO, who doesn't believe what I'm telling you in this book because I'm "just" *Jason McDonald SEO guru of San Francisco, California*, print out the guide on paper. Next, you can roll up the guide, and start beating him or her on the head, explaining: HERE'S A CRAZY IDEA. TO GET TO THE TOP OF GOOGLE CAN WE PLEASE JUST DO WHAT GOOGLE TELLS US TO DO? If you print the guide with an inkjet and moisten it prior to the beating, you may also be able to get the Google logo to bleed off onto their forehead.

Seriously, the guide is a great basic, official guide to On Page SEO and should be required reading for anyone on your team involved in search engine optimization.

Hate reading? Here are some videos:

VIDEO. Watch a video tutorial of TITLE, META DESCRIPTION and KEYWORDS "meta" tags for SEO at **http://jmlinks.com/17r** as well as a video on how to do a page tag analysis at **http://jmlinks.com/5u**.

I also highly recommend you read my "SEO Page Tag Template" at **http://jmlinks.com/18t**. The end result of page tags is to understand that page tags communicate your keywords to Google, so your first **TO-DO** is pretty obvious: weave your keywords into your page tags, starting with the all-important TITLE tag.

Basically:

Target keyword > embed in TITLE, META DESCRIPTION, HEADER, IMG ALT and VISIBLE PAGE CONTENT

Now, do NOT overdo this! *"A little salt is good for the soup, but too much salt ruins the soup."* You want to take a specific landing page, and focus Google's attention around one, and only one, keyword phrase.

Focus One Page on One Keyword Target

As you build out your landing pages and blog posts (leaving aside for a moment your homepage), let's discuss **focus**. Generally speaking, you want *one page* on your website to match *one target keyword pattern* on Google. To see this in action take a look at Nationwide's Pet Insurance website at **https://www.petinsurance.com/**, more specifically how they have:

Dog insurance at **https://www.petinsurance.com/dog-insurance.aspx** and *cat insurance* at cat insurance at **https://www.petinsurance.com/cat-insurance**.

Visit those pages and RIGHT CLICK > VIEW SOURCE. You'll notice that the tag structure, starting with their TITLE TAGS focuses on one, and only one, type of keyword or pet. So they have a "dog insurance" page that is all about "dog insurance" (and no "cat insurance"), and they have a "cat insurance" page that is all about "cat insurance" (and no "dog insurance). Indeed, their homepage is focused on "pet insurance" (the umbrella term) with downward "one-click" links to each landing page. And each page has tag structure that communicates cleanly and efficiently to Google what the page is about.

That's just how Google likes it.

Remember: Google is a company founded by engineers and run by engineers, you know, the kind of dweeby nerds that got beat up in High School with pocket protectors and a highly organized set of multicolored pens. You know, the guys and girls who were on Chess Club because they liked rules and didn't like chance. Those people. The ones with few friends. Well, today they rule the world, and they like websites that would win neurotic organization awards for neurotic organization. Everything has a place and everything is in its place. The dogs are on the dog page, and the cats are on the cat page, and the pets on the pet page.

It's Google's world. You and I just live in it.

Audit High-Ranking Pages and "Reverse Engineer" Their Page Tags

Now that you know how Page Tags "talk" to Google, revisit some top-ranking pages especially by companies like Geico, Progressive, or eSurance that clearly practice high-stakes SEO. Revisit Google searches like "motorcycle insurance," "car insurance," or even "Segway insurance," and see how the winning websites are "speaking Google" via Page Tags.

The insurance industry is an excellent place to look for SEO Olympians! They're playing high stakes competition, and they do everything right.

For example, revisit a high-ranking page such as the page on Progressive.com for "Segway Insurance" (**https://www.progressive.com/segway/**) view the source code via CTRL+U / COMMAND+U, do a CTRL+F / COMMAND+F and search for "Segway Insurance," and notice how that target keyword phrase ("Segway Insurance") has been strategically embedded into the tag structure and visible content. Compare it with other top-ranking pages such as **https://www.esurance.com/insurance/segway** and notice how they do the same. These pages are using Page Tags to communicate to Google that they want to rank for "Segway Insurance."

VIDEO. Watch a quick video tutorial of a page audit at **http://jmlinks.com/5v.**

Now, toggle back to your sad, pathetic web pages, and notice how inefficiently they are talking to Google. Notice how disorganized and unfocused they are. Notice how the keywords are not embedded in the Page Tags, or if they are, how it's all done in a messy or disorganized way. Then go onto Amazon or Netflix and watch the 1984 movie, "Revenge of the Nerds." It's time to get your website, starting with your landing pages, into pocket-protector, multicolored pen in each correct color-coded case, sort of order.

Toggle back to your web pages and have your "Aha" moment and realize that you need to revise their keywords / page content vis-à-vis their page tag structure to "speak Google." *#nerdalert.*

» WEAVE KEYWORDS INTO PAGE TAGS

In summary, now that you know that the TITLE tag is the most important tag, that Google likes the header tag family, that each web page should have at least one image tag with the ALT attribute defined to include a keyword, and should link across to other web pages based on your target keywords, you are ready to write a strong SEO page or re-write an existing page to better communicate keyword priorities to Google.

Page Tags and Keywords for All Pages Except the Homepage

We will deal with the homepage separately, because the homepage is both incredibly important to SEO and has unique responsibilities. But, for all pages EXCEPT the homepage, here's how to write SEO-friendly content for one, and only one, specific page and matching keyword target:

1. **Define your target keywords**. Using your keyword worksheet as well as the various keyword tools, define the target keywords for the specific page. A best practice is to focus on a single keyword per individual landing page or blog post.
2. **Write a keyword-heavy TITLE tag**. The TITLE tag should be less than 80 characters, with the most important keywords on the left. The *first 59 characters* will generally appear on Google as your headline.

3. **Write a keyword-heavy META DESCRIPTION tag**. The META DESCRIPTION tag has a 90% chance of being the visible description on Google, so write one that includes your keywords but is also pithy and exciting. Its job is to "get the click" from Google. Character limit is 300 characters, but focus your most important content in the first 155 characters.
4. **Write a few keyword-heavy header tags**. Start with an H1 tag and throw in a couple of H2 tags around keyword phrases.
5. **Include at least one image with the ALT attribute defined**. Google likes to see at least one image on a page, with the keywords around the ALT attribute.
6. **Cross-link via keyword phrases**. Embed your target keyword phrases in links that link your most important pages across your website to each other around keyword phrases.
7. **Write keyword dense text**. Beyond just page tags, Google looks to see a good keyword density (about 3-5%) and keywords used in natural English syntax following good grammar.

Presto! You now "speak Google."

DON'T OVERDO IT!

Finally, don't *overdo* it! That's called *keyword stuffing* and it's dangerous. A little salt is good for the soup, but too much salt ruins it. So don't fall into either extreme. Know your keywords and write keyword-heavy content that's good for Google, including putting your keywords into strategic tags. But don't go crazy and think that just by stuffing keywords in willy nilly, you'll succeed. Google isn't stupid.

Write with Pizzazz

Also, as you write your TITLE and META DESCRIPTION tags, remember to write both "for humans" and "for Google." For Google, you need to get the target keyword into the tag. For "humans," you need some pizzazz that says "Click me! Please click me! This is a great fit for what you're looking for!"

Take a look at the Progressive listing on Google for "motorcycle insurance," for instance, and notice not only that it has the target keyword but also has some marketing pizzazz. Here's a screenshot:

Get A Motorcycle Insurance Quote From The #1 Insurer | Progressive
https://www.progressive.com/motorcycle/ ▾
Ride with the #1 **motorcycle insurance** company starting at just $75 per year.* See all the savings and protection we offer. Get a quote online.
Motorcycle Insurance Coverage · Scooter Insurance · Sport Bike Insurance · Mopeds

Is Progressive really the "#1 insurer?" Can you really "Ride with the #1 motorcycle insurance company?" Not really, but there's no Google police against this puffery, so they've written tag content that has the target keywords in it and also hypes their website as the best place to click to for "motorcycle insurance."

As you write your own tags, therefore, don't be modest. Be a marketer.

» USE WORDPRESS FOR KEY SEO TAGS

You don't have to be an HTML expert to properly use page tags for SEO. Modern CMS systems like WordPress, Squarespace, or Drupal will do most of the heavy lifting for you. You just have to know that in terms of HTML output you need to get your keywords into the proper tags. Since WordPress is the dominant platform, let me give you an example using WordPress. We'll use my page on "AdWords Expert Witness," which targets my rank on Google and Bing for my services as an expert witness in litigation on AdWords (usually for trademark infringement). It's an easy-to-understand keyword target that is very high value even if it's low volume.

With that target keyword in hand, I log in to WordPress and edit the page. I'll assume you have the Yoast plug in installed as well. First, I scroll down and find the Yoast plugin at the bottom of the page. I find the "Snippet preview" in Yoast and click "Edit

Snippet" and then write an "SEO Title," which becomes the TITLE tag and a "Meta Description" which becomes the META Description tag. Here's a screenshot:

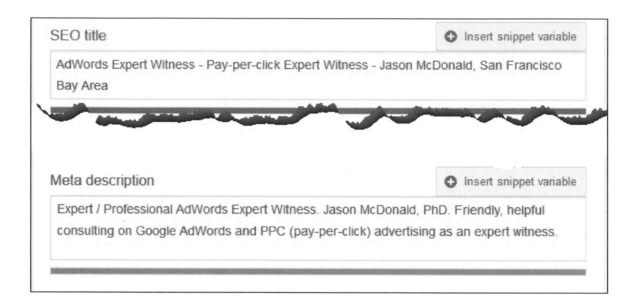

Next, I scroll back up to the top of the page in WordPress and write a "Post Headline" which will become an H1 tag. Here's a screenshot:

Note also that the "Permalink" or URL contains the target keyword phrase of "AdWords Expert Witness" shown as *adwords-expert-witness*. Then, as I write content, I pepper and salt phrases like "AdWords expert," "litigation," "expert witness," and "Google ads" throughout the copy. As I create sub-headers, I select the header family on the menu. For example, here's a screenshot for "AdWords Expert Witness – Deliverables:"

By selecting "Header 2" in WordPress, I make sure that the HTML output is:

```
<h2>AdWords Expert Witness - Deliverables:</h2>
```

Finally, I make sure that I have at least one image on the page and I select the "ALT" attribute and put the keyword into it. Here's a screenshot of that:

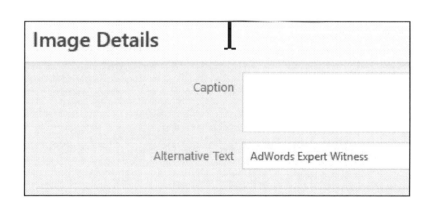

In this way, even if you have only a rudimentary knowledge of HTML yet know the key HTML tags for search engine optimization, you can use a modern CMS system like WordPress or Squarespace to make sure that you get your keywords into the right tag positions. As you output pages, then "View Source" and verify that the output you are getting has the proper tag structure. You can check out my page targeting "AdWords Expert Witness" at **http://jmlinks.com/47f**.

» A Visual Test for Keyword Density

As you are writing new pages or analyzing existing ones, however, keep in mind that **keyword density** on the Web is more **redundant** than in normal English writing.

Few SEO experts and even fewer average marketers really realize just how *redundant, repetitious, repeating, reinforcing,* and *reiterating* strong prose is for Google! Furthermore, it's not just about stringing keywords in comma, comma, and comma phrases. The Google algorithm, post-Panda, clearly analyzes text and looks for natural syntax, so be sure to write in complete sentences following the rules of grammar and spelling.

Write keyword heavy text in natural English syntax sentences, while avoiding comma, comma, and comma phrases. What keyword density is "just right?" The best answer is to do your searches and look at who is actually ranking already.

Let's revisit "Motorcycle Insurance" as an example. Here's a screenshot of the Geico motorcycle insurance page, using CTRL+F in Firefox to highlight the occurrences of the phrase "motorcycle insurance":

Get your motor running and get a **motorcycle insurance** quote

A free online **motorcycle insurance** quote from GEICO could help you save money. No matter what you ⟨ bike, or a sweet custom ride, you can turn to us for great rates and great coverage. We even offer scoote road knowing that the Gecko®'s got your back!

Protecting more than just your bike

When you carry comprehensive or collision coverage, you could also get protection for your accessories. Accessories coverage may include: saddlebags, backrests, seats, chrome pieces and CB radios. Learn

"We kept hearing that **motorcycle insurance** *out. We were very sur way lower than our cu coverage. The switch*

Second, how keyword dense is a page? Well, according to Chrome, the page has 15 occurrences of the phrase "motorcycle insurance" (using CTRL+F) and according to SEO Centro's Meta Tag Analyzer (**http://jmlinks.com/37w**) it has a density of 1.07% for "motorcycle insurance." Third, the #1 ranking page (Progressive's at **https://www.progressive.com/motorcycle/**) has 12 occurrences, and density of .96%. So we can see we need well-written text that has about a 1% occurrence of the target phrase.

> **Keyword density**, in short, is higher than if you were to write the pages "for humans" but not so high as to incur a Google penalty.

A less technical way to look at Web content is what I call the **visual pinch test**. Find pages for very competitive Google searches (such as "motorcycle insurance" or "reverse mortgage" or "online coupons"), highlight their keywords by using CTRL+F (PC) / COMMAND+F (Mac) in Firefox, read the text aloud and pinch yourself every time the keyword is used. At the end of the page, you should be in pain! If you are not in pain, the density is too low. If you're in the hospital, it's too high. In terms of metrics, a good rule of thumb is about 1-2% density, but remember also that it's not just numeric density but the occurrence of keywords in normal sentences that matter.

Page Content: What Comes First?

Google likes text, but people like pictures. There is a trade-off between the heavy, redundant text favored by Google and the clean, iPhone like picture websites favored by humans. The usual solution is to put the eye candy for humans towards the *top*, and the text-heavy stuff for Google towards the *bottom*. Revisit many of the pages on Geico.com or Progressive.com and you'll notice how the eye candy for humans is at the top, and the redundant text for Google is at the bottom.

Another page that does this in a really obvious way is the Fillmore Florist homepage at **http://www.sfflowershop.com/**. Scroll to the bottom of that page. Here, let me show you the horror. Here's a screenshot of the text on the bottom of their homepage with a huge list of all the cemeteries and funeral homes in San Francisco:

LOCAL CEMETERIES & FUNERAL HOMES

Cypress Abbey Company, Cypress Lawn Cemetery, Cypress Lawn Cremation Society, Cypress Lawn Funeral Home, Duggan Dan Bill & Matt, Duggan Duggan & Duggan, Duggan Serra Mortuary Cremation Services, Duggan's Serra Mortuary Cremation Services, Eternal Home Cemetery, Golden Hills Memorial Park Inc, Greenlawn Memorial Park, Hills Of Eternity Memorial Park, Hills-Eternity Jewish Cemetery, Holy Cross Catholic Cemetery, Home Of Peace Cemetary, Hoy Sun Memorial Cemetery Inc, Japanese Cemetery, National Cremation Service, National Cremation Svc, Orthodox Memorial Park Eastern, Salem Memorial Park, San Francisco Funeral Flowers, Sci, Serbian Cemetery, Sierra Enterprises Inc, Societa Italiana Di Mutua, Stonemar Partners, Woodlawn Memorial Park, Chinese Cemetery Association, Golden Gate National Cemetery, Nixon's Undertaking Service, San Francisco Nat Cmtry 903, United States Government, Colma Cremation & Funeral-Svc, Noftsger Richard A, A Algado Undertaking, Mortuary Designs International, Oravitz-Komlos Lauretta, Ashley & Mcmullen, Hoy-Sun Memorial Cemetery, Inc, Carew Leo V, Giovannini Carol Mrs, Gray Halsted N, Lee Jefferson H, Anderson

They know that people search for florists near such-and-such cemetery or funeral home, and they've stuffed these phrases into their homepage.

Now, this text and their homepage text as a whole are pretty gross and violate Google's terms of service post-Panda by having comma, comma, comma, comma phrases ad infinitum. But their website nonetheless ranks well on Google for searches like *same day flower delivery San Francisco*, most humans never scroll down to this garbage on the homepage, and instead look at the eye candy at the top.

That said, there's a trade-off here because Google isn't stupid. It clearly sees words at the top of your page as more important than words at the bottom. In this way, you can see that the Geico page for "motorcycle insurance" accomplishes the same strategy of "eye candy" for humans at the top and "keywords" for Google at the bottom with more style.

Revisit it at **https://www.geico.com/motorcycle-insurance/** and notice how they have visuals at the top and text at the bottom yet have the target keyword "motorcycle insurance" in an H1 tag high on the visible text. Geico creates SEO-friendly content with a lot of style and grace. That's what you want to do, too.

The Panda Update

Periodically Google updates its algorithm, to improve the search results and combat what is called "Web spam." One of the most important algorithm updates was called **Panda**, and Panda specifically targeted *keyword stuffing*, which is the overuse of keywords on a page such as you see on the Fillmore Florist page. In this post-Panda world, the key thing to do is to hit a "sweet spot" of just enough keyword density but not so much as to trigger a penalty. Even more important, don't think of **keyword density** as a simple numeric percentage, but rather as the strategic weaving of keywords into HTML tags and text. Here are post-Panda principles to writing SEO-friendly content:

1. **Know your keywords**. Keywords remain as important as ever! In addition to your focus keyword, however, look for **related** or **adjacent** keywords. A page targeting "motorcycle insurance" for example should have sentences that also contain words like *riding, rate, quote, Harley-Davidson*, etc. Use Google Autocomplete and Google related searches functions to find "adjacent" words and weave them into your content. Write like people talk, and write at about 6th-grade level.

2. Use **natural syntax** and **good grammar**. Write using good *subject, verb, object* structure. Gone are the days when you could just write *keyword, keyword, keyword*. I recommend you should read your page content out loud: it should sound heavier than normal English in terms of keywords, but not so heavy as you sound crazy. Grammar- and spell-check your final visible content.

3. **Avoid comma, comma, comma phrases**; another way of saying write normal, natural prose (but still containing your keywords!). Google is aware of the obvious tricks such as sentences with twenty-five commas, and white text on a white background. Don't be stupid. It can work, but it can create a penalty and you'll disappear from Google until you fix it.

4. **Don't be too perfect**. Don't have an optimized, perfect TITLE and META DESCRIPTION and ALT ATTRIBUTE for an IMAGE, etc. – mix things up a bit.

Post-Panda, the trick is to be keyword heavier than normal English, but still retain good, natural syntax. *A little salt is good in the soup; too much salt ruins it.*

A good litmus test is:

- Does your page contain the target keywords in the key HTML tags yet with some variety and adjacent keywords? And,
- Is your numeric keyword density between 1 and 2%? And,
- If a "normal" person reads your page, will he or she be unaware that it has been optimized for SEO yet hear the keyword phrase loud and clear? And,
- Does the page actually convey useful information to the human reader?

If the answer is YES to these questions, you'll probably survive Panda. If the answer is NO, you are either underoptimized (*keywords do not appear in key tags*) or overoptimized (*density is too high, text is clunky and weird to "normal" humans*).

Another easy rule-of-thumb. Do your target searches and look at the content of the current "winners." Find the middle ground characterized by the winners in your industry and be as text heavy and dense as they are, but not aggressively more so.

Keywords No Longer Matter?

Finally, you may read on the blogosphere that "keywords no longer matter." This is an incredibly stupid and dangerous idea, based largely on ignorance and on Google propaganda about so-called semantic search. "Just write for humans and don't worry about SEO, or SEO-friendly page tags," is a common refrain among the ignorant.

Indeed, with recent chatter about Google's **RankBrain** algorithm update, there is more and more talk about AI (Artificial Intelligence) and voice search. The idea is that Google is getting better at a) inferring meaning from how people talk, and b) predicting how a search for one thing (e.g., "pizza") leads to a search for another thing ("directions to Jason's Pizza Emporium of Palo Alto"). RankBrain and voice search, however, are far from impacting most searches on Google (especially "transactional" search terms), and are not quite ready for prime time. For those of us with small businesses, we can focus on writing good, keyword-heavy prose in the proper HTML and SEO-friendly format. Follow the instructions above for SEO-friendly prose that is also easy for humans to read, and you'll be fine. To learn more about RankBrain, see **http://jmlinks.com/35c**.

Even more important, remember that keywords still matter and are not going away anytime soon. Here's why.

First, people type keywords into Google and speak keywords into their mobile phones and these words are the "connection points" indicating what they want Google to go out an "find" for them. Secondly, language in and of itself is *sui generis* based on keywords, and Google isn't going to change language. We don't beat around the bush. Rather, we say things like, "Honey do you want **PIZZA** tonight?" to our spouses and "Excuse me, do you know where the **TOILET PAPER** is?" to the employees at the supermarket. So keywords mark what we want in actual human language. They are not going away!

Third, the *keywords META tag* is ignored but this confusion between a META tag and keywords causes even more confusion. It's the META tag that's ignored, not keywords. And, finally, this idea that "keywords don't matter" is based on a false choice: either you write FOR PEOPLE or you write FOR GOOGLE, when in fact, you can write for both.

Aim for the sweet spot of keyword density high enough for Google but not so high as to be unreadable, or "stuffed" in the parlance of SEO. A little salt is good for the soup, and too much salt ruins it. But you need salt to make soup! Google isn't abolishing "keywords" any more than cooks are going to abolish salt!

To use another analogy: as I always tell my wife on our yearly road trips: speed a little, honey, but don't be the fastest car on the Interstate. If you don't speed, you won't get there first (or near first), but if you drive the red car, right past the cop at 120 mph, you'll get pulled over. Don't *underdo* your keyword density, and don't *overdo* it either (welcome to post-*Panda* SEO content).

And don't believe everything you read on the blogosphere. A lot of it is pure dribble.

» THE ANSWER BOX

Search is moving towards voice search as more and more people talk into their mobile phones or speak into devices such as Apple Siri, Amazon Alexa, and Google home. So search is moving towards "natural speech," which means that as you research your keywords and write your content, you want to think more and more about how people talk and about how people answer questions with natural syntax.

Take a high-value search such as "How do I repair my credit?" Try searching that on Google. You'll see what's called the "Answer box" showing prominently in the first position (or what's come to be called "Position Zero"). Here's a screenshot of the top-ranked website formatted into what is called the Answer Box on Google:

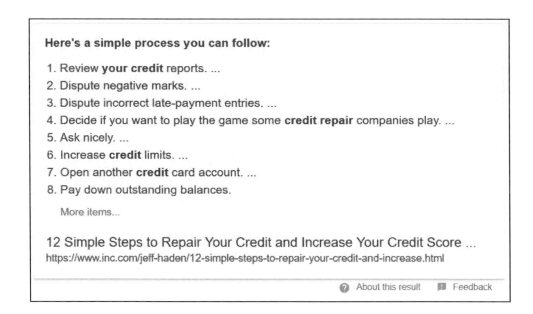

Check out the winning web page on INC.com at **http://jmlinks.com/47d**. Next, notice their HTML tag structure vis-à-vis target keywords and how they use tags such as the H2 tag and numbers like "1," "2," "3," etc. They are "answering" the question posed to Google almost "as if" you as a human were asking them a question and they as a human were answering back. The trend is thus towards semantic question and answers "as if" you were having a conversation with web searchers.

Also note that just below this answer, you'll see what are called PAA's or "People also ask." Here's a screenshot:

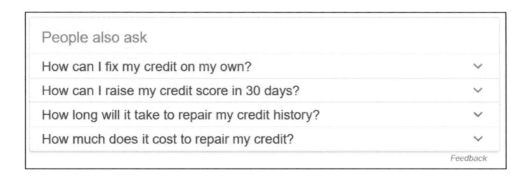

Each of these is it's own "answer" to a common "question."

Clearly, Google wants to go in the direction of natural Q&A speech and it's rewarding websites that answer back in an organized fashion with a higher ranking. The magic words to learn more about this trend are "featured snippets" or "position zero." You can Google "How to rank for position zero?" or "How to rank in featured snippets?" and you'll find blog posts and YouTube videos explaining the steps. The long and short of it is:

1. **Research** your keyword targets and **state them in question format**.
2. **Answer** these questions by placing the appropriate keywords in the key HTML tags. Write content that regurgitates the question and answers it back "as if" you were having a conversation.
3. Use **tags** such as the Header tag family, TABLES, and lists to indicate a step-by-step structured response.
4. **Build links** and do **Off Page SEO** (which we'll discuss in Chapter 5.1).
5. **Rank** for "Position 0" by **out-doing your competitors** in terms of SEO.

For an in-depth explanation of "featured snippets" and how to rank for them, visit **http://jmlinks.com/47e**. As you work with Google to build out the new AI (Artificial Intelligence) web, just remember that "Genisys is Skynet." Say to your Google device, "Hey Google! What is the date Skynet becomes self-aware?," and you'll understand.

» DELIVERABLE: A COMPLETED PAGE TAG WORKSHEET (FOR ONE PAGE)

The first **DELIVERABLE** for Step Three is a completed **page tag worksheet** for one specific landing page, other than your homepage. Take either a new page or an existing page of your website, and compare it against the desired target keyword. (Note: each page should have one, and only one, keyword target. Using the "page tag worksheet," audit the page for how well it communicates the keyword target to Google. For the worksheet, go to **http://jmlinks.com/seo19tz** (reenter the passcode "seo19tz"), and click on the link to the "page tag worksheet." Note: you'll want to do this at least for all of your major landing pages.

As you work on your On Page SEO, here are two free, useful tools to help you analyze your keywords vs. tag structure and visible content.

SEO Workers at **http://jmlinks.com/5w**.

SEO Centro at **http://jmlinks.com/13p**.

Input an individual web page from your website into one of these tools and check it against its keyword target. The page's target keyword / keyphrase should be clearly and prominently indicated in the tool; if not, you are not correctly signaling keyword priorities to Google. For more nifty tools to help with Page Tags, refer to my SEO dashboard at **http://jmlinks.com/seodash** and scroll down to the subsection called Page Tags.

Obviously, your **TO-DO** here is to audit the content of not just one page on your website but rather each and every page on your website, especially your landing pages, and upgrade them to SEO-friendly HTML for Google. Note as you do this that each landing page should focus on *one*, and *only one* keyword group, as Progressive.com does with a unique landing page for auto insurance, another one for motorcycle insurance, and yet another one for Segway insurance. By having a **single keyword focus** per landing page you will vastly improve your chances of ranking on Google.

» SET UP YOUR HOMEPAGE

Page tag SEO applies to your homepage, but your homepage is so important you should handle it in a very specific way. Your homepage is your "front door" to Google and the **most important page** of your website. Google rewards beefy, keyword-heavy homepages that have a lot of text. Think carefully about every word that occurs on this page, and about the way each word is "structured" by embedding it into good HTML page tags. Here are your important "to do's" for your homepage:

Identify your customer-centric, top three keywords. These three "most important" words must go into your homepage <TITLE> tag, the most powerful tag on your website!

Repeat the <TITLE> tag content in the <H1> tag on the page. There should be at least one <H1> but no more than three per page.

Identify your company's major product / service offerings. Re-write these using customer-centric keywords, and have <H2> tags leading to these major landing pages, nested inside of <A HREF> tags. Be sure to include the keywords inside the <H2> and <A HREF> tags!

Have Supporting Images. Google rewards pages that have images with ALT attributes that are keyword heavy. Don't overdo this, but have at least one and no more than about seven images on your homepage that have keywords in their ALT attributes.

Create keyword-focused one-click links. Link down from your homepage to defined landing pages around target keyword phrases.

- **Write lengthy, keyword-rich content for your homepage.** You need not just structural elements, but lots of beefy prose on your homepage that clarifies to Google what your company is "about."

For good homepage ideas, look at Healthy Paws Insurance (**https://www.healthypawspetinsurance.com/**), eSurance (**https://www.esurance.com/**), as well as some of SEO-savvy Bay Area medical malpractice attorneys such as **http://www.danroselaw.com/**. Now, some of this is a bit overdone, but the point is to see that effective SEO homepages have a lot of text, contain the target keywords, and embed the keywords in key tags often with links "down" to specific landing pages.

VIDEO. Watch a quick video tutorial on effective SEO homepages at **http://jmlinks.com/18g**.

Or, choose your own industry, do some high-level searches on Google or Bing, and reverse engineer the homepages of the winners at SEO. Then, proceed to audit your own homepage: how effectively does your own homepage "speak Google?"

In auditing your homepage, it should:

- Have a **TITLE tag** that succinctly explains your business value proposition, and includes at least three highly valued keywords in the first 59 characters.
- Have a **META description** tag that explains your business value proposition, contains your keywords, and is written in a pithy, exciting way to "get the click" from Google to your website. The character limit, of course, is 300 characters.
- Follow the **principles of Page Tag SEO** by weaving your keywords into the main tags such as the H1 / H2 family, the A HREF anchor tag, the IMG alt tags, etc.
- Have **keyword-dense, well-written text** that explains what you do and contains your target keywords.
- Have "**one-click**" links down to your most important landing pages.

It should also be visually appealing to humans, and lead to a desired action such as a sale or a registration form. Don't forget the carbon-based life forms!

A Warning about Too Many Changes

One final warning. Don't change your TITLE tags frequently. Google will penalize a site that has such-and-such Homepage TITLE tag on day 1, and then another on day 7, and still another on day 44. A good rule of thumb is to decide on your TITLE tags for your homepage and key landing pages. Run them by your boss and team members, and sleep on it. Then deploy them, and **do not change them again** for at least ninety days. This rule is really for the TITLE tags, but not the content itself. Ironically, Google actually rewards Homepages that have "new" content such as featured blog posts, so optimize your TITLE tags and leave them alone but feel free to update your content, especially blog posts and press releases.

» DELIVERABLE: A HOMEPAGE PAGE TAG AUDIT

In the next Chapter, we'll learn a bit more about how website structure influences Google and SEO, but we can begin the process now by doing a **page tag audit** for your homepage. The most powerful tag on your website is the homepage TITLE tag, so start there. Drill down to the text content on your homepage and verify that it contains the priority keyword targets identified in your keyword worksheet.

> **WORKSHEETS.** For your **DELIVERABLE**, analyze your homepage's existing Page Tag vs. target keyword status, and devise a "quick fix" strategy to improve keyword placement in important tags. For the worksheet, go to **http://jmlinks.com/seo19tz** (reenter the passcode "seo19tz" to register if you have not already done so), and click on the link to the "homepage worksheet."

»» CHECKLIST: PAGE TAG ACTION ITEMS

Test your knowledge of page tags! Take the *Page Tag quiz* at **http://jmlinks.com/qzpt**. Next, here are your page tag **Action Items**:

❑ **Learn** the basics of HTML **Page Tags** and SEO. Which tags are the most important?

  ❑ Download and read the *Google SEO Starter Guide*. Verify that you are implementing its recommendations on your website.

❑ **Audit** at least one "landing page" for SEO; ultimately, audit all of your key landing pages for Page Tags. For each -

  ❑ **Identify** the keyword target and closely related keywords.

  ❑ **Verify** that the **keyword target** is in the TITLE, META DESCRIPTION, IMG ALT, A HREF, and HEADER tags.

    ❑ Write **keyword-heavy visible content** that is also easy-to-read for humans and follows grammatically correct English, including having related phrases and words just like people talk.

❑ **Audit** your **homepage** for SEO.

  ❑ Know your **keyword targets** and closely related keywords. *Usually, the Homepage identifies the MOST IMPORTANT two or three keywords for the website.*

  ❑ **Verify** that the **keyword target** is in the TITLE, META DESCRIPTION, IMG ALT, A HREF, and HEADER tags.

  ❑ **Write keyword-heavy visible content** that is also easy-to-read for humans. Be sure to get the five or seven key phrases that you want to rank for on your homepage, including helpers words and qualifiers such as cities or locations.

  ❑ **Create "one-click"** links FROM the homepage TO the landing pages around keyword phrases.

Check out the **free tools**! Go to my *SEO Dashboard > Page Tags* for my favorite free tools for tags. Just visit **http://jmlinks.com/seodash**.

3.2

WEBSITE STRUCTURE

Website structure – that is, the "organization" of your website - is a major part of **Step #3**. Whereas **page tags** approach SEO from the perspective of individual web pages, website structure turns your attention to how your *entire* website communicates keyword priorities to Google. How you name your files, how you "reach out" to Google, how you link your homepage to and from your landing pages, and how you optimize your landing pages all combine to make a *good* SEO strategy, *great*!

Let's get started!

TO-DO LIST:

» Define SEO Landing Pages

»» Deliverable: Landing Page List

» Write a Keyword Heavy Footer

» Create a Blog and Start Blogging

» Use Keyword Heavy URLs over Parameter URLs

» Leverage the Home Page for One Click Links

» Be Mobile-friendly, Fast, and Secure

» Join Google and Bing Webmaster Tools

»» Deliverable: Website Structure Worksheet

»» Checklist: Website Structure Action Items

» DEFINE SEO LANDING PAGES

We've already touched several times on the key concept of **landing pages**. From the perspective of SEO, a landing page is a page that targets one, and only one, specific core keyword. For example, you see this clearly on Geico.com with specific pages for "motorcycle insurance," "car insurance," and even "ATV insurance." Revisit their sitemap at **http://jmlinks.com/47g** to browse their landing pages, but as you do so turn your perspective not to the individual pages and how they are SEO-optimized but to how the entire **website structure** works as a symphony of focus vis-à-vis Google.

Landing pages are not simply about "page tags." It's not simply about optimizing them one-by-one. It's about integrating them into the structure of the website to communicate interrelated themes to Google and to prioritize which keywords are the most important to the website. Technique we will discuss are a) "one-click" links from the homepage to the key landing pages, b) "one-click" links from a keyword footer to the landing pages, c) both HTML and XML sitemaps, and d) using blog posts to inject freshness to core landing pages by upward links. In addition, external link-building to key landing pages is yet another tool in the SEO toolbox.

Pet Insurance

In order to visualize SEO-friendly website structure, let's turn our gaze towards the pet insurance industry. Notice, right out of the gate, that in terms of keyword patterns or search queries on Google we have:

> *pet insurance* at **http://jmlinks.com/37x**,
>
> *dog insurance* at **http://jmlinks.com/37y**, and
>
> *cat insurance* at **http://jmlinks.com/37z**.

So we have one ambiguous keyword phrase and two non-ambiguous phrases, and all of the three are pretty transactional. By the time someone is searching for "cat insurance," he's done with education and he's ready to buy (or at least get a quote). Among the high-ranking websites for these patterns we have:

https://www.petinsurance.com/

https://www.healthypawspetinsurance.com/

https://www.aspcapetinsurance.com/

Now, each has done a very good job at identifying their target keywords and weaving them into the proper HTML tags (TITLE, IMG ALT, A HREF, etc.), as well as writing good SEO-friendly copy that contains not only the target keywords but related words. Let's look at their **website structure** or **organization** and make some observations, using Healthy Paws as an example. We have:

A **Home Page** with optimized TITLE tag and SEO-friendly text, focusing on the more generic "pet insurance" at **https://www.healthypawspetinsurance.com/** and then a

A **Landing page** on "Dog Insurance" with optimized TITLE tag and SEO-friendly text at **https://www.healthypawspetinsurance.com/dog-and-puppy-insurance**

A **Landing page** on "Cat Insurance" with optimized TITLE tag and SEO-friendly text at **https://www.healthypawspetinsurance.com/cat-and-kitten-insurance.**

Notice as well how the Home Page has "one-click" links down from the Home Page to each Landing Page. Here's a screenshot:

Dog Insurance

Learn more about our pet insurance for dogs and puppies.

Cat Insurance

Learn more about our pet insurance for cats and kittens.

And here are some excerpts of the HTML code linking from the Home Page down to the landing page for "dog insurance:"

```
<img                    class="right                    mobile-hide"
src="/Images/V3/HomePage/icon_healthy_paws_dog_and_puppy_insurance
.png" alt="Our dog and puppy insurance" />


<h2   class="greenTitle   mobile-hide"   style="margin-left:   0;">Dog
Insurance</h2>


<img        class="mobile-show"        style="display:        inline-block;"
src="/Images/V3/HomePage/icon_healthy_paws_dog_and_puppy_insurance
.png" alt="Our dog and puppy insurance" />


Learn   more   about   our   <a   href="/dog-and-puppy-insurance">pet
insurance for dogs</a> and puppies.
```

Take a look as well at the footer of the website and notice how each and every page has textual links to the key landing pages, as indicated by keyword phrases. Here's a screenshot:

Pet Insurance

Dog Insurance

Cat Insurance

And here's the HTML code:

```html
<div class="bold">Pet Insurance</div>
<ul class="nodisc footerLinks">
    <li>
        <a href="/dog-and-puppy-insurance" track="Ftr - Dog Insurance">Dog Insurance</a>
    </li>
    <li>
        <a href="/cat-and-kitten-insurance" track="Ftr - Cat Insurance">Cat Insurance</a>
    </li>
```

Well done, well done, well done! Everything is working together as a team – Homepage, Landing Pages, and Footer to send clear signals to Google about the keyword target.

For your homework, take a moment and do the search "Pet insurance" on Google and then visit some of the top ranking websites – petinsurance.com, healthypawsinsurance.com, and aspcapetinsurance.com. Notice how each of them has this same structure of an optimized "Home Page," optimized "Landing Pages," and cross-links between them around the target keyword phrases. Don't miss the use of the site-wide footer as well.

THERE AREN'T A THOUSANDS WAYS TO AN SEO-FRIENDLY WEBSITE. THERE'S JUST ONE WAY.

As you return to your own website, audit it to verify that you have a well-defined homepage and then specific landing pages that represent that core keyword families you identified in your keyword worksheet. A common mistake is to think that there are thousands of ways to build an SEO-friendly website, when – in practice – there is just this one simple structure of *homepage > landing pages* plus a keyword footer, and a blog alongside.

Let's dive into the blog for a moment. Most strong websites have a blog as Healthy Paws does at **https://www.healthypawspetinsurance.com/blog/**. Notice as well that they have blog "categories" that touch on their keyword themes:

Pet Care Blog

Dog Health   Funny Pets

Cat Health   Claim Stories

Pet Care   Pet Insurance Reviews

Pet Stories

Thus the blog adds to their SEO symphony be reinforcing to Google the keyword themes and reminding Google that they have new or fresh content. A good blog post also links up or "link sculpts" up to the key landing pages, thus injecting freshness into the Google algorithm vis-à-vis the most important keyword themes. Hence, you need a blog to complete your SEO-friendly website structure.

Localized Landing Pages: a Special Case

If your business has a local element, it is often useful to create localized landing pages for individual cities or towns that are "helper words" for your keywords. For example, Stamford Uniform and Linen (**http://www.stamfordlinen.com/**) wants to dominate Google not only for keyword phrases such as "Stamford Linen Service" (where the business is located) but for those in nearby towns where they lack a physical store, such as "Hartsdale Linen Service" or "Greenwich CT Linen Service." One method to accomplish this is **localized landing pages**.

Check out the company's homepage, scroll to the bottom and notice the "one-click" links to landing pages for target cities plus the keyword search "uniform rental service." One of their target cities is Hartsdale, Connecticut, even though they are technically located in Stamford. Indeed, Stamford is part of the "suburban sprawl" outside most American cities, where one city (Stamford) blends into others like Greenwich, New Canaan, and Hartsdale. People search by city and Google optimizes results by nearby locations.

What can a business do then that needs to optimize for fragmented city-specific searches? **Create localized landing pages**, that's what they can do. (Now, this is a tactic that is close to a violation of Google's terms of service, called "doorway pages," so if you use this strategy you need to make sure that each page has unique, valuable content specific to the needs of the target city. Don't overdo this! You can get away with a few landing pages of this type, but not with hundreds. *See below for further discussion*).

A good tactic is to give "driving directions" from various cities to your home office, therefore giving each city-specific page a reason to exist and making it read as useful for humans. At the same time, you can optimize it for SEO.

For example, take a look at the Hartsdale page at **http://www.stamfordlinen.com/hartsdale/**. Also notice how each landing page is unique, with content at the bottom of each city that is unique and different from the others in the set. In addition to writing unique content for each page, you can also identify and city "local historical facts" about the city, or perhaps "famous people" from the city. You need to create unique and valuable content for each city-specific landing page.

Try some Google searches such as "Stamford Linen Service," "Hartsdale Linen Service," or "Greenwich CT Linen Service" to see how effective localized landing pages can be!

Another site that uses this effectively is Jonathan D. Sands. Check out his sitemap at **http://jmlinks.com/13q**. You'll see localized landing pages for cities such as Larchmont, Mamaroneck, and New Rochelle reflecting localized search patterns such as "Larchmont Personal Injury Lawyer" or "Mamaroneck Personal Injury Lawyer." Mr. Sands office is actually located in Mamaroneck, NY, but his SEO is trying to capture localized search patterns for nearby cities.

Doorway Pages and Localized Landing Pages

Caution: localized landing pages can be considered "doorway" pages by Google, especially post-Panda. You can read the official Google perspective on doorway pages at **http://jmlinks.com/6a**. The trick for localized landing pages is:

- **Be conservative**: create only a few landing pages for specific cities. Less is more.
- Make sure each has **unique** and valuable **content**.
- **Imagine you are a Googler** reading this page: does it have a reason to exist, other than being optimized for SEO?

To see a company that has gone overboard on this tactic, visit **http://www.certstaff.com**. Go to any page of that website and scroll to the bottom: you'll see page upon page of city-specific landing pages. This is a dangerous tactic, and sets that company up to be penalized, and completely removed from Google. Be careful! Less is more! Yet, it's working for certstaff.com. Try a search for "Fort Lauderdale Javascript training" and you'll find them in position #1 on Google. Ditto for "Unix classes Oklahoma City" and so on and so forth.

> **VIDEO.** Watch a video tutorial on SEO landing pages at **http://jmlinks.com/5z**.

»» DELIVERABLE: A LANDING PAGE LIST

Inventory your existing or to-be-created landing pages to reflect your major keyword patterns as described in your **keyword worksheet**. Using the "website structure worksheet" in combination with your **keyword worksheet**, create a list of your high priority landing pages. Each page will then be optimized via page tags and ultimately "one-click" from the homepage, using a keyword heavy syntax. I recommend a tab on your keyword worksheet that identifies no more than ten SEO-friendly landing pages for your website.

» WRITE A KEYWORD-HEAVY FOOTER

A second tactic I recommend is to write a **keyword-heavy footer**. Take a look at Progressive.com, scroll to the bottom, and check out their footer. Notice how the footer has direct links to major pages, all around the phrase "insurance" as in "motorcycle insurance." Or, take a look at my site **https://www.jasonmcdonald.org/** or **https://www.westpawdesign.com/**. Again, scroll to the bottom and see that target SEO keywords have been embedded in the footer with direct links to landing pages. Or take a look at Attorney Sands website at **http://jmlinks.com/13q** and again, you'll see a keyword-heavy footer.

Here's a screenshot of the West Paw Design footer, with "one-click" links to keyword-specific landing pages:

TOYS	BEDS
Dog Toys	**Dog Beds & Mats**
Zogoflex® Dog Toys	Montana Nap®
Zogoflex Air® Dog Toys	Heyday Bed®
	Big Sky Blanket®
	Replacement Bed Parts
Fabric Dog Toys	

And here's one for Stamford Linen:

In both cases, there are keyword-focused links from the footer to the more important landing pages.

Your keyword footer should be short, well-written, and contain only your most important keywords. Link FROM the keyword footer TO your target landing pages. The footer increases the site-wide density of your website for your target keywords and allows for "link sculpting" – linking around strategic keywords to your key landing pages. Here's another tip. I find the best success writing subject / verb / object footers, that is footers that speak in complete sentences vs. just throwing keyword links on the page. I also find that even if the key landing pages are in the top, visible navigation "for humans," I find best success when I have a redundant keyword footer "for Google" in the bottom navigation.

Using your Keyword Worksheet and the "landing pages" tab, make sure that as you create new pages for your website as well as blog pages that you link FROM these pages TO your landing pages around keyword-specific phrases. Again, do not overdo this. Just as a general rule, cross-link your pages to each other around important keyword phrases.

Once you have your basic structure of *Home Page > Landing Pages*, and *Footer > Landing Pages*, it's time to create a blog. Blogs are critical for both SEO and for social media marketing, as a good keyword-heavy blog allows you to comment on keywords that matter to you and your customer. In terms of social media marketing, a blog gives you a place to put content that is of interest to your human readers and customers (See my *Social Media Marketing Workbook* on Amazon at **http://jmlinks.com/smm** for more on this topic).

In terms of SEO, a blog allows you to do the following:

1. A blog allows you to write short SEO-friendly posts on **long tail keywords**. Take a look at the West Paw Design blog at **https://www.westpawdesign.com/scoop/**. Notice how the company blogs on topics of interest to pet owners, and also optimizes its blog posts on keyword topics such as "Dog-Friendly National Parks" (**http://jmlinks.com/35d**). Also notice how the blog links over to key landing pages, especially those that are product-oriented. Or, take a look at the Mentor Graphics blogs at **https://www.mentor.com/blogs/** and notice how that hi-tech company uses its blogs to write engineering articles yet touch on keywords that matter to it such as "Sensor Modeling and Signal Conditioning Circuit Design" (esoteric keywords for a techie industry) (**http://jmlinks.com/13s**).

2. A blog gives "freshness" to your website, with Google rewarding sites that have frequent postings. Indeed, I recommend that you automate your homepage so that it constantly rotates your three most recent blog posts onto the homepage as at **https://jm-seo.org/**. Scroll down to "News and blogs" to see my most recent three blog posts.

3. A blog allows you to link "up" to your strategic landing pages, and pass "freshness" to those landing pages. Your landing pages will not change frequently, but by blogging on related topics you can communicate to Google that you are fresh and alive. For an example of this, read my blog post on "SEOs, San Francisco, and Eating Your Own Dog Food" at **http://jmlinks.com/38a**.

Blogs are covered in Chapter 4.1 on content, but in terms of website structure, realize that having a blog and posting SEO-friendly, keyword-heavy content to your blog on a regular basis is a "must" for success at search engine optimization. I recommend you commit to at least four blog posts per month on your keyword themes.

» USE KEYWORD HEAVY URLS OVER PARAMETER URLS

URLs or web addresses are what you see in the URL or address bar at the top of the browser. Google pays a lot of attention to URLs; URLs that contain target keywords clearly help pages climb to the top of Google. Here's a screenshot of the Progressive landing page URL for "Motorcycle Insurance":

I have highlighted the URL in yellow.

Try a few competitive Google searches such as "Reverse Mortgage Calculator" (**http://jmlinks.com/13t**) and notice how the URLs that are on page one often contain the target keywords. Here's the #1 result for "Reverse Mortgage Calculator" at **http://www.reversemortgage.org/About/Reverse-Mortgage-Calculator** and here's the #3 result at **http://reversemortgagealert.org/reverse-mortgage-calculator/**.

What's the takeaway? If possible, choose a **domain** that contains your target keywords. Beyond that, make sure that your URLs (**file names**) contain the target keywords.

Consider these two examples:

> **Example 1 / Geek File Name** - *http://www.yourcompany.com/files/llk1/2/kyoklaol.html*. No "clues" to Google as to what is "contained" inside these directories and files.

> **Example 2 / English File Name** - *http://www.sf-attorney.com/medical-malpractice/obstetrics.html*. The domain, directories, and file names all indicate that this is a medical malpractice attorney, specializing in suing OB/GYN doctors.

By the way, what goes for URLs also goes for **images**: name your images after keywords just as you name your URLs after keywords. Rather than naming an image "image215.jpg" have your graphic designer name your images after your keywords such as "medical-malpractice.jpg."

Re-read the *Google SEO Starter Guide* (**http://jmlinks.com/googleseo)** and you'll notice that Google says, "Improve the structure of your URLS" (pg. 8) and "Optimize your use of images" (Pg. 18), so – again – *just be crazy and do what Google is literally telling you to do*: put keywords in your URLS and IMAGE file names / alt tags!

As part of the **DELIVERABLE** for Step #3, conduct an inventory of your website URLs and image file names (as well as ALT attributes). Are they keyword heavy? Do the visible keywords match the keyword themes from your keyword worksheet?

Parameter URLS

Just as important, **avoid parameter URLs**. Parameter URLs are URLs that contain numeric, crazy, geeky codes such as the question mark (?), percent sign (%), equals sign (=), or SessionIDs (often marked SESSID=), these indicate to Google that these are "temporary" pages not worth indexing. Static, keyword heavy URL's far outperform URLs that tell Google a website is database-driven via geeky parameter URLs.

PARAMETER URLS = KISS OF (SEO) DEATH

As examples of sites that use parameter URLs, visit **http://www.zilog.com** or **http://dl.acm.org**. Both sites have URL's full of session IDs, question markets, etc. Refer back to the *Google SEO Starter Guide* (**http://jmlinks.com/googleseo**) and read the section on Parameter URLs. On page 8, Google says:

> URLs like (1) can be confusing and unfriendly. Users would have a hard time reciting the URL from memory or creating a link to it. Also, users may believe that a portion of the URL is unnecessary, especially if the URL shows many unrecognizable parameters. They might leave off a part, breaking the link. Some users might link to your page using the URL of that page as the anchor text. If your URL contains relevant words, this provides users **and search engines** with more information about the page than an ID or oddly named parameter would (2) (*emphasis added*)

Here's an example URL on Zilog.com:

> *http://zilog.com/index.php?option=com_product&task=product&businessLine=1&id=77&parent_id=77&Itemid=57*

To Google, that URL looks like a mess of information; therefore, this page is going to receive a negative ding in the search algorithm for its target keywords.

Avoid parameter URLs at all costs as Google severely deprecates them in its search results!

If you do have parameter-based URLs, **insist** that your webmaster convert them to "pseudo-static" URLs. You can Google "pseudo-static" URLs for articles on this topic. If you are using WordPress make sure that the "permalink" setting has keyword-heavy URL's. Just to make our lives more miserable, there are blog posts even by Google that say parameter URLs are OK. Don't believe everything you read on the blogosphere! Try searches that matter to your company and count the number of parameter-based URLs that are ranking on page one of Google. I guarantee it won't be many, if any. If you get into an argument with a geeky Web nerd who says the official Google blog said such-and-such about parameter URL, take out your copy of the *Google SEO Starter Guide* and smack him on the head.

PARAMETER URLS: JUST SAY NO.

Siloing and Link Sculpting

Bruce Clay, one of the gurus of the SEO industry, has coined the term "SEO Silos" to explain how keyword structure should determine website architecture. You can read an excellent article by him entitled, "SEO Siloing: How to build a website silo architecture," at **http://jmlinks.com/37u**. Secondarily, Matt Cutts of Google wrote a landmark blog post in 2009 on "PageRank Sculpting" (**http://jmlinks.com/38b**). The point of this discussion of URL structure and internal linking has been to emphasize the following:

1. Your website URL's should be **keyword-heavy** and reflect the core keywords as determined on your keyword worksheet. It goes without saying that you refrain from using parameter-based URLs.

2. If at all possible, "like" content should be put into "like" **directories** (e.g., all the content on "cat insurance" should "live" in a directory called *abc.com/cat-insurance* as in *abc.com/cat-insurance/get-a-cat-insurance-quote* and *abc.com/cat-insurance/kitten-insurance*, etc. This is what Bruce Clay means by "siloing."

3. If siloing is not possible, then links on your website FROM any given page TO your landing pages should be around the keyword phrase, i.e., any blog post that mentions "cat insurance" should link around the phrase "cat insurance" to *abc.com/cat-insurance*. This is what Matt Cutts is implying by "PageRank **Sculpting**."

In addition, you should refrain from linking outwards to other websites, except when they are in your keyword community and are quite important. A Brahman Cattle breeder, for example, should like to Brahman.org (the National Association of Brahman Cattle breeders) and a San Francisco pizza restaurant should link to both SFGov.org (the City of San Francisco) and the American Pizza Community (**http://www.americanpizzacommunity.com/**) *which promotes pizza as a shared meal in communities everywhere* and is "in" the keyword community of pizza.

In summary, how you structure your URLs, how you link to and from your internal pages, and how you link outwards are strong signals to Google as to your keyword targets. So do all of this in a very organized, systematic, and judicious way. Don't take all of this too seriously and drive yourself crazy, however. Do the best you can, the point being to use your keyword themes to structure your links. *And eat a lot of pizza, especially with friends, because a) pizza is good, and b) friends are good.*

» LEVERAGE THE HOMEPAGE FOR ONE CLICK LINKS

Google interprets your homepage as the most powerful page on your website, and as we saw in the Page Tags Chapter, you want to have lots of keyword-heavy text on the homepage. In addition, you should embed our most important keywords into the homepage TITLE tag. Beyond that, you should leverage your homepage as a "one-click" gateway to your landing pages. It's as if your HTML communicated this message to Google:

Home Page > One Click to Landing Pages = *Hey Google! These keywords are important to us!*

Google also looks at the directory structure, namely the presence of keywords in URLs and how "far" those URLs are from the homepage or "root" directory. So, in addition to naming your directories and files after your keyword families and high priority keywords, and placing "one-click" links from your homepage, create a directory structure that is "**shallow**" or "**flat**."

http://www.yourcompany.com/medical-malpractice/sue-doctors.html (2nd level)

is seen by Google as "more important" than

http://www.yourcompany.com/1/files/new/medical-malpractice/sue-doctors.html (5th level)

Thirdly, your homepage needs to communicate "freshness" to Google by having at least three *fresh* press releases and/or three new blog posts. Having new, fresh content that is "one click" from the homepage signals to Google that your website is alive and updated (vs. a stagnant site that might be out of business), so it's a best practice to rotate press releases and/or blog posts through the homepage as "one-click" links.

VIDEO. Watch a video tutorial on SEO-friendly homepages at **http://jmlinks.com/18g**.

For the past few years, Google has emphatically trumpeted the "mobile revolution." Most searches now occur on mobile devices such as phones and tablets, and Google has declared itself a "**mobile-first**" company. On November 4, 2016, for example, Google announced "Mobile-first indexing" on the official Google Webmaster Central Blog (**http://jmlinks.com/38y**). The idea is that they will look, first, at how your site looks on a mobile phone and that will become THE index for both the desktop and mobile versions of Google. Sites that are not mobile friendly, and/or slow may be penalized with poor rank on Google, or even drop out of Google altogether. For a good article on how to prepare for the "mobile first' index see **http://jmlinks.com/39c**.

Here's what you need to do. First, make sure you are using a **responsive** website design. If you're using WordPress, a so-called "responsive" WordPress theme will accomplish this pretty easily. Just verify that your theme is responsive. If you're using another platform, you'll need to verify that your platform is responsive. Squarespace, for example, is already responsive (**http://jmlinks.com/38z**). (Use the free AdWords preview tool at **http://jmlinks.com/39g** and change the device type to *mobile device* to check out how your site looks on a phone). Second, make sure your website is fast – as fast as is possible. Use a tool like WebPageTest (**http://jmlinks.com/39a**), Google's own PageSpeed Insights (**http://jmlinks.com/39b**), or SEOSiteCheckUp.com's (**http://jmlinks.com/39d**). Inside of Google Analytics, you can click on *Behavior > Site Speed* to get detailed information on your site's speed over time. Contact your web hosting company and purchase *everything* that speeds up your website! The cost is inconsequential compared with the negative impact of a slow website.

Finally, if you are a big site such as a publisher, you can explore Google's move to promote **AMP** (Accelerated Mobile Pages) at **http://jmlinks.com/39e**. For most of us, if we are a) responsive, and b) fast, our websites will survive the transition to "mobile first" just fine. Don't panic.

Be Secure. Be https.

As for **security**, Google is also promoting the transition from *http* and to *https* (secure). A site like the JM Internet Group (**https://www.jm-seo.org/**) is secure and marked by *https*; a site like the JM Links Website (**http://jmlinks.com/**) is not secure and marked by *http*. (The "s" stands for *secure* or *encrypted*). All things being equal, the *https* sites may begin to outperform non-secure *http* sites (non-encrypted). Google is even threatening to "warn" users in Chrome about non-secure elements on websites! To learn more about *http* vs. *https*, visit **http://jmlinks.com/39f**. The bottom line is that you should begin planning a transition to *https*, though in my opinion this is not (yet) a critical SEO factor for most small business websites that are not eCommerce. If you are eCommerce and collecting credit card or payment data, it goes without saying that you should be *https* or secure.

» JOIN GOOGLE (AND BING) WEBMASTER TOOLS

Google rewards websites that make its job easier! Set up sitemaps for Google (and Bing), and participate in their official programs for Webmasters. Sign up for Google Search Console (formerly called "Webmaster Tools") for your website (**http://jmlinks.com/6c**) as well as Bing Webmaster tools (**http://jmlinks.com/6d**). Then follow the steps below to alert Google to your Google-friendly files as follows.

First, create an **HTML sitemap** that makes it easy for a search engine spider to go from Page 1 to Page 2 to Page 3 of your website. If you use Javascript / CSS pulldowns for navigation, your HTML sitemap is a critical alternative path for Google to index your website. Second, use the free tool at **http://jmlinks.com/6c** to create your XML sitemap. If you are using WordPress, look for a plugin that creates an HTML sitemap as well as an XML sitemap. Third, create a robots.txt file that points to your XML sitemap. (Note: if you are using WordPress, just search popular plugins for XML sitemaps and robots.txt functionality). Test your *robots.txt* file to verify that Google can easily index your website.

Fourth, after you have created these files, submit your **sitemap.xml** file via Webmaster tools. Pay attention as well to your "crawl errors" and "HTML suggestions." All things being equal, sites that participate in Webmaster tools will beat out sites that do not. Here's a screenshot of how to submit an XML sitemap via Google webmaster tools:

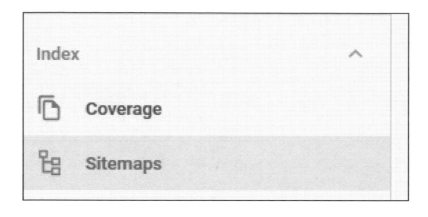

Click on Sitemaps and follow the instructions to submit your XML sitemap.

Fetch as Google

Another feature available in the Google search console is "fetch as Google" located at *Search Console > Crawl > Fetch* as Google. (Note: this feature is only available in the "old" version of Search Console at this time of writing, so transition back from the "new" to the "old" version by clicking "Go to the old version" at the bottom left to access this.)

What fetch-as-Google does is alert Google to new or revised content on your website, thus increasing the speed at which your site gets indexed in Google and is available to rank high.

If you create a new page on your website, or edit an existing page, for example, you can log in to the Google search console and "submit" your new URL to Google. In this way, you get into the Google index faster and can more quickly climb to the top of Google. Here's a screenshot:

Fetch as Google

See how Google renders pages from your website. Learn more

http://www.jm-seotips.org/   Desktop ▾   FETCH   FETCH AND RENDER

Leave URL blank to fetch the homepage. Requests may take a few minutes to process

This feature is also useful to get a new blog post indexed. First, write a new blog post. Second, log in to Google Search Console, and go to "Fetch as Google." Third, submit your URL to Google. This accelerates the indexing of a timely post to your blog.

To find out if content is indexed, use the *site:* command on Google. Enter a URL of your website after site: (no space) on Google. To see an example, go to **http://jmlinks.com/13u** which confirms that the blog post at **https://www.jm-seo.org/2016/08/google-local-impness-description/** is "in" the Google index. If not, then I could use "fetch as Google" to alert Google to index / reindex it.

Set a Preferred Domain

You should also set a "preferred" domain (available under the gear icon, top right of the screen, under "site settings."). This is because you want to tell Google to use **http://jm-seotips.org** not **http://www.jm-seotips.org**. This prioritizes one format for SEO. Here's a screenshot:

Site Settings

Preferred domain	⊙ Don't set a preferred domain
	⊙ Display URLs as **www.jm-seotips.org**
	⦿ Display URLs as **jm-seotips.org**
Crawl rate	⦿ Let Google optimize for my site (recommended)
	⊙ Limit Google's maximum crawl rate

Similarly, via your Web hosting company, make sure that the one you do NOT want redirects to the one you do want. For example, if you go to **https://jm-seo.org/**, it redirects you to **https://www.jm-seo.org/**. The magic word here is the "htaccess" file, which you can read about at **http://jmlinks.com/6f**. Generally, I'd ask your resident computer nerd or the tech support at your web hosting company to make sure one, and only one, format is in use.

To test this, choose one preferred version such as **https://www.jm-seo.org/**. Then create an email to yourself or text file of the three alternate versions, click on them and make sure that they all redirect to the current version:

https://jm-seo.org > https://www.jm-seo.org/

http://jm-seo.org > https://www.jm-seo.org/

http://www.jm-seo.org > https://www.jm-seo.org/

Also take your domain as in **jm-seo.org** and search on Google using the *site:* command as in *site:jm-seo.org*. Verify that all the results returned are to your one, and only one, preferred version. Check this out at **http://jmlinks.com/47h**.

Turning back to Search Console (again in the "old" version only), click down from Search Traffic to **International Targeting** and set your country to United States (if you are in the USA), or to whatever country you are in (if you are somewhere else).

Other To-dos in Webmaster Tools

There are some other features of value in Webmaster tools. Scrolling down the left menu in Google Search Console, let me point out the following:

Messages. If you are penalized by Google (or Bing), you may see a warning message when you log in. Plus, you can be emailed alerts for web problems such as manual penalties or hacking.

Search Appearance. Drill down into some information about how Google sees your website structure, including so-called "microdata."

Search Traffic. Google will give you some data about which keywords you rank for, as well as links to your site from other sites. In addition, it has a "mobile usability" check up feature to give suggestions as to how friendly your website is to mobile users.

Google Index. Here, you get information on how indexed your site is by Google, blocked resources, and how to remove URLs from the public index.

Crawl. Google gives you information on how it is crawling your website, including errors as well as the important "fetch as Google" function described above.

Security Issues. If you've been hacked, Google will alert you and give you tips on how to recover.

You should also link Google Search Console to your Google Analytics account. For the help file, visit **http://jmlinks.com/47j**.

Bing's Webmaster tools has similar features. In particular, Bing's information on inbound links to your site and keyword discovery tools are meritorious as is Bing's SEO Analyzer which gives feedback on how SEO-friendly a URL is.

VIDEO. Watch a video tutorial of how to use Google Webmaster Tools (Search Console) at **http://jmlinks.com/17u**.

» DELIVERABLE: A COMPLETED WEBSITE STRUCTURE WORKSHEET

At this point, you have the major components of the Chapter **DELIVERABLE**: a **website audit** using the "website structure worksheet," namely:

1. **Your homepage**. Optimize your Home Page TITLE tag, META DESCRIPTION tag, IMG ALT's, and visible text. Link down to your key landing pages.

2. **Your target landing pages**. These are your product or service pages that match common keywords searches your customers do on Google. Inventory the ones that you have as well as the ones that you need to create, and then outline the SEO-friendly content you will write (or rewrite) and weave into the correct tag structure.

3. **Create a Keyword Footer**. Write a short paragraph with keyword-optimized links to your key landing pages.

4. **Your Blog**. Set up a blog, and started to blog on your keywords.

5. **Your URL structure**. Avoid parameter (numeric, special character) based URLs in favor of keyword heavy URLs, and build a "shallow" website organization.

6. **Your Google-Friendly Files**. Make sure you've signed up for Google (and Bing) webmaster tools and Google Analytics, including an HTML sitemap and robots.txt file.

7. **Participate in Google (and Bing) Webmaster Tools**. You should have registered for Webmaster Tools and crossed your t's and dotted your i's in terms of sitemaps (both XML and HTML) and preferred domain.

DELIVERABLE. Complete the "website structure worksheet." For the worksheet, go to **http://jmlinks.com/seo19tz** (reenter the passcode "seo19tz"), and click on the link to the "Website Structure Worksheet."

»» CHECKLIST: WEBSITE STRUCTURE ACTION ITEMS

Test your knowledge of website organization! Take the *Website Structure quiz* at **http://jmlinks.com/qzws**. Next, here are your structure **Action Items**:

❑ **Define**, based on your keyword worksheet, your 3-10 SEO landing pages.

    ❑ If appropriate, create *localized landing pages* but make sure that they have useful content for humans (!). Do not overdo this!

❑ Organize your **website structure** from the Home Page to the key landing pages to the blog; write a keyword footer.

❑ Make sure you have **"one-click" links** to the landing pages from the Home Page.

❑ Make sure you have **"one-click" links** to the landing pages from the keyword footer.

❑ Set up a blog and start blogging (more in the next Chapter).

❑ Verify that you have *non-parameter URLs*

❑ Verify that you are mobile-friendly ("responsive") and fast.

❑ Silo or "link sculpt" to/from your key landing pages based on keyword themes

❑ Link out to a few key industry-specific websites.

❑ Set up and join Google Search Console and Bing Webmaster Tools

Check out the **free tools**! Go to my *SEO Dashboard > Website Structure Tools* for my favorite free tools for website organization. Just visit **http://jmlinks.com/seodash**.

4.1

CONTENT SEO

In **Step #1**, you defined your goals; in **Step #2**, you identified your keywords; and in **Step #3**, you structured your pages and website to talk to Google about your target keywords. In **Step #4**, you begin to populate your SEO-friendly website with keyword heavy content.

Content, after all, is king.

But let's be clear. Just throwing content up on your website willy-nilly won't help your SEO! Why? Well, for one, we've already learned that *well-structured content* (SEO-friendly page tags, SEO-friendly website structure) is critical for success at SEO. For two, that content needs to be well-written and include your keywords in sufficient density. And, for three, Google increasingly looks at not only grammar and related words but whether the human user actually finds it interesting, so you need to write content that's good for Google AND good for humans.

In **Step #4**, we will expand on this by creating an **SEO Content Marketing Strategy** ("Content SEO" for short) built upon your keyword targets.

Content SEO is all about creating web pages that *match* Google search *queries* with compelling, relevant *content,* be that on a specific web page, a press release, or a blog post. **Content SEO** is all about creating an on-going "content marketing machine" (*daily, weekly, monthly content*) that produces compelling SEO-friendly content for your website. And, in the new synergy between SEO and *social media marketing,* **Content SEO** is also about creating content that real people want to read, and want to share on Twitter, LinkedIn, Facebook and other social networks.

Let's get started!

To-do List:

» Dispose Yourself of the False Content Dichotomy

» Identify Keyword Themes

» Create a Content Map

» Set up a Blog and Start Blogging

» Create a Content Marketing Plan

»» Checklist: Content Action Items

»» Deliverable: A Content Marketing Plan

» Dispose Yourself of the False Content Dichotomy

Allow me to get up on my soapbox here for a moment. As you've read this book, so far, you've surely realized that I make a big deal about **keywords**. I strongly advocate that you research your keywords and that you identify five to ten core transactional keywords for your website. I also recommend, as we shall see in more detail in a moment, that you focus on keyword families or clusters of keyword, including educational search queries, especially for your blog.

SEO stands or falls, in my view, with keywords.

However, you will undoubtedly read on the blogosphere that Google has "moved beyond" keywords and that Google can "figure out" what you mean (or what the searcher intent) is. Just recently, for example, I read Neil Patel's article, "Why You Shouldn't Do Keyword Research for Your Blog Posts (And What to Do Instead)" (**http://jmlinks.com/38c**). As a good teacher, I want to expose you to this newer, sexier, and easier theory of how to succeed at SEO: just write great content for Google and let Google do the rest. It goes under the ruse of "content marketing," and it's wrong.

In this view, you can abandon worrying about keywords (and about your rank on keyword queries as well). You can just write "for humans" and not worry about Google, SEO, and the tried-and-true methodologies of researching keywords, inserting keywords into the proper HTML tags, writing keyword-heavy text and yet not overdoing it in the age of Google Panda. Neil Patel is a smart guy (probably smarter than I am), and there are many gurus who follow this new thinking. Well, like there was the "New Math," there's the "New SEO." (And like the "New Math" or the "New Coke," I don't think this is going to end well).

First and foremost, this idea of writing just "great content for Google" is based on a **false dichotomy**, a false choice. Either you write for Google or you write for humans, either you embed your keywords in HTML tags or you write for Google, and so on and so forth. In my humble opinion, you can do *both* and you *should* do *both*. It's a "false choice" to think you can't research keywords and yet write great content, or that you shouldn't pay attention to the keywords people search for and write content accordingly.

Furthermore, SEO is an endeavor that can be measured. Do some searches that matter to you. Look at the top three winning results. Check to see if they have placed those keywords into key tags, and written content that at the very least spits back the keyword phrase to Google. Or, as you work on your SEO, create keyword-heavy content that follows the system I am teaching and content that follows this "New SEO" of letting Google think for you absent keywords. Then check which content ranks, and which content does not. In fact, in everything that follows in this Chapter, I am assuming that you are going to do your best to write content that humans actually read, humans actually find engaging, and humans actually find motivates them to take your desired action, whether that's a sales lead or an eCommerce sale.

> I believe in "content marketing." I just believe that you can do so by combining the more traditional SEO focus on keywords with the newer focus on writing great content that's engaging for your human audience. I believe in "both/and" not "either/or" when it comes to content.

Once you've disposed yourself of the notion that you should abandon keywords and create content "just for humans," you're ready to dive into SEO-friendly content marketing.

» IDENTIFY KEYWORD THEMES

Every successful website has keyword **themes** just as every successful company or organization has a **focus**. You don't produce *everything*, nor do your target searchers search Google for *everything*. You **focus**, and they **focus**. If you are Safe Harbor CPAs (**http://www.safeharborcpa.com/**), a CPA firm in San Francisco, for example, your target customers search Google for things like "San Francisco CPA Firms," "Business CPAs in San Francisco, CA," or keyword specific searches such as "CPA Firm for IRS Audit Defense in SF," or "FBAR Tax Issues." Guess what? Safe Harbor CPAs has matching content on its website for each of those queries, including an active blog, and that's no accident!

If you are a Houston probate attorney, you'll need lots of content about "Houston" and about "probate" plus related terms like estate planning, guardianships, and wills. Take a look at **http://www.fordbergner.com/** and – guess what – that site has well-optimized content, including an up-to-date blog, on exactly those keyword themes.

Both sites also have lots of content on their blogs about "adjacent" or "educational" keywords as contrasted with more purely transactional keywords. If you take a look at the Bergner blog, for example, you'll see blog headlines such as:

What to do with an IRA when estate planning

What Rights Do You Have as a Beneficiary?

Estate Planning: Tips To Pass on the Family Farm

Not Every State Handles Guardianships as Well as Texas

etc.

If **keyword discovery** is about organizing your SEO strategy around keyword themes, then **content SEO**, in turn, is about creating a strategy to produce the type of content that "matches" your keyword themes on an on-going basis.

MATCH CONTENT TO SEARCH QUERIES

The first step is to match your keyword themes as identified on your keyword worksheet with content that needs to be produced. Among the most common themes are:

Branded or Navigational Searches. These are searches in which customers already know your company, and simply use Google to find you quickly. In the example of Safe Harbor CPAs, a branded Google search is literally "Safe Harbor CPAs," while for Ford Bergner Law Firm it is "Ford Bergner." **Matching content**: your "about you" page on the website.

Reputational Searches. Customers often research reviews about a company, product, or service online before making that final decision to make a purchase. Google your company name plus "reviews" and make sure that what they see about your company is positive; you'll be creating and encouraging content to proliferate positive content about your company's reputation. **Matching content**: people don't search for *testimonials* about a business; they search for *reviews*. So rename your *testimonials* page on your website to *reviews* for better SEO. Also claim and optimize your company profiles on various reviews sites like Google, Yelp, CitySearch, Judy's Book, etc., and encourage happy customers to write reviews.

Anchor Searches. These are searches in which a core customer *need* matches a core *product or service*. In the example of Safe Harbor CPAs, an anchor search would be "San Francisco CPA Firms," or "Tax Preparation San Francisco." For a large company like Progressive Insurance, the anchor searches are "Auto Insurance" or "Motorcycle Insurance." **Matching content**: your landing pages.

Educational Anchor Pages. Besides transactional keyword searches, there are often common and repeated "educational searches" for which people want long-form content. An example would be an explanation of the difference between *follicular unit extraction* and *follicular unit transplantation* as techniques for hair transplants. Or, another example would be an explanation of *how to contest a will under Oklahoma law*. **Matching content**: FAQ (Frequently Asked Questions) documents, eBooks, and long-form blog posts.

Keyword Specific Searches / Long Tail. Searches that are usually (but not always) long tail searches (multiple search keywords), and reflect a very focused customer need or educational query. For example, "How to defend against an IRS audit?" or "Rights and responsibilities of a trustee in Texas" vs. just "CPA Firm" or "Probate attorney." **Matching content**: blog posts.

Keyword Specific Searches / Micro Searches. Short but micro-focused search queries such as "Tag Heuer Repair," or "Breitling Repair," or "AdWords Coupons." These are short but very specific search queries. **Matching content**: blog posts or micro landing pages.

News and Trending Searches. These are searches reflecting industry news, trends, and buzz. For example, with recent IRS initiatives to crack down on overseas assets, a search such as "FBAR" reflects an awareness of foreign asset disclosure requirements. Similarly, if you were a networking company, growing awareness of computer security would make blog posts on "cybersecurity" a good bet to attract interested customers. **Matching content**: blog posts, press releases, and video summaries (with matching YouTube videos)

These are not the only types of keyword queries and matching content that might exist; just the most common. Your **TO-DO** here is to track trending topics, and blog on them quickly to "get ahead" of the news cycle. Use tools like Google Alerts (**https://www.google.com/alerts**), Feedly (**https://feedly.com**), and Buzzsumo (**http://www.buzzsumo.com**) to monitor trending topics in your industry.

Evergreen Content and Link-bait Content

Many SEO content experts also distinguish between *evergreen* keywords (keywords that are always valuable such as "CPA San Francisco") vs. *time-sensitive* content (such as "2019 Tax Changes). And don't forget the difference between *educational* search queries and *transactional* search queries ("knee pain" vs. "best knee surgeon in San Francisco"). Finally, there is *link bait* content (such as infographics, or tutorial posts), designed to attract links, and of course *social media content*, especially content that is designed to be highly shareable on networks like Facebook or Twitter. Brainstorm content that has a long shelf-life, and that will attract user interest and inbound links.

Here's a screenshot from Backlinko (**http://jmlinks.com/18v**) showing an "Evergreen" FAQ on how to build links for SEO:

And here's a long form post on "How to contest a will in Texas" (**http://jmlinks.com/38d**) from Sheehan Law of Austin, Texas:

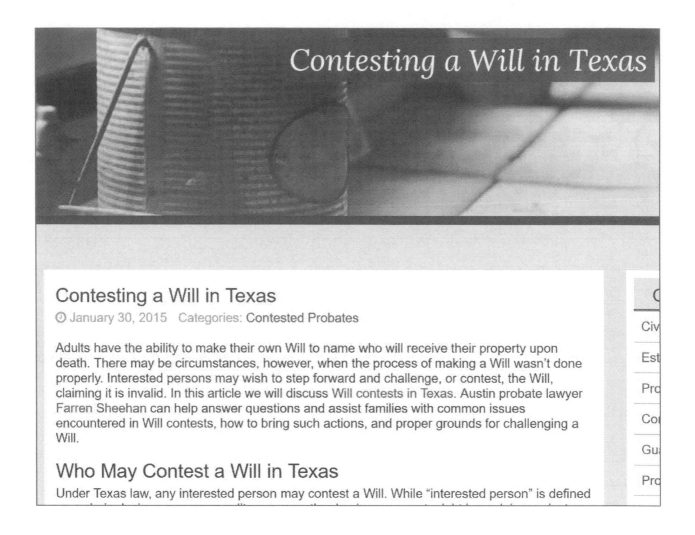

Regardless of the target keywords, the basic goal is to map out the types of content that are most relevant to you and your customers, and to start a content marketing process that generates highly relevant content on a regular basis. So your process is:

1. **Identify** a target keyword phrase, and match it to branded, educational, evergreen, anchor content, etc. Note: another way to think of this is to brainstorm "customer needs" or "customer pain points." What do your customers want to learn about? What interests them that relates to your company, product, or service? What hurts or scares them? What do they desire or want?

2. **Brainstorm** the type of content you need to produce that best matches the keyword query such as a long-form blog post, an FAQ document, or a short and quick blog about a trending topic.
3. **Produce** the content on a regular and systematic basis.
4. **Promote** the content, often by syndicating it as a Press Release, sharing it on social media, or even advertising it on Google, Facebook, or Twitter.

For your first **TO-DO**, review your **keyword worksheet**, brainstorm your keyword patterns, and group your keyword families into patterns that reflect **branded search**, **reputational search**, **anchor search**, **esoteric search**, and **news search** and other patterns.

» CREATE A CONTENT MAP

Now that you have your keyword themes, it's time to brainstorm the types of content you are going to create that will match the relevant keyword theme. Your second **TO-DO** is to create a **content map**. In a sense, you are "reverse engineering" the process of Google search: taking what people search on Google as your **endpoint**, and creating the type of content that has a good chance of appearing in Google search results as your **starting point**. Your **content map** will map your keyword themes to the relevant locations on your website.

Here's a table mapping out how keyword themes are generally reflected on website locations:

KEYWORD THEME	WEBSITE LOCATION	COMMENTS ON CONTENT SEO
Branded Searches	Home Page, About You, Testimonial Pages	Branded search is all about making sure you show up for your own name as well as commonly appended helper words like "reviews." Make sure that at least

		some TITLE tags communicate your name, and your "about" page is focused on branded search. Don't forget branded search for key company employees (JM Internet Group vs. Jason McDonald, for example).
Anchor Searches / Transactional Searches	Home Page, Landing Pages, Product Pages (High Level), FAQ documents, eBooks	Anchor or transactional search terms generally reflect your product categories in the format that customers search. Revisit *progressive.com*, for example, and you'll see how each anchor search query is reflected in a focused **landing page**. In addition, the site navigation and links are "sculpted" around keywords to pull Google up to the target landing pages. Besides landing pages, FAQ documents, Q&A documents, or infographics can match these anchor keywords.
Very Specific Searches	Product subpages, blog posts.	Your esoteric searches are generally long tail searches, and/or searches for very niche, focused products or services ("micro" searches). These are less competitive than anchor searches and are well served by content on product subpages on an e-commerce website as well as blog posts.
News Searches	Press releases, blog posts	Every industry has news, buzz, and timely topics! The place to put this content is generally either in a press

		release on your website, and/or a blog post.
Educational Searches	Blog posts, FAQ document, possible eBooks	These are when the potential customer is in "learn mode" as in the "causes of hair loss" rather than "Best Hair Transplant Surgeon in Miami."

For your second **TO-DO**, take your keyword themes and map out where they should be reflected on your website into your **content map** or **content calendar**. I recommend doing this in Excel. Check your rank on Google searches vs. relevant search queries for each type – if you are not on page one, or not in the top three positions for a query… you have work to do! If possible, create a content or editorial calendar and divvy up who in your company will be responsible for writing which content. The goal is to make a "content marketing machine" so that you are constantly feeding fresh content to your website and to your social media. Think *factory production*, not *William Shakespeare*!

In some cases, you may have *missing* elements (for example, you don't have blog or don't produce press releases); in others you may have the elements there *already* (product specific pages, for example) but their content is not SEO-friendly (has poorly defined TITLE tags, content does not reflect logical keyword target, etc.). Regardless, you are mapping your keyword themes to the logical locations on your website with the goal of getting into a rhythm or content creation process of creating SEO-friendly content on a regular basis.

Social Media & SEO

Google increasingly pays attention to social media, especially shares on Twitter. In addition, what people "share" on social media is also often what they "search for" on Google and what they "link to" on their blogs. So keep an eye on social media as you research and build out content for your website and blog.

What types of content interests your customers? What types of content are they likely to share? Use a tool like Buzzsumo (**http://www.buzzsumo.com/**), input your keywords, and identify the most shared content on Facebook, Twitter, LinkedIn, etc. This tells you what type of content is popular, and therefore you can produce that content yourself.

Here's a screenshot from Buzzsumo showing the most shared article on "hair transplant" for the past year:

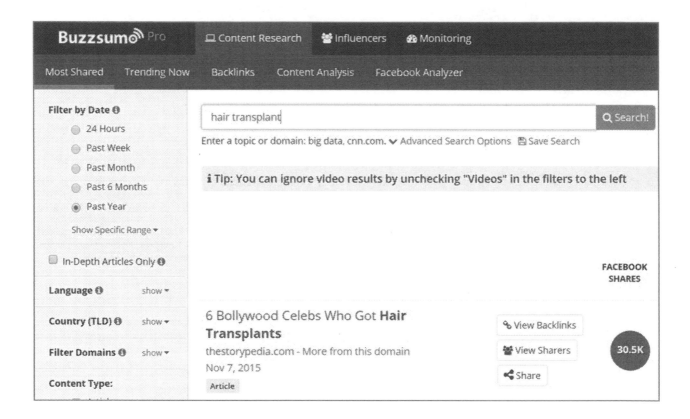

Another useful tool is Google trends (**http://jmlinks.com/38f**). David Meerman Scott coined the term "newsjacking" to describe a method of first identifying trending topics and second creating blog or social content that "newsjacks" that content for your own purposes. Watch his video at **http://jmlinks.com/38g**.

Click Backs and Google

Finally, related to the trend towards social media, is the idea of "click backs." Google monitors your every move (*we all know that, or at least we should*). They know your behavior on Google, on websites via the Analytics tracking code, via AdWords cookies, via YouTube, and via your Android phone. They know everything. Don't believe me? Google, "Is Google God?," and you'll end up at the ChurchofGoogle.com at **http://jmlinks.com/47k.**

Google knows when you do a Google search, click over to a website, and quickly "click back." They know you didn't find what you wanted, so to speak, and there is evidence that they may penalize sites that have "thin content" as measured by quick or frequent click backs to Google. In this way, and parallel to efforts to monitor social media, Google is likely already penalizing sites that have low-quality content, content that is just a few paragraphs, and content that is not engaging to users. This trend is likely to get stronger in the future.

Indeed, these intertwined trends – social media and Google monitoring – speak to upping your content marketing game by producing long-form content, content that is truly engaging and content people love to read. Quality and engagement are metrics not just on social media; they are now metrics for SEO-friendly content as well.

Is it easy to produce high-quality content? Well, no, it isn't. But did I title this book, "The Ridiculously Easy Guide to SEO?" No, I didn't. We're all competitors in the content game, however, so just remember that you only need to produce content that is better than your competitors, not perfect content.

» Set up a Blog and Start Blogging

To succeed at SEO, you must have a blog! Blogs are great for social media marketing, and for SEO, your blog helps in these important ways:

- **Micro-specific Content**. Whereas your major landing pages must reflect "anchor" searches, your blog can have a nearly infinite number of pages tied together by keyword themes. Your blog gives you the easy ability to create a lot of content and match that content on the many small, fragmented and long-tail searches that make up today's search behavior. Often you might not win on the "major" searches but you can make up for this by winning on the "micro" searches, many of which will be low volume but high value. (In addition, your blog gives you content to share on social media).

- **Freshness**. Google rewards sites that have new, fresh content. Having a blog gives you an easy way to churn out fresh content and send a freshness signal to Google: we're alive, we're alive, we're alive… I recommend at least four blog posts per month for this reason, and rotating three blog posts on your homepage as I do on **https://jm-seo.org/**. Another good blog is Albertson & Davidson, California probate lawyers, at **http://jmlinks.com/47m**. Try Googling various educational searches in your industry plus the word "blog," and look at what competitors who are ranking on Google are blogging about.

- **Website Size**. Size matters (at least to Google)! Given the choice between *pizza restaurant* No. 1 with 10 web pages, and *pizza restaurant* No. 2 with 1000 pages, Google will prefer the larger website: *it must be more important because it has more content*. A blog allows you to expand the size your web content.

As for blogging platforms, the best, by far, is **WordPress**. If you do not already have a blog, touch base with your Web developer and insist that he or she set up a blog for you. Major providers such as GoDaddy have easy-to-use, out-of-the-box WordPress packages. As you blog on WordPress, be sure to "tag" each blog post with keyword themes that reflect your keyword targets (as identified on your keyword worksheet).

Take a look at our blog at **http://jmlinks.com/15k** for examples of best blogging practices for SEO, including tagging blog posts based on keyword themes. Here's a screenshot of our WordPress "tag cloud," located at the far left of every page on our blog:

TAGS

AdWords AdWords Books Arizona Austin Book Reviews Books Business California Content Marketing Directory Display Network Free Tools Google Google Algorithm Google Analytics Google Local Houston Keyword Planner Keywords Local SEO Los Angeles Marketing Metrics Mobile-friendly Mobile SEO New York New York City Photography Remarketing Retargeting San Francisco SEO SEO Books SEO Tips SEO Training Small Business Social Media Social Media Marketing Texas Top Tens Tucson Twitter Marketing Viral Marketing WordPress SEO Yelp

Notice how our WordPress tags reflect our target keywords such as AdWords, SEO, and Social Media Marketing as indicated with a bigger font, meaning more blog content. To learn more about WordPress tags, please visit **http://jmlinks.com/6n**.

Also, as blogging evolves between SEO and social media marketing, consider "vlogging," that is video blogging on YouTube, Facebook, and/or LinkedIn. You can "repurpose" content by having a textual blog version and a video blog version. The more the merrier!

Blog Hosting

For SEO purposes, it is better to host your blog on a subdirectory (not subdomain) on your own site (**http://www.company.com/blog** not **blog.company.com**) than on another site (**http://company.wordpress.com/**). However, the "Perfect is the enemy of the Good" (Voltaire), so if you can't host on your own domain, host on another platform. For a quick blogging platform, I prefer Blogger (**http://www.blogger.com**) to WordPress.com (**http://www.wordpress.com**), as the former is very SEO-friendly while the latter (ironically) is not, and has many obnoxious lock-ins to prevent you from porting your blog to your own site at a later time. (Note: just to confuse you,

Wordpress.org is the site for the free software (good), whereas *WordPress.com* is a revenue-generating site (bad)).

VIDEO. Watch a quick video tutorial on SEO-friendly blogging at **http://jmlinks.com/17t** vs. how to blog for social media marketing purposes at **http://jmlinks.com/16p**.

In a nutshell, a blog post that is *meant for SEO* is meant to be "searched for" and to assist you in propelling your website to the top of a relevant search query on Google; a blog post that is *meant for social media marketing*, in contrast, is aimed at being "shared" by real humans on sites like Facebook or Twitter. Both are important and valuable reasons why everyone needs a blog!

Start Blogging

Having the structure of a blog means nothing if you aren't blogging! I recommend at least four blog posts a month, each about 3-5 paragraphs in length and each focusing on your keywords. Be sure to identify a keyword target for each blog post plus weave the keyword target into the important HTML tags as well as write content that is good for humans *and* good for Google. *(See the next Chapter for an in-depth discussion of blogging.)*

At this point, begin to outline a blog calendar that identifies the topics you want to blog on and who is going to do the blogging. Wrestle up team members, from the CEO and other executives, to the product marketing managers, and even the sales rep's. The more people you involve in the blogging process the easier it will be to create the quantity you need.

»» CHECKLIST: CONTENT ACTION ITEMS

Test your knowledge of content marketing! Take the *content quiz* at **http://jmlinks.com/qzcs**. Next, here are your content marketing **Action Items**:

❑ Revisit your **keywords**, looking beyond landing pages to which keywords match which content types as for example how an "educational search query" can match a blog post or an evergreen FAQ document.

❑ Build a **content map** or **content calendar**, laying out the matches between keyword themes or types and content to be produced.

> ❑ Research which content tends to be *shared on social media* in your industry with an eye to the "social media" aspect of SEO and content.
>
> ❑ Assign **content production** to team members, such as who will write which blog posts or which types of anchor or evergreen content.
>
> ❑ If you haven't already, set up a **blog** on your website. Begin to brainstorm your blog topics and *assign who is going to write what* with respect to your blog.

Check out the **free tools**! Go to my *SEO Dashboard > Content* for my favorite free tools for content marketing. Just visit **http://jmlinks.com/seodash**.

»» DELIVERABLE: A CONTENT MARKETING PLAN

Now that you have a **content map** of your website vs. your keyword themes on your **keyword worksheet**, you are ready to produce your **DELIVERABLE**: a **content marketing plan**. Your content marketing plan will consist of these basic phases.

Phase 1: Quick Fix. Based on your keyword worksheet including the content map, conduct an inventory of existing pages. Adjust their TITLE tags, META DESCRIPTION tags, and content to bring that content into alignment with your logical Google searches. I usually also write a "keyword footer" and place on all website pages to increase keyword density and allow for link sculpting. Don't forget to optimize the content of that all-important homepage!

Phase 2: Content Inventory. Are you missing anything? Often times, there will be a very important keyword pattern that has no corresponding landing page, for example. Or your site will not have a blog, or you will have never set up a press release system. Inventory what you are missing and start to prioritize what needs to be done to get that content on your website. Commonly needed elements are:

- **Blog**. I recommend at least four blog posts per month; these can be on easy, man-on-the-street type themes but you really need to commit to at least four, and make sure that they are relevant vis-a-vis your keyword themes.

- **Press Releases**. As discussed in Chapter 4.2, I recommend at least two per month and (if possible), using the CISION / PRWEB system (**http://www.prweb.com/** or Newswire (**https://www.newswire.com**)) to syndicate them (cost is approximately $350 / month).

- **Landing Pages**. Make sure that each major search has a corresponding landing page. In addition to your transactional landing pages, make sure that you brainstorm educational searches and create long-form content such as FAQ (Frequently Asked Questions) documents. These are great "link bait," i.e. ways to attract inbound links to your website.

- **Anchor or Evergreen Content**. Consider writing the "ultimate" guide to major topics in your industry, provocative "hot button" issues, and other timely topics. This type of content is great to a) attract links, and b) to acquire customer email addresses and contact information. Most companies need to commit to one, and only one, type of anchor content.

Phase 3: Content Creation Process. Once you have done the Quick Fix to the website and created any missing landing pages, set up a blog, and/or set up a press releases system, you need to create a content creation schedule and process. This is an assessment of who will do what, when, where, and how to create the type of on-going content that Google and Web searchers will find attractive.

WORKSHEETS. For your **DELIVERABLE**, fill out the "content marketing worksheet," specifically each phase. For the worksheet, go to **http://jmlinks.com/seo19tz** (reenter the passcode "seo19tz"), and click on the link to the "content marketing worksheet."

4.2

BLOGGING

Nothing is as easy or as powerful for SEO as blogging! While landing pages reflect your anchor keyword terms, and press releases can build inbound links via syndication, blogging allows you to sculpt content for narrower keyword queries as well as to respond quickly to industry buzz and trends. In addition, frequent blogging - like frequent press releases- sends a powerful signal to Google that your website is "fresh." Every website should have a blog!

Let's get started!

TO-DO LIST:

» Why Blog?

» Make a Blog Calendar

» Set Up Your Blog for Best SEO

» Write SEO-friendly Blog Posts

» Rank for Featured Snippets

»» Checklist: Blogging Action Items

»» Deliverables: Blog Calendar and Your First Blog Post

» WHY BLOG?

Why Blog? Blogging is one of the most powerful, highest return-on-investment (ROI) activities you can engage in, after you've SEO optimized your homepage and your landing pages. Here's why. First, an active blog sends out a "freshness" signal to

Google, Bing, and Yahoo saying "I'm alive, I'm alive, I'm alive." Google prefers sites that have new, fresh content.

Why? Well, you have to look at the world from Google's perspective. Google's goal is to return highly relevant, active websites for any search query. So, if a user searches for a *pizza restaurant in Okmulgee, Oklahoma*, Google has a set of pizza websites to consider. It will choose the one that has optimized for the keywords "Pizza" and "Okmulgee," plus has active inbound links, plus has many reviews on Google, and – all things being equal – the one with the more active blog. Why? Because Google is concerned that the other pizza restaurant – the one without an active blog – is out of business. If it's June 3, 2019, and the last blog post on Website A was May 3, 2019, and the last blog post on Website B was June 1, 2017, and the last blog post on Website C was… *well Website C doesn't even have a blog*… then Website A is the winner (all things being equal).

AN ACTIVE BLOG TELLS GOOGLE, "YOU'RE ALIVE!"

Second, after freshness, a blog allows you to write content on micro or long tail search keywords. To use our pizza example, the primary keyword might be "Pizza" or "Pizza Okmulgee," but there may be some searches for "best pizza restaurants in Okmulgee for kids' birthday parties." These are *high value, low volume* searches. A quick blog post on how to select the best pizza restaurant in Okmulgee for kids birthdays is an easy way to get to the top of Google for these micro, or long-tail search phrases. So, an active blog allows you to create a lot of content on lots of varied themes. It costs next to nothing, and can be free advertising on long tail keyword queries. How great is that?

Third, an active blog increases the volume of content on your site. All things being equal the bigger site will win on Google. If, for example, Pizza restaurant A has ten pages, and Pizza restaurant B has one hundred pages, then Pizza restaurant B must be better in Google's eyes (all other factors being equal). Bigger means better; more content means a more serious website. Use the *site: command* plus your domain to check how many pages you have indexed on Google, and then use the *Search Tools > Anytime > Past Month* drop downs to find out if you have new content that is being indexed by Google. Here's a screenshot:

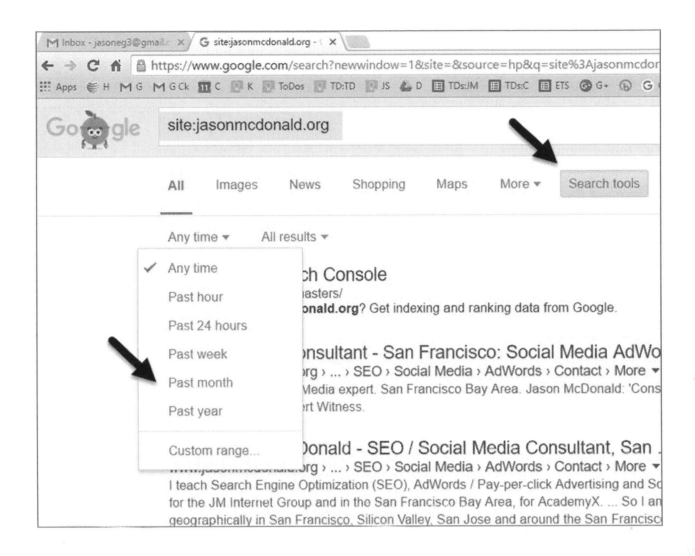

Remember it's *site: **no space** and your domain* as in *site:jasonmcdonald.org* in the Google search bar. To see this in action, visit **http://jmlinks.com/14d**.

Fourth, a blog allows you to pass link juice up to your landing pages. When you blog on *best pizza restaurant in Okmulgee for kids*, you can link "up" to the landing page for *Pizza* and the landing page for *Okmulgee Pizza* when you use those phrases in your blog and link directly from them, again passing "freshness" and "link juice" up to those landing pages. Finally, a blog (especially long-form blog posts) can act as "link bait." When you write an interesting, in-depth blog post on an industry topic, especially trending or puzzling topics, people are likely to find it and link to it, thereby attracting links to your website. In addition, people often share blog articles on social media, helping you both for SEO (by getting social mentions of your URLs and website) and social media marketing (by creating sticky, interesting, shareable content that gets your brand in front of more customers).

In summary, you just gotta blog!

» MAKE A BLOG CALENDAR

As you begin to blog, remember to stick with your keyword themes. Don't blog on just anything – blog on topics that contain your keywords. Stay on topic. A good way to brainstorm topics to blog on is to take a "seed keyword" or phrase like "how to contest a will" and then look at the related searches at the bottom of Google. Here's a screenshot:

```
Searches related to how to contest a will

how to contest a will and win              how to contest a will after probate

how to contest a will without a lawyer     what happens when you contest a will

how to successfully contest a will         how much does it cost to contest a will

who pays to contest a will                 who can challenge a will
```

There's no excuse for writer's block, as Google related searches will give you a clickable list of interesting topics.

As an SEO Content strategist, look around your company and identify blog topics as well as other company employees who can contribute to the blog. Unlike press releases, blog posts can be much more informal, opinionated and quick. So whereas you might generate just two press releases per month, set a goal of at least one blog post per week, if not more. I generally recommend two press releases per month and four blog posts per month as a solid website goal. The word *blog*, after all, comes from *web log*, and is meant as a running commentary on what's going on on your website, at your business, and in your industry.

You Can't Really Overblog

Think of Captain Kirk on the Starship Enterprise: *"Captain's log, Stardate 4.2.51535, Spock and I have beamed down to the planet to investigate. I will check out the beautiful women, and Spock will be taking soil samples."* Kirk logged, and logged, and logged his way across his five-year mission, and he was pretty shameless. So don't be shy: blog, blog, blog, blog, blog! You can't really overblog as long as you write decent content, and if you don't toot your own horn, who will?

> *As long as your blog content is fresh, original, and keyword-heavy, all blogs posts will help your SEO. The more the merrier!*

A Blog Calendar

Depending on your company size, a blog calendar can help you keep track of possible blog topics and themes. You can also assign out the blog posts to different members of your team. Don't try to do all the blogging yourself.

Here is a sample blog calendar for a hypothetical roofing company in Dallas, TX.

SAMPLE BLOG TOPIC:	WHEN TO POST:
We complete a roofing job.	Write a blog post about each roofing job, when completed, with information on the city where the job was located, the type of roofing material used, and customer reaction. Goal is to help with geotargeted searches.
Our day-to-day in a host city for a job.	Because geographic search terms are important for a roofing company,

	create city-specific blog posts such as your favorite "taco joint" in the city, or variances in city roofing codes.
Industry trends and events	Any time there is an industry trend, such as a new roofing material, chime in with an opinion. Ditto for any industry events or events in the Dallas, Texas, area.
New website content	Blog about our website, explaining what new content we are creating and why.
Partnership Announcements	Identify potential blog opportunities with our partners.
Industry Awards or Milestones	Any time we win an industry award or cross a milestone (such as the 1000th follower on Twitter), it's time for a blog post!

You'll see many similarities between successful SEO blogging and SEO press releases. The difference is one of degree: blogging is quicker, more informal, and more a quantity play vs. the more formal, higher quality status of press releases. Commit to writing four blog posts per month, and stick with it.

If you're freaked out about creating this much content, you can go to a site like Fiverr.com and enter "blogging" and easily find lots of decent writers who can write at least a rough draft. Give them a keyword prompt, tell them you want five to seven paragraphs, and then do the final SEO-friendly edits yourself. (I do find that most bloggers don't understand SEO, so it's easier to do the final SEO optimization myself).

The best blog platform by far is WordPress (**http://wordpress.org/**). Ask your web designer and/or ISP to install WordPress on your site. If you are building a new site, use an ISP like GoDaddy that makes WordPress a "one-click" installation. If you are running WordPress, be sure to install the Yoast SEO plugin (**https://yoast.com/**) so that you can easily optimize the blog post TITLE and META DESCRIPTION tags.

And, if you don't have the budget for WordPress, I recommend Google's blogger platform at **http://www.blogger.com/**. Regardless of your platform, follow these basic principles for successful SEO blogging:

Host your blog on your own site. Blogging helps with site freshness vis-a-vis Google as well as acts as link bait. So it makes little sense to host your blog on another site. If at all possible, host your blog at your own domain in the subdirectory position as for example, **http://www.company.com/blog**. (Subdirectories are better than subdomains, by the way: *company.com/blog* is better than *blog.company.com*).

Check each blog post for good SEO. As you write a blog post, check to make sure that your blogging platform allows for basic "On Page" SEO: a keyword heavy TITLE tag, META DESCRIPTION tag, the use of the header family, one image with the alt attribute defined, and keyword-heavy cross links.

Make sure your blog allows for keyword heavy tagging and cross-indexing. Make sure that your blog allows you to "tag" a post with keywords and that these "tags" act as URL cross-links.

Verify that your blog URLs are keyword heavy. Numeric, parameter-centric URLs are very bad for SEO, so make sure that your blog generates keyword-heavy URLs for each post.

At the homepage level, a best practice is to have "one-click" links from your homepage down to at least three, rotating blog posts. You can use the "Display Posts Short Code" plugin in WordPress (**http://jmlinks.com/47n**) to accomplish this easily. Here's a screenshot from the homepage of **https://www.morenoranches.com**, a Brahman cattle breeder, showing new blog posts to their site, and a list of upcoming events:

LATEST NEWS

Why Brahman Cattle?

Brahman cattle are known as one of the superior breeds in the cattle industry thanks to the many attributes and [...]

READ MORE >

Why Use Moreno Ranches' Brahman bulls?

At Moreno Ranches, we have some of the best award winning and performance oriented Brahman bulls, and offer genetic products [...]

READ MORE >

BRAHMAN CATTLE EVENTS

Oct 7-10 | National Brahman Show | Dallas, TX
Nov 26 | Cyber Monday Online Sale | www.morenoranches.com
Dec 8-9 | Heartland Classic Show | Wauchula, FL
Dec 13 | 12 Days of Christmas Online Sale | www.morenoranches.com

And here's a screenshot from my JasonMcDonald.org website, homepage, again showing three recent blog posts:

My Blog(s), My Press Release(s), My So-called Life

- When It Comes To Social Media Marketing I Can Talk About It, Talk About The Talk, And Walk
- Facebook's Really Bad Horrible No Good Rotten Day July 26, 2018
- Twitter CAN Actually Be Used For Marketing – If You Know What You Are Doing July 14, 2018

- Read more posts on my blog... Or, read posts from other blogs I write –
  - Jason+ | JM Internet Group Blog

The blog posts freshen the website, allow for micro or long tail keyword targeting, increase the size of the website, and give something to share on social media. You just gotta blog!

Tag Your Blog in WordPress

Many people do not correctly "tag" each blog post, yet tagging is incredibly important to SEO-friendly blogging! (Note: I'm talking about WordPress "tags" not HTML "tags." Unfortunately we use the same term for both things). Make sure that your blog tags match your keyword themes, and make sure that when you write a blog post each post gets tagged. One of the better blogs to emulate is by Nolo press (**http://blog.nolo.com/**). Here's a screenshot of the tags at the bottom of the page for a post on bankruptcy forms:

WordPress has two types of tagging: "categories" and "tags." From an SEO perspective, both accomplish the same thing: lumping your posts into SEO-friendly cross-linked URL's. Both are strongly encouraged because both give Google an SEO-friendly URL structure to grab onto. Here's a link to the Nolo blog "Chapter 7" tag: **http://jmlinks.com/14j**. Notice how the practitioners at Nolo are churning out blog post after blog post on their keyword theme of "Chapter 7," and related keywords! And notice the URL structure itself, which mimics the target keywords and signals to Google that this blog has quite a bit of content on bankruptcy:

http://blog.nolo.com/bankruptcy/tag/Chapter-7/

Another example of a really good SEO-friendly blog can be found on Thomas Upchurch Law. Check out their blog at **http://jmlinks.com/14g**. Notice how he blogs on his target keyword themes such as "estate planning" and "will contests." To find good blog examples in your own industry, go to Google and do a search for your keywords as in "probate" plus "blog" and then browse the top websites. For an example search, visit **http://jmlinks.com/14h**.

» WRITE SEO-FRIENDLY BLOG POSTS

Blogging is a complementary SEO content strategy to your anchor landing pages, your homepage, your product pages, and your press releases. Whereas anchor landing pages focus on your evergreen anchor keyword terms, your blog can focus on more keyword-specific, timely topics. Blogging is especially useful for posting content that responds to quick industry trends. Here is a wrap up of the steps towards writing an SEO-friendly blog post:

1. **Identify the target keywords.** A good blog post is laser-focused on a very narrow keyword, so do your keyword research first! Use Ubersuggest.io, Google autocomplete, and the Google Keyword Planner to identify keyword topics and related keywords to your targets.
2. **Follow "On Page" SEO best practices.** Make sure that your post follows all of the "On Page" rules such as a keyword heavy TITLE, META description, at least one image with an ALT attribute that contains the target keyword, etc.
3. **Consider an action or purpose.** Have a defined action for each blog post, usually by embedding a link from the blog post "up to" one of your defined anchor landing pages. Another use of blog posts such as "Top Ten Things that Can Go Terribly Wrong at Your Wedding" is link bait or share bait; people will link to informative, provocative, shocking blog posts and/or share them on social media.

4. **Tag your blog post.** Identify keyword themes for your blog that match those of your keyword worksheet and recognize that each blog post is part of a keyword cluster, supporting the entire website's SEO themes.

VIDEO. Watch a video tutorial on SEO-friendly blogging posts at **http://jmlinks.com/17t**.

For a template on an SEO friendly blog post, visit **http://jmlinks.com/14e**. For a fun blog topic generator, check out **http://jmlinks.com/14f**.

» RANK FOR FEATURED SNIPPETS

It's no secret that Google is going all out for **voice search**. As Google's own *Google home* begins to compete with Amazon's *Alexa* and Apple's *Siri*, there's a gold rush towards voice searches on the phone and in the home. "Hey Google! How do you tie a tie?" or "Hey Google! How tall is Donald Trump?" or "Hey Google! What are the best movies of 2019?" are becoming common searches as we "talk" to computers on our phone and in our home.

Accordingly, Google has rolled out what are called **featured snippets**. For example, here's the featured snippet for "How to tie a tie" (**http://jmlinks.com/38h**).

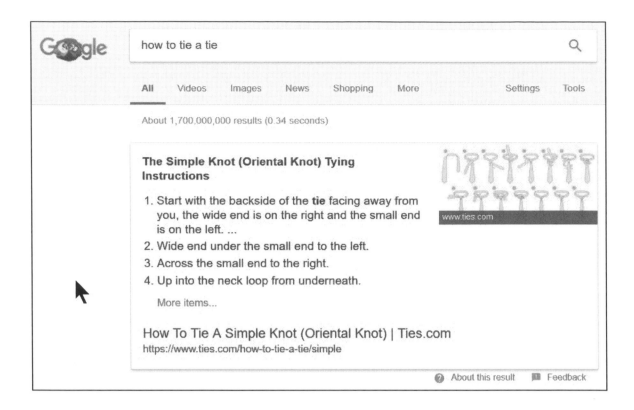

Featured snippets or also often called "Answer Boxes," and they are prominent text that occurs on some types of search queries.

Featured snippets frequently occur for searches that are *educational* in nature such as "how to" do something, as well as ratings and reviews, such as "best" of such-and-such as in "best SEO conferences." They also tend to occur for financial, mathematical and other type of "requirement" queries such as "what are the best home mortgage rates" or "improve my credit score." But they occur for transactional queries such as "What are the top selling cars of 2018?" and so forth.

Related to featured snippets is a subordinate box called "People Also Ask" or *PAAs*. If you search for "improve my credit score," for example, you'll also see a box labeled "People also ask." Here's a screenshot:

People also ask
How do you increase your credit score?
How can I improve my credit rating?
How can I improve my credit score without a credit card?
How do you increase your credit limit?

Each of the PAAs is essentially a featured snippet in its own right, so the rules of ranking are essentially the same (though not the same answer shows for a featured snippet in its own right vs. a PAA to a related snippet!).

How to Rank for Featured Snippets

It's not easy to rank for a featured snippet, but when you do you get a lot of traffic from Google. Here are the steps to rank for a featured snippet:

1. Identify **relevant search queries** for your company that are also likely to generate a featured snippet such as "how to," "best," or "step-by-step" questions. Pay special attention to those queries that are already generating featured snippets in your industry.
2. **Write and optimize a blog post** vis-à-vis the target featured snippet query, using HTML for numbered or bulleted lists, tables, and other designations that clearly indicate to Google this is "organized" or "step-by-step" content.
   a. Along the way "regurgitate" the **question**(s) and **answer**(s) to Google, as in "How do make chicken soup," you ask? Well, first, you bring the chicken stock to a boil, second, you add in the vegetables." Imagine you are a Google Home, Alexa, or Siri device that is being asked a question

such as "How do you make chicken soup," and you are "answering" step by step.

3. Use all your **Off Page SEO tactics** such as mentioning your post on social media, featuring it on your homepage, building external links to it, etc. Conduct an "Off Page" SEO audit and look for opportunities to promote your potential featured snippets.

Don't get discouraged. it's not easy to rank for featured snippets, but it is incredibly valuable. Featured snippets are relatively new and not everyone even agrees on what factors decide which queries generate them, and which factors determine who wins "Position 0," ("Position Zero"), which is another term for featured snippets. For more information on featured snippets, see **http://jmlinks.com/38k**.

»» CHECKLIST: BLOGGING ACTION ITEMS

Here are your blog **Action Items**:

❏ **Set up your blog** if you haven't already; I recommend the WordPress platform. Be sure to enable "WordPress tags" so you can "tag" individual posts on your keyword themes.

❏ Create a blog **content calendar**, laying out the matches between keyword themes or types and blog posts to be produced.

❏ **Research** which content tends to be *shared on social media* in your industry with an eye to the "social media" aspect of SEO and content.

❏ Assign **blog content production** to team members, such as who will write which blog posts and how frequently. Set a goal of at least four blog posts per month.

❏ **Write each** SEO-friendly **blog post** with an eye to what Google wants (keyword-heavy, SEO-friendly tags and content) and what humans want (interesting, fun content that answers their needs or questions).

❑ After you write a blog post, use Google Search Console's **fetch as Google** feature to notify Google to index your content. Then, use *site:yourdomain.com/blogpost.html* to verify that your content is being indexed.

❑ Make sure that your **homepage** has your **three most recent blog posts** on it with "one-click" links down to them and that each blog post links "up" to your target landing pages.

❑ Try to rank for **featured snippets**. They're the new, new thing!

Check out the **free tools**! Go to my *SEO Dashboard > Blog Tools* for my favorite free tools for blogging. Just visit **http://jmlinks.com/seodash**.

» DELIVERABLES: A BLOG CALENDAR AND A SAMPLE BLOG POST

The **DELIVERABLE** for this Chapter is your blog calendar. This can be as simple as a Word document or Google document that serves as an "idea list" of when to generate a blog post. The goal is to avoid writer's block and get into a rhythm of generating at least one blog post per week, if not more. The second **DELIVERABLE** is your first SEO-friendly blog post, uploaded to your own site and tagged with appropriate (keyword) tags. Use the "page tags worksheet" to step through an SEO-friendly blog post from keyword target to final content.

4.3

PRESS RELEASES

After you've created your landing pages, anchor or evergreen content, and begun to blog, it's time to shift gears towards *Off Page* SEO. We'll cover Off Page theory in greater detail in the next Chapter, but for now just realize that you want people to talk about your website across the Internet. Press releases function as a bridge between On Page and Off Page SEO: like blog posts, they live on your website and add fresh content, but like social media mentions and links, they become references external to your website that draw Google's attention to your website.

Here are the reasons why Google likes press releases. First, websites that have new, fresh content are clearly more "alive" than websites that never get updated. We live in a fast-paced world, and users want the *latest* iPhone software, the *latest* news about Donald Trump, and the *latest* nutritional supplement. Google wants to give users the latest and greatest on any topic as well. Second, fresh content signals to Google that your website and business are still alive vs. the many "walking dead" websites that are businesses dead or dying in this age of economic turmoil. And third, press releases have a unique SEO advantage: **syndication**. Free and paid syndication services like PRLog, NewsWire, and Cision's PRWeb connect with blogs, portals, other websites and even Twitter feeds to push your press releases across the Web, creating inbound buzz and backlinks which Google interprets as signs of community authority. Press release SEO, in short, gives a three-for-one benefit!

Let's get started!

TO-DO LIST:

» What is a Press Release?

» Make a Press Release Calendar

» WHAT IS A PRESS RELEASE?

Have you ever heard the quip about the weather, that everyone talks about it, but no one does anything about it? Or, if you don't like the news, go out and make some of your own? Well, there's some truth in these adages: you need to toot your own (marketing) horn to be successful, and press releases allow this in spades.

But what is a press release, and how does it differ from a blog post? Think of a blog post as a much shorter, more informal, off-the-cuff type of content vs. a more formal press release in which your company FORMALLY ANNOUNCES something NEW AND EXCITING. A common example would be when you launch a new product. If you're the Ford Motor Company, for instance, and you're announcing the new and improved 2019 Mustang, then it's time for a press release, usually written in the format of:

> ***Detroit, Michigan*** *– January 2, 2019. The Ford Motor Company, the leading producer of American-made sports vehicles, is proud to announce their new 2019 Mustang. With a venerable history as an American "muscle" car, the new 2019 Mustang will also be eco-friendly with its hybrid engine.*

> etc. etc.

> Basically Ford has some NEWS and it's ANNOUNCING that news to the world via a press release.

In fact, you can browse the official press releases of the Ford Motor Company at **https://media.ford.com/**. You can browse other sample press releases at

http://jmlinks.com/13x and **http://jmlinks.com/13y**. In fact, it's a good idea to take a keyword like "organic" and search for it on PRWeb.com to find press releases in your industry. To see a sample for "organic," visit **http://jmlinks.com/47q**. Replace "organic" with one of your keywords in the search bar and find out which competitors are already issuing press releases. Notice how company after company is "tooting its own horn" by announcing "news," and realize that you can, too.

» MAKE A PRESS RELEASE CALENDAR

What can make a good press release? **Almost anything**. Keep your keyword worksheet in mind and look for press release opportunities around your company, products, or services that match up with your SEO keyword targets. I recommend you create a **press release calendar** of opportunities.

> *Tip. Many people are too "shy," acting as if they and their company don't have any "legitimate" news. Don't be shy! If you don't toot your own horn, no one will toot it for you. And remember that for SEO purposes, you're really aiming your promotion at Google, so if "real people" read your press releases, that's great, but your real objective is to use press releases to influence Google to rank your website higher. If they influence Google, you should be happy!*

For your first **TO-DO**, open up a Word document, title it "Press Release Calendar," and write down a list of possible press release topics and dates of the release. For example:

SAMPLE PRESS RELEASE TOPIC:	WHEN TO RELEASE:
New product or service	Every time you have a new product or service, generate a press release.
Annual Trade Show	Generate a press release before the annual trade show, as well as after

	announcing your participation to celebrate your success.
Personnel Changes	Generate a press release for every major corporate hire.
New website content	Generate a press release after any major blog post, list of "top seven resources," infographic, etc., and even when you update a landing page or anchor content.
Partnership Announcements	Generate a press release after any cooperative partnership with a company or supplier.
Industry Awards or Milestones	Any time you win an industry award or cross a milestone (such as the 1000th follower on Twitter), it's time for a press release!

Your **press release calendar** will help keep you focused, and tie your press release opportunities to your keyword worksheet. The goal is to avoid writer's block and get into a rhythm of at least two press releases per month. Have a company meeting and divvy up the responsibilities by assigning writing a press release to different people in the company for different events, or for different months. Make your SEO a "team sport," rather than attempting to do it all yourself.

Steps to Writing an SEO-friendly Press Release

Once you have an idea in hand, here are the steps to create a press release:

1. Identify the **press release idea**. Realize that a press release can be not only a new product or a new technology but something as simple as your participation

in a trade show, an event that you may be having, a new hire, new inventory, or even your commentary on an industry trend. **Literally, anything new can become a press release!**

2. Connect the press release idea to a **target keyword** from your keyword worksheet. The point of generating press releases, after all, is to improve keyword performance.

3. Include an *http://* format link to your website in your press release, preferably near the target keywords. For example, have a sentence that says something like *"To learn more about our amazing car insurance, visit* ***http://www.ourcompany.com/car-insurance."***

4. Create your **press release** following "**SEO best practices**" for on page SEO as explained in Chapter 3.1. Be sure to include your keywords in the Headline / Title, and in the actual content of the release itself.

5. **Upload** the press release to your website, be sure that your website has a press release section with each press release on an independent URL, and include a "one click" link from the homepage to the press release.

6. Leverage free and/or paid **syndication services** such as PRLog.org and PRWeb.com to proliferate mentions of your press releases around the Internet.

To browse sample press releases that follow the correct procedures, visit http://jmlinks.com/47p.

» UPLOAD YOUR SEO-FRIENDLY PRESS RELEASES

Double-check your press release to make sure that it follows "On Page" SEO best practices. Here's your checklist:

ITEM	SEO PAGE TAG STRUCTURE
Pithy, exciting headline	<TITLE> tag
First paragraph with "main idea"	<META DESCRIPTION> tag and first paragraph.

Target URL	A target URL on your website, to which you want to attract Google. Embed this in the first paragraph, and have it as a "naked" URL (http://) format in the third paragraph.
Several paragraphs describing your news and an image.	Write keyword heavy copy and include at least one image with ALT attribute.
Contact information for more info.	Embedded URL early in the press release, set up in http:// format plus contact information at the end of the release

In other words, follow your HTML page tag template to optimize your press release in terms of its on-page SEO. Be sure to embed your target keywords in your <TITLE> tag, and use best SEO practices like the H1 family, <B>, <STRONG>, ALT attributes, for images etc. Write **keyword-heavy** text for the press release body! Make sure that it has a snappy <TITLE> and a snappy META DESCRIPTION / first paragraph so that people will be interested in "reading more."

At the website structure level, your best practice is to have a directory called "news" as in *http://www.yourcompany.com/news/* and to host each press release in HTML linked to from a primary news gateway page. I also recommend that you run at least three press releases on your homepage, with "one-click" links down to each new press release. All of this freshens your website and pulls Google into your new content.

VIDEO. Watch a quick video tutorial on how to write an SEO-friendly press release at **http://jmlinks.com/18f.**

Good examples of press releases can be found **http://jmlinks.com/13z** and **http://jmlinks.com/14a**. Duct Tape Marketing has a nifty tool to help you write a press release at **http://jmlinks.com/14b**. Here's a screenshot:

Press Releases After the Penguin Update

Before the Penguin update to Google, you could use Press Releases to "optimize" your inbound links. (Remember that the Penguin update is a Google algorithm penalty for suspicious inbound links). For example, you'd create a bunch of press releases all linking back to your site around the phrase "industrial fans" or "motorcycle insurance." This manipulation did not make Google happy, so the search giant pressured the major services to add the NOFOLLOW tag to their releases, which nullified much of this benefit, as part of Google's so-called Penguin algorithm update.

Thus, for a short while, press releases had little impact on SEO. However, there is always another turn of the screw. Now, despite the fact that press release URL's remain "nofollow" in most circumstances, Google does tend to reward sites that issue them. (*Trust me: I know this based on client experiments; the reason probably being that in many industries, Google has so few links to choose from among competing sites that the sheer quantity of press release links can be sufficient to help a site get to the top*).

Google denies this (**http://jmlinks.com/47r**), and you'll read on the blogosphere that press releases don't work. You'll also read that the moon landing was faked and that the earth is flat. The trick here is to be skeptical, experiment, and don't go crazy issuing five thousand press releases in one month.

SET A GOAL OF ONLY TWO PRESS RELEASES PER MONTH

In addition, if you use ONLY the *http://* format for your clickable links, there are still a small percentage of sites that retain the DOFOLLOW link structure. So be sure to include links FROM the press release BACK to your site in the format of **http://www.company.com**. The reality is that Google is often forced to choose not between two GREAT sites to rank for a search query but between two just OK sites; if yours is the site with a few inbound links via Press Releases, including *nofollow* links, you can often win.

> *The perfect is the enemy of the good (Voltaire).*
>
> *You don't have to run faster than the bear, just faster than your buddy (Unknown).*
>
> *Google might publicly say one thing, but the reality might be something altogether different and this includes the value of nofollow links.*

To see examples of Press Releases issued by the JM Internet Group with examples of proper link formatting, visit **http://jmlinks.com/6q**. As is so often true in SEO, "A little salt is good for the soup, but too much salt ruins it." In other words, I recommend that you create two – *but no more than two* – press releases per month for syndication, that you use the http:// format in your links, and that you write them in proper English with real or quasi-real news in them. Strive for them to be "good for humans" and "good for Google," and they work.

» LEVERAGE PRESS RELEASE SYNDICATION SERVICES

Once you've created your press release and uploaded it to your own website, you are ready to leverage press release syndication services. The best **free** service is PRLog.org (**http://www.prlog.org/**) and the best **paid** services are Newswire (**https://www.newswire.com**) and PRWeb.com (**http://www.prweb.com/**), owned by Cision. You can learn more about the available packages from Newswire at **http://jmlinks.com/35e**. Cision is just as good at a technical level, if not a bit better, but their website is really hard to follow, so just call them at 866-459-2598 and inquire about their press release packages. They also run PRWEB at **http://www.prweb.com/** which has self-service options.

If you have budget, I highly recommend setting up a paid account on one of these services. With a yearly package, the cost per release is about $175. A paid service gets you many times the benefit of the free services like PRLog.org.

After you've set up your account on one of these services, open your press release in one browser window. In another window, log into the press release syndication service and begin the process of submitting a release. Copy and paste the following from your press release into the syndication service -

> **Headline.** Make sure it includes your target keywords!
>
> **Quick Summary.** Write a pithy, exciting one-to-two sentence summary. This will usually become your META DESCRIPTION tag on the syndication service.
>
> **News Body.** Copy and paste your news body. Be sure to embed a URL after the first or second paragraph, and write in the simple *http://* format (since embedded links may not be retained in syndicated press releases).

URL / Active Link. Make sure that your press release has at least one prominent link to your website, and **make sure it is in the http:// format**. News is especially good at getting Google to index new web pages on your site!

Contact Information. Include a description of your company with a Web link and email address for more information. This is another link-building opportunity.

Tags. Select appropriate tags for keyword / content issues as well as target geographies.

Finally, commit to publishing press releases on your website and using news syndication on a regular, consistent basis. It's better to publish one release per month, consistently, than six releases in one month and nothing for six months. For an online press release template, visit **http://jmlinks.com/6r**. To see sample press releases on PRWEB as written by the JM Internet Group visit **http://jmlinks.com/14c**.

VIDEO. Watch a quick video tutorial on how to syndicate press releases at **http://jmlinks.com/18f**.

WORKSHEETS. For the corresponding worksheet, go to **http://jmlinks.com/seo19tz** (reenter the passcode "seo19tz" to register if you have not already done so), and click on the link to the "press release worksheet."

Measure Your Results

As you churn out press releases, measure your syndication by doing Google searches for the headline of your release in quotation marks. For example, our press release headlined, "JM Internet Announces Social Media Marketing Book for Small Business Now Available as Audiobook" garnered approximately 123 results on Google (**http://jmlinks.com/38m**). Here's a screenshot:

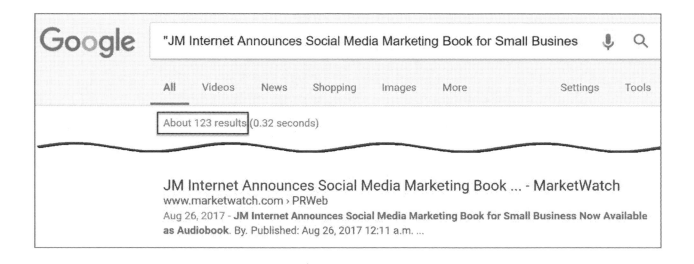

Each paid service will also generate reporting that shows the "pickups" of your press releases. In this way, you're getting the benefit of syndication links back to your website, pickup on real sites on the Internet, and even social media pickups on Twitter, LinkedIn, and Facebook. You can even go into Google Analytics and measure referrals from various websites that ran your press release, in that way seeing which actual websites real people read and click over from.

»» CHECKLIST: PRESS RELEASE ACTION ITEMS

Here are your press release **Action Items**:

❑ **Identify** press release **opportunities** around your company such as new products, participation in trade shows, new hires, or even pseudoevents such as new blog posts.

❑ Create a **press release calendar** of two press releases per month.

❑ **Write** each press release *following SEO best practices* and post to your website.

❑ **Syndicate** your press release via a service such as PRLOG, PRWEB, or NEWSWIRE and include an *http://* format link in the release.

❑ **Measure** your results, especially replication across the Internet, by searching for your press release by the headline in quotation marks

Check out the **free tools**! Go to my *SEO Dashboard > Press Releases* for my favorite free tools for press release issues. Just visit **http://jmlinks.com/seodash**.

» DELIVERABLES: A PRESS RELEASE CALENDAR AND A SAMPLE PRESS RELEASE

The first **DELIVERABLE** for this Chapter is your press release calendar. This can be as simple as a Word document or Google document that serves as an "idea list" of when to generate a press release. The goal is to avoid writer's block and get into a rhythm of generating at least two press releases per month. The second **DELIVERABLE** is an SEO-friendly press release, uploaded to your own site and pushed out via a syndication service such as PRLOG.org or PRWEB.com. Use the "press release worksheet" to guide you to success.

SURVEY OFFER

CLAIM YOUR $5 SURVEY REBATE! HERE'S HOW –

- Visit **http://jmlinks.com/survey**.
- Take a short, simple survey about the book.
- Claim your rebate.

WE WILL THEN –

- Rebate you the $5 via Amazon eGift.

~ $5 REBATE OFFER ~

~ LIMITED TO ONE PER CUSTOMER ~

SUBJECT TO CHANGE WITHOUT NOTICE

RESTRICTIONS APPLY

GOT QUESTIONS? CALL 800-298-4065

5.1

LINK BUILDING

Steps #1 to #3 are "On Page" SEO: things you do to your own website. **Step #4** is about **content**: *content marketing*, *blogging* and *press releases*. In **Step #5**, we fully cross the Rubicon, shifting our attention 100% to the actions of others through "Off Page" SEO. Just as *references* matter to an effective job search, external *links* matter a great deal to effective SEO.

Step #5 in the **Seven Steps to SEO Success**, therefore, is to "go social." Google pays incredible attention to how others talk about your website, whether in the format of inbound HTML *links* or inbound *social mentions*. We'll turn first to **links**, the more traditional of the two, and in the next Chapter look directly at **social authority** and **social mentions**. In Chapter 5.3, we'll turn to **reviews**, which for local companies, are a key aspect of "Off Page" SEO.

Remember that a link *from* a directory, blog, web portal, or other industry site *to* your website is counted as a **vote** by Google that your site is important. The *more* links (votes) you have, the *higher* you show on Google search results for your target keywords. But how do you get links? In this Chapter, we outline the basics of effective link building for SEO.

Let's get started!

TO-DO LIST:

» Understand Links and Off Page SEO

» Beware the Penguin

» Define Your Link Objectives

» Solicit the Easy Links First

» Identify Directory, Blog, and Other Link Targets

» Reverse Engineer Competitors' Links

» Create Link Bait

»»» Checklist: Link Building Action Items

»»» Deliverable: Link Building Worksheet

» UNDERSTAND LINKS AND OFF PAGE SEO

Google's genius was to be the first search engine that effectively counted links as votes. Prior to Google, search engines basically looked at page content, and it was therefore very difficult to figure out which site was better if the page content itself contained the keywords. Google realized that you could look at how websites linked to other sites, in a kind of grand vote scheme on the Internet.

For example, why do I rank so well for the searches *SEO expert Bay Area*, or *AdWords Expert Witness*? Among the reasons is that I have many sites linking to JasonMcDonald.org. BAIPA.org, for one, links to my website, JasonMcDonald.org at **http://jmlinks.com/6u**. In this way, BAIPA.org is "voting" that my website is important. Similarly, the Authors Guild (*Authorsguild.net*) (**http://jmlinks.com/18w**) also links to me. These "votes" reinforce my On Page SEO and propel me to the top of relevant searches on Google. The same is true for Progressive.com and Geico.com for searches in the insurance industry; these sites have many *other* sites linking back to them, thus "voting" to Google that these are the "most important" sites for a query like "motorcycle insurance."

Links are Like Votes

In short, a site with *more links to its website from other sites* than its competitors have is seen by Google as more important, and ranks higher on Google, all other things being equal.

LINKS ARE LIKE VOTES

Think of *links* like *votes in an election*, and you'll begin to understand how it works.

Quantity. How do you win the US Presidential Election? Get more votes. Generally speaking, the candidate who wins the popular vote becomes president. (*OK, not always – but, at least, that's what we tell our kids!*) If two websites are competing, the website with more links must be more important and therefore wins. (**Link quantity**)

Quality. Not all votes are alike, however. The voter must correctly vote for a candidate by marking his or her name correctly on the ballot. (*Think hanging chads in Florida and confusion about voter intent in 2000*). If two websites are competing, the website with more links that contain the keyword target will win (**Link syntax**).

Authority. Not all votes are equal. In the 2016 Presidential election, the votes of people in Michigan counted a lot more than the votes of people in California. Indeed, if you look back to 2000, the votes of the justices on the Supreme Court counted the most, throwing that election to George Bush, even though Al Gore had won the popular vote. (**Link authority** or **PageRank**).

In general, therefore, links are like votes, and you want to secure as many external websites as possible linking to your website. But that's not the whole story; it's more complicated than simple quantity (*just like votes in a US Presidential election*), so you need a more detailed understanding of how Google counts links.

Let's dive in to the three variables at play in the game of link-getting or "link-building," as it is called in the industry.

#1 Link Quantity

All things being equal, the website that has *more* websites linking to it will rank higher on Google. If, for example, Website A in the "industrial fan" industry has 1,000 sites that link to it, and Website b has only 500 sites that link to it, Website A will rank higher on Google.

#2 Optimized Link Syntax

An *optimized link* contains the target SEO keyword. If, for example, Website A has many (or more) links that have the blue linkable text around the phrase "industrial fans" vs. Website B that has more links that say only **http://www.myfans.com/** or "click here," then – all things being equal, Website A will outrank Website B for the query "industrial fans" on Google.

If you're confused as to what an optimized link is, here's an example of a link "to" Progressive.com from Progressivecommercial.com at **http://jmlinks.com/47s**. Here's a screenshot:

And here's the HTML code:

```
<div class="grid-10 clearfix">
    <ul class="bulletList two-columns">
        <li><a href="https://www.progressive.com/auto/" target="_blank">Car Insurance</a></li>
        <li><a href="https://www.progressive.com/homeowners/" target="_blank">Homeowners Insurance</a></li>
        <li><a href="https://www.progressive.com/motorcycle/" target="_blank">Motorcycle Insurance</a></li>
        <li><a href="https://www.progressive.com/boat/" target="_blank">Boat Insurance</a></li>
        <li><a href="https://www.progressive.com/rv/" target="_blank">RV Insurance</a></li>
        <li><a href="https://www.progressive.com/snowmobile/" target="_blank">Snowmobile Insurance</a></li>
        <li><a href="https://www.progressive.com/segway/" target="_blank">Segway Insurance</a></li>
        <li><a href="http://investors.progressive.com/" target="_blank">Investors</a></li>
        <li><a href="https://www.progressive.com/careers/" target="_blank">Careers</a></li>
        <li><a href="https://progressive.mediaroom.com" target="_blank" data-gatrackdirect>Newsroom</a></li>
        <li><a href="https://www.progressive.com/lifelanes/subject/commercials/" target="_blank">TV Commercials</a></li>
    </ul>
</div>
```

This means that the link itself is telling Google to rank progressive.com/motorcycle for "Motorcycle Insurance." Anytime you are on a website, hover your mouse over a link, and that link is a keyword – that is an "optimized link" that is signaling to Google the keyword context for the referenced website. That's link **syntax**.

#3 Domain Authority or PageRank

If quantity matters, and quality or syntax matters, there's a third element: **authority**. Links from more powerful sites count for more than links from less powerful websites. It stands to reason, for example, that a link from the New York Times (NYTimes.com) is worth more than a link from the Tulsa World (Tulsaworld.com). Accordingly, the Google algorithm quantifies this difference in authority.

While Google doesn't share its algorithm, third-party tools like AHREFS.com allow you to peek behind the curtain and see the relative Domain Authority of different websites.

For example, NYTimes.com has a Domain Authority of 94, while TulsaWorld.com has a domain authority of 81. My website, JasonMcDonald.org, has a DA of 26. In other words, not all links are created or valued equally: a link from the NYTimes.com is worth an incredible amount, a link from TulsaWorld.com is also great, and link from my website to yours is good but not in the same league, not at all.

Google calculates this **Domain Authority** (or "PageRank" as it is referred to historically) based on the number of links not just to any domain but to specific web pages or URLs on that domain. It's self-referential: the more websites that link to a URL, the more important that URL is, and the more "authority," "PageRank," or "Link Juice" that URL has to pass to other URLs on the Internet. It's sort of like the popular kids in High School. How do you know they're popular? Because the other popular kids like them, and those popular kids have the "authority" to pass their popularity to new kids who come to the school. Dogs chase their tails, popular kids beget more popular kids, and the most important websites on the Internet lend credibility to the other "very important" websites.

If, in other words, Website A has more links from more *authoritative* websites than Website B, then – all things being equal – it will outrank Website B.

Relevance Matters

Authoritative isn't just raw domain authority, however – it's *relevance*, too. For a Brahman cattle breeder, a link from Brahman.org (DA of 51) may be worth more than a link from NYTimes.com because of the relevance of the linking website. Keywords, in other words, re-enter the picture. Because Brahman.org talks about Brahman cattle (and not organic potatoes), it's a highly relevant AND authoritative website for websites that want to rank for terms like "Brahman bulls." By contrast, if you want to rank for "organic potatoes" a link from the Potato Association of America (Potatoassociation.org), especially their page on "organic potatoes) at **http://potatoassociation.org/industry/organic-methods** is an extremely relevant AND authoritative link for you to get.

In sum, the cool kids in school that are jocks are relevant if you want to be a cool athlete, and the cool kids in school that are theater people are relevant if you want to be an actress. It's the same thing on the Web with respect to links. Authoritativeness and relevance work together.

Summing Up

Before your head explodes with all this complexity, let's keep it simple. You want other websites to link to you -

1. in high **quantity** (more is better);

2. with the **right syntax** (try to get your keywords in the link text itself, rather than just an http:// link or a "click here" link); and

3. from **high Domain Authority** websites (NYTimes.com is worth more than TulsaWorld.com), as well as from sites that are **relevant to your industry** (a link from Brahman.org is worth more to a Brahman cattle ranch website than a link from Pizzaexpo.com).

In summary, **links** are like **votes**, and you want **quantity**, **quality**, and **authority**. As you solicit links from other websites, remember, however, that you won't always get a *trifecta* or perfect *quantity*, *quality*, and *authority* from a link, so get what you can. As Voltaire said, "The perfect is the enemy of the good."

Solicit Links (And Don't Sweat the Small Stuff)

It Gets Complicated

This is only a simple model of how links work in the Google algorithm. The reality is more complicated. For instance, what if Website A has a higher quantity of links to it, but Website B has better syntax vis-à-vis the target keyword? Or, what if Website A has better syntax, but Website B has a few links from very high authority websites? Or what if Website A has many, high quality links but Website B has a few, high quality links and better "On Page" SEO? The Google algorithm takes all these factors into account; so remember, it's not just *one* factor that propels you to the top of Google but the algorithmic *summation* of these weighted factors vs. your competitors.

Because "it's complicated," just remember – in general – to always be on the lookout for links to your website as you also remember that success at SEO is "everything working together" factor-by-factor.

A Word about NoFollow

Here's another wrinkle about links and link-building. At a technical level, the **rel="nofollow"** attribute tells Google to ignore a link; these types of links are devalued by Google. So if you see *nofollow* in the HTML source code it's a sign that given link is not as valuable. Here's a screenshot of the Pokemon page on Wikepedia, for example, with an outbound link to the official Pokemon website:

External links

- Official Japanese website of *Pokémon* (Japanese)
- Official US website of *Pokémon*
- Official UK website of *Pokémon*

And here's the HTML source code showing the link, including the *nofollow* attribute, therefore nullifying the link:

```
<a               rel="nofollow"             class="external            text"
href="http://www.pokemon.com/">Official      US      website      of
<i>Pokémon</i></a>
```

You can see it at **http://jmlinks.com/6w**. What this means is that the link FROM Wikipedia TO pokemon.com does NOT help its SEO because the nofollow attribute tells Google NOT to count the link as a vote. Commonly, as you look for links to get to your website, be sure to look at the source code and if you see the *nofollow* attribute then these links are not valuable. The most common "nofollow" links are links from blog comments, links from social media sites, and links from some associations or directories.

Note: a link that does NOT contain the *nofollow* attribute is commonly referred to as a *dofollow* link, although there isn't technically a *dofollow* attribute.

Don't freak out, however, and don't overthink it. You don't have to be an HTML source code genius to understand links! Just realize that, generally speaking, links in comments on blogs are all *nofollow*. Craig's list, Wikipedia, and many directory links are also *nofollow*. Many links on social media are also *nofollow*. Press release links are commonly *nofollow* too. These links are not as valuable as links that do not have the *nofollow* attribute (called *dofollow* links in SEO lingo).

However… in SEO there's always another twist of the screw…

Do Nofollow Links Matter?

The first take-away is that *nofollow* links do *not* help SEO. This is the official Google position and commonly held position in the SEO community. However (*there's always a however in SEO*), my opinion is that *nofollow* links actually *do* count, and can help your SEO. Think of links like a stock portfolio: you want diversity in your links – some *nofollow*, some *dofollow*, some in the HTTP format, some in your brand name, and some in your keyword syntax. *Nofollow* links are like "penny stocks" – one-by-one, not very valuable but in totality, they can indeed be valuable.

Google, in short, probably devalues the weight of *nofollow* links to the tune of 90% or 95%, but they still seem to carry some weight. No one knows for certain but because Google has terrified so many sites into making blank *nofollows* across all outbound links, Google has created a problem for itself. For many smaller sites (competing for many narrow keywords), there aren't many links that differentiate site #1 from site #2. This is often the case for many small businesses. You might have ten links, and your competitor might have seven. And if all (or most) of these links are nofollows, then Google still has to decide. Presto! *Nofollow* links suddenly count. For a fascinating study of the power of *nofollow* links visit **http://jmlinks.com/47t**.

Just Get Links

Again, before you give up in despair at all this technical mumbo-jumbo: just remember to **get links**. Ask customers, suppliers, and other business contacts whom you know to add a link FROM their website TO your website. It can be as simple as asking the janitorial company that cleans your office, or the pizza company that delivers your office pizza, to go on their website and add a link FROM their site TO your site. Or, to ask a customer who has a blog to write a product review about her experience, and have her include a link in that blog post FROM her blog TO your website. Or, ask Mom, Dad, Uncle Jay, your best friend… anyone who has a blog to write up an article about you, and link TO your website.

Register for professional associations that include links to your website. Set up your social profiles on Twitter, Facebook, Google+ and other sites. Ask everyone you know who has a website to write something about your company and link over to it.

Just get links!

Just like in real-world elections, the most important part of successful link building is sheer **quantity**. Politicians don't always sweat the small stuff; they kiss a lot of babies, and shake a lot of hands in their quest for high quality votes. So should you in your quest for links!

POLITICIANS KISS BABIES & SEOs SOLICIT LINKS

For further step-by-step directions on how to solicit links, I highly recommend the MOZ guide at **http://jmlinks.com/14n** and the BackLinko SEO link-building tactic list at **http://jmlinks.com/38r**.

» BEWARE THE PENGUIN

Google's "Penguin" update, launched in April 2012, is an on-going algorithm attack against artificial link-building. While officially Google says that you should NEVER "build links" but rather just wait "passively" for links to come to your site, a passive strategy will get you nowhere.

You can, must, and should "build links."

However, you have to be aware of Penguin, and solicit links in a smart fashion. First, let's consider what Penguin penalizes, and then let's turn to the "big picture" of link-building, post-Penguin.

First, Penguin penalizes a large quantity of in-bound links from "low quality" websites as well as "overoptimized links." "Low quality" websites are generally artificial blogs — blogs that are poorly written, contain non-related content, and are clearly created "for search engines" and not for people. A good example of this scenario is Indian-based SEO companies that built thousands upon thousands of blogs (called a private blog network), and then (for money) will link back to your site around a target keyword phrase such as *Miami divorce attorney*, or *organic baby food*. It is easy for Google to detect this chicanery and penalize sites with this sort of a link footprint.

In fact, if you are solicited by SEO companies offering link schemes that directly involve posting links to your website on low quality blogs or low quality directories, do **NOT** fall for these schemes! They will hurt you much more than help you.

What are Overoptimized Links?

"Overoptimized" links are links from other websites to your website that all include the same keyword phrase over and over. A "divorce attorney," for example, might create / pay for / solicit links from blogs all around the exact phrase "divorce attorney." He would end up with, for example, 1000 blogs all linking back to his website, all having the format of:

blah, blah, blah, blah, blah divorce attorney (linking to: http://www.divorceattorneywebsite.com) blah blah blah blah blah blah blah

Now, to have 1000 links all exactly alike, all linking back to the same website is "unnatural," isn't it? So what Penguin did was look at the "link footprint" of websites and identify "unnatural" link footprints. It then penalizes these sites by taking them off of Google or harshly pushing them from Page 1 to Page 101.

Penguin looks for "unnatural" link profiles: many links from low quality blogs or directories as well as many optimized links. You can use the Remove 'em tool at **http://jmlinks.com/6x** to check your own link footprint.

Link Diversity

Second, when building links post-Penguin, you should a) never solicit links from low quality blogs and/or easy, free directories, and certainly not get links from sites the blatantly advertise "links for sale," and b) pay attention to the (over)optimization of your link structure. A good general rule of thumb is 1/3 *http://* links, 1/3 *branded* links (links to your company name), and 1/3 *optimized* links. In HTML code these are written as:

> Check out Jason McDonald's SEO consulting website at **https://www.jasonmcdonald.org/** (naked or http link).
>
> Check out **<a href= "http://www.jasonmcdonald.org/ ">Jason McDonald's</a>** SEO consulting website. (branded link)
>
> Check out Jason McDonald, an amazing **<a href= "http://www.jasonmcdonald.org/ ">SEO consultant</a>** in San Francisco. (optimized link)

Link diversity means having people link to you in different formats, and to get links from a variety of sources: trade associations, blogs, directories, non-profits, etc.

Fortunately, for most companies, too many links and *too many* overoptimized links are the least of their problems; most companies just have *too few* links. But, that said, if you engage in serious link-building, you must "beware the Penguin" and build a "natural" yet robust inbound link profile. Build links at your own risk!

Outbound Links from Your Website

Finally, Penguin penalizes websites that are "too perfect." Pre-Penguin, many SEO experts would advise you never to link out FROM your website TO other websites. This advice is no longer correct; a website that has zero outbound links looks suspicious to Google. Similarly, many websites would use the *nofollow* attribute on all outbound links, or to "sculpt" links internally. After Penguin, this kind of behavior is a dead giveaway that you are attempting to manipulate Google. So, don't be "too perfect:"

> Do not refuse to link outbound to other websites because a website with zero outbound links looks suspicious to Google.
>
> Do not "nofollow" all your links to other websites, as the use of "nofollow" on all outbound links can also look suspicious to Google.
>
> Do not "nofollow" certain internal links in an attempt to link sculpt, as this also looks suspicious to Google.

Therefore, post-Penguin, I advise you to strategically link out to highly reputable websites in your industry. A breeder of Brahman cattle, for example, should link out to sites like the National Brahman Association (brahman.org) as well as other websites in the cattle industry. A San Francisco attorney might link to the city of San Francisco (SFgov.org). The objective is to convince Google that you are a good "Net citizen," and you are linking *out* as well as receiving links *in*. Just keep your outbound links to a minimum, and make sure that they are to highly reputable sites in your own industry.

You may also hear a warning that "reciprocal links" will cancel each other out – if the Brahman cattle breeder is listed on Brahman.org, and he also links over to Brahman.org, this will "cancel out" the "link juice," for instance. While this might theoretically have some truth in it, in practical terms I do not find this to be so. Yes, it is better if people only link to you (and you do not reciprocate), but I just wouldn't stress this too much. In all of this, I am assuming you have a) relevant links, and b) you aren't massively engaging in reciprocal link schemes. So much of proper link building is proper scale. Did I ever mention to you, that "A little salt is good for the soup, but too much salt ruins the soup?" Don't overdo any type of link-building.

Google's Hypocrisy

As we conclude this explanation of what links are, why they matter, and the basic ideas on how to build links *post-Penguin*, let me stop for a moment and talk about Google's hypocrisy. Google famously had the phrase "Don't be evil" as their corporate motto, which besides being pretentious, has probably turned out to be yet another empty platitude by yet another big corporation. Google, like all big corporations, keeps its eyes on profits, and has a very effective corporate marketing machine working hard to create a brand image of efficiency and honesty. Google isn't any better, or any worse, than any other big corporation.

In terms of links, the official propaganda of Google is that no one should ever build links. (Read it at **http://jmlinks.com/14r**). In Google's opinion, we should all just passively wait until links "spontaneously" emerge on the Web, and then Google will "objectively" evaluate the link footprint of competing websites and choose the "best" website to place at the top of its results.

I'm sorry to destroy your illusions, but if you've read this far in this book, you should realize, by now, that the idea that Google results are "objective" is pretty ridiculous. It's a competitive war between companies to get to the top, and in any serious keyword competition, everyone is working very hard to "manipulate" Google. Your competitors (at least the smart ones) are building links, and you pretty much have to, too, even though Google's official public line is that you should NEVER solicit links.

Everyone, quite simply, has to violate the rules without any clear guidance as to what the "real" rules are. Google simply looks the other way, and occasionally smacks down a vendor or two when it gets out of hand. You can either be 100% compliant with Google's policy on links (*and end up spending a fortune on AdWords*), or you can violate Google's policy and succeed.

It gets worse. Google even encourages companies to "turn in" competitors that are violating its policies. Watch an official video on this at **http://jmlinks.com/14t**. You can even "turn in" a competitor via the official Google webspam form at **http://jmlinks.com/14u**. Here's a screenshot:

Google

Search Console

Help us maintain the quality of Google search results.

We work hard to return the most relevant results for every search we have users' best interests at heart. Some site owners attempt to "buy

Google uses a number of methods to detect paid links, including alg submissions, and we'll use your data to improve our algorithmic dete

Report paid links

Website selling links:

[   ]

Website buying links:

[   ]

Nefariously, the effect of all these activities is to encourage users to turn in other users as well as what to create "negative SEO" when one competitor "fakes" noncompliance by another competitor (and turns them in) to destroy their website performance. It's a mess, and far, far from "don't be evil" in terms of its impact. Yet Google, happily making millions, doesn't seem very concerned about the devastating impact its policies have on websites, or on the "unintended consequences" of its policies.

Now, I'm not saying go 100% to the dark side via black hat SEO and build or buy fake links. And I'm not saying I have a solution for how this could be done differently. I'm not Google, and I don't have a zillion dollar budget to figure out a solution. *It's Google's world; we just live in it.* But what I am saying is put your best foot forward, solicit real links from real websites, and you'll go a long way towards succeeding. But don't publicly announce what you're doing, and don't wave a red flag under Google's nose.

Similarly, with respect to the *nofollow* attribute in Web links, Google publicly says that it nullifies the value of all links, but in my experience, this isn't exactly true. Some *nofollow* links do seem to help. And, even more ominously, there are many, many examples of websites that are heavily violating Google's policies on links, and doing very, very well. Enforcement of any rules is sporadic at best, and Google takes periodic action against high profile violators to "frighten" the SEO community into compliance. See, for example, the "Rap Genius" incident in which Google made an "example" of Rap Genius as a site that had gone "too far" in soliciting links at **http://jmlinks.com/14s**. There are many, many sites that are violating Google's policies just as badly, but Rap Genius was singled out, and made an example.

Be Skeptical. Experiment and Do What Works

The bottom line is that you should be skeptical about what Google says are the rules, and what the rules are. You should be skeptical about what you read in the blogosphere about these policies. And you should be silent when, and if, your website is doing well in terms of SEO for fear that a competitor will turn you into Google. You should not get greedy and "go too far." The art of SEO is figuring out what actually works despite what Google says, despite what you read, and staying pretty silent about it. Just as you might drive on Highway 101 in California – speed, but don't be the fastest car on the freeway. As for the posted speed limit, it's not the "real" limit, but who knows what the "real" limit is? You certainly can't ask the Highway Patrol!

So, now that we've taken a little side journey into Google's misleading and contradictory policies on links, let's return to some relatively safe tactics to build links to your own website (at your own risk, of course).

» DEFINE YOUR LINK OBJECTIVES

Now that you know the game – that *links are like votes*, it's time to define your objectives. We'll assume you've SEO-optimized your homepage, landing pages, keyword footer, and that you've begun to blog and issue press releases. Those tasks are done, or underway. In terms of links, therefore:

- Links are like votes, i.e. quantity.
    - **Objective**: *get people to link to you.*
- Link syntax matters, i.e. quality. It matters whether links are around your keyword phrases and/or come from content that talks about your keyword themes.
    - **Objective**: *get links that contain your keyword phrases.*
- Link PageRank or Web Authority matters, i.e. authority. Some sites (e.g., NYTimes.com) or more authoritative than others (e.g., TulsaWorld.com).
    - **Objective**: get authoritative sites to link to you.
- Link Footprint matters, meaning you want a "natural" footprint of about 1/3 naked http links, 1/3 branded links, and 1/3 optimized links from quality websites.
    - **Objective**: increase inbound links to your website but do so in a "natural" way in terms of the footprint.

In terms of authority, also realize that in any given industry, certain industry hubs are considered very authoritative. If you are selling Brahman cattle, for example, **http://www.brahman.org/**, the website of the American Brahman Breeders Association is the most authoritative website for the keyword Brahman cattle. If you are a pizza restaurant, getting the "American Pizza Community" (**http://www.americanpizzacommunity.com/**) to link to you is your goal. Every industry has certain key websites, key associations, key directories, key bloggers, key trade shows, etc., and your **objective** here is to identify the most authoritative websites in your industry and get them to link to you!

Don't Get Discouraged

Now that you know the link game, don't get discouraged. People commonly think, "Dratz, no one will link to us… we are so boring… or our industry is so dumb that no one will link to anyone." However, you don't have to run faster than the bear, just faster than your buddy! You're not running for President of the United States, it's more likely that you're running for school board in Okmulgee, Oklahoma, an election decided by tens or hundreds of votes. Your competitor faces the same challenges as you, so if you just pro-actively solicit links – even just a few links – you'll usually win.

He might have two links to his website, and you'll have three. You win.

He might have ten links to his website, and you'll have twelve. You win.

Let's turn, now, to **link-building**: systematic strategies for getting other websites to link to your website for SEO. (For an in-depth list of ideas to help you brainstorm your link-building tactics, check out the BackLinko guide at **http://jmlinks.com/14p**. Another good one is Quick Sprout's *Advanced Guide to Link-building* by Neil Patel at **http://jmlinks.com/38n**.)

» Solicit the Easy Links First

Your **ecosystem partners**, i.e. those companies you do business with on a regular basis, are your easiest link targets. If you attend an industry trade show as an exhibitor, for example, ask for a link back to your company website from the trade show website. If you buy a lot of stuff from a supplier, require a link back to your company website from their website as a condition of doing business. If you sponsor a local charity like the *Breast Cancer Walk Pittsburgh*, ask for a link back to your company website from the charity website. If your boss teaches a class at the local university, help him set up a link from his profile page back to your company website. If anyone in your company gets interviewed or is able to write a guest blog post on another website, make sure that they get a link back in their author profile! If Grandma or Grandpa (or the friends, family, or contacts of key employees), has a website or blog, ask them to link to you.

You get the idea: create a **culture of link solicitation** in your organization, so that on a day-in and day-out level everyone in your company is soliciting links, and (over time) getting them.

Don't forget your **social media profile** links! If local search is important to you, make sure that your company is included in Google My Business, Yelp, Citysearch and other local listing sites. Be sure to set up a Twitter, Google+, Facebook and other social media profiles for your companies and include links in those profiles.

VIDEO. Watch a video tutorial on easy link-building tactics at **http://jmlinks.com/17w**.

Your first **TO-DO** is to open up the "link building worksheet," and fill out the easy link target section. For the worksheet, go to **http://jmlinks.com/seo19tz** (reenter the passcode "seo19tz" to register if you have not already done so), and click on the link to the "link building worksheet."

» IDENTIFY DIRECTORY, BLOG, AND OTHER LINK TARGETS

Quality directories, blogs, and other websites found on Google make great link targets. How do you find them? For **directories**, do a Google search for keywords such as "AddURL + Your Keywords," "Directory + Your Keywords," and/or "Catalog + Your Keywords." As you browse these sites, make note of their **Domain Authority** (*use MOZ.com or AHREFS.com, and the Domain Authority metric*) and **keyword themes** that align with your own target keywords. Use the Solo SEO link search tool (**http://jmlinks.com/14q**) for a quick and easy way to look for possible link targets.

A marriage counselor in Bethesda, Maryland, for example, might search Google for:

*marriage counselor directory (view this search at **http://jmlinks.com/6y**)*

directory of therapists

relationship therapist directory

directory Maryland businesses

directory woman-owned businesses

Her goals are to a) identify quality directories that have *dofollow* outbound links, b) figure out how much it costs and/or what are the procedures to be listed, and c) acquire those directory links. **Remember**: if it's absolutely easy to get in, every SEO will do it and the directory will be low quality or contaminated. **You want serious directories that**

either cost money and/or have real qualifications to be included. Do not list yourself in free directories. Quality is important!

Identify Relevant Blogs

To find **blogs**, type your target keywords plus the word "blog" into the Google search box. For example, our marriage therapist might type in "marriage therapy blog" at **http://jmlinks.com/19h.** You're looking for blogs that will allow a guest post and/or blogs that are interested in your keywords. Remember to also pro-actively ask customers if they have a blog, and if they do, solicit them to write something about your company, product or service. Then you have to devise an idea / solicitation that they'd like to include on their blog, plus include a link back to your website.

A common tactic is to give out product samples, for free, in exchange for a product review and link back on the blog. (Again, with an eye to Google's sensitivity about links, don't "overdo" this – find high quality, legitimate bloggers, and don't publicly announce your product-review-link program!). Do NOT go to a public blog exchange and buy links – that's way too obvious, and too dangerous!

Complementary Competitors

Finally, do searches for your major keyword phrases. As you search, segregate your **direct competitors** (sites so similar to your own that there is no way that they would link to you) from your **complementary competitors**. These are sites like blogs, personal websites, portals, directories, Wiki entries and the like that "show up" on your searches but may have a complementary reason to link to you. A wedding photographer, for example, might search for not only directories of wedding suppliers but also florists, priests, caterers, bakers, and facilities that would likely exchange links due to the complementary nature of their businesses.

Sponsor Non-Profits and Include Links

Another great tactic is non-profit link-building. Solicit non-profit links: identify relevant non-profits, and pay them as a "sponsor" with a link from their website to your own. As with all link-building tactics, do not overdo this.

A good way to do this is to search Google using the site: command, as in:

site:*.org "your keywords"

For example: site:*org "organic food" (**http://jmlinks.com/7d**).

For example: site:*.org "organic food" "link to your website" (**http://jmlinks.com/7e**).

You thus identify non-profits in your keyword community, and can even drill down to those that allow paying sponsors to link back to their website. Voila: a link-building strategy based on helping non-profits!

VIDEO. Watch a video tutorial on how to identify nonprofits for link-building at http://jmlinks.com/18e.

To-dos for Link-Building

Your second **TO-DO** is to fill out the section of the "link building worksheet" focusing on blogs, portals, and directories. For the worksheet, go to **http://jmlinks.com/seo19tz** (reenter the passcode "seo19tz"), and click on the link to the "link building worksheet."

» REVERSE ENGINEER COMPETITORS' LINKS

Wouldn't it be wonderful to be able to "reverse engineer" who links to your competitors, and then solicit links from those websites? You can easily do this.

Many fabulous tools exist to "reverse engineer" inbound links of competitors. Most offer a limited "free" version, and for about $99 / month, you can access a robust paid version. I recommend signing up for at least one month, spending the $99, and doing some in-depth link research. You can download all the data into Excel spreadsheets, and then cancel your account.

Your objective is to identify complementary websites that link to a competitor but who may also be willing to link to you. Type each competitor's homepage URL into these tools, and then surf to the appropriate websites, making note of the PageRank (domain authority), content, and contact information for your "Link Building" target list. Here are my three favorites:

Link Explorer by Moz (https://moz.com/link-explorer). Type your competitor's homepage into this tool, or the URL of a highly ranked site on Google. Browse to see who is linking to your competitors.

Ahrefs (http://ahrefs.com/). Similar to Open Site Explorer, this tool allows you to input a competitor URL and reverse engineer who is linking to that competitor.

Open Link Profiler (http://www.openlinkprofiler.org/). This tool tracks new links to your website (or to competitors), and requires no registration and no payment. It's totally free!

Here's a screenshot of Open Link Profiler's analysis of **http://www.progressive.com/** showing that that site has over 20,239 linking domains totaling to over 710,460 inbound links. No wonder *progressive.com* dominates searches for insurance!

VIDEO. Watch a video on how to use the AHREFS tool and other link discovery tools to "reverse engineer" competitors at **http://jmlinks.com/18d**.

At the end of this process, you should have a defined list of "link targets" sorted by PageRank (Domain Authority) and their keyword themes with your "keyword community." Your third **TO-DO** is to take this list, and then go one by one through the results, soliciting links from the various targets. If summer is here, link solicitation is a great task for a cheap intern! Or, go to a site like Fiverr.com (**http://www.fiverr.com/**) and identify a cheap outsourced worker to do the "grunt" work of your link solicitation system.

» CREATE LINK BAIT

Link bait takes link building to the next level. Link bait is the art of creating content that is so compelling that people will *spontaneously* link to it, without you even having to ask. Let's run through some common link-bait ideas.

Content Bait

People love in-depth content, so write an in-depth "Frequently Asked Questions" document or article that fits the needs and interests of your industry. If you're a probate lawyer, for example, write a beefy article to your blog on "How to avoid probate." Beefy, in-depth, good content becomes link bait for journalists, bloggers, and influencers on social media looking to point their audience to the "ultimate guide" on a key topic. Here's a great example. BackLinko has written the "definitive guide" to Link Building (which is, in and of itself, link bait) at **http://jmlinks.com/7b**.

Ego Bait

Have a customer of the month contest (if your customers have websites), have a supplier of the month award (if your suppliers have websites). Email, call, and even give gifts to blogs, portals, and other content sites that might be willing to cover you and your company. In link building, remember you are dealing with other people, so look at the situation from their perspective: what's in it for them? If you "feature" them with an award, they'll often spontaneously link to you – plus your "award contest" can get press, publicity, and links.

Product Sample Bait

Give away free samples of your product only to people who have a blog, and/or are willing to share your site on social media. Ask them to write honest product reviews, and require a link back in the blog article.

Scholarship Bait

Identify a noble cause (preferably relating to your keyword targets), and create a scholarship program for deserving students. Next, require an essay as part of the application (which will be great content for your blog, and ego bait). Then, identify relevant colleges and solicit them to link "out" to your scholarship. It's win win: the student gets a scholarship, and you get links from quality .edu domains to your website.

Ultimate (Free) Guide Bait

An ultimate guide or free eBook can be excellent link-bait. Write the definitive eBook on "top ten new technologies" for your industry, write a provocative FAQ document with "how to" templates, or tell an emotional story. HubSpot has done a fantastic job of this. Check out their eBooks at **http://jmlinks.com/38p**.

Badge Bait

Consider creating **badges**: customer of the month, best tool for such-and-such, partner companies, verification of a certification test, and so on and so forth.

Have you ever noticed how many Yelp results show up high on Google search? Have you ever thought of how many companies have Yelp badges on their websites, with links up to their Yelp listings? Now that you know something about link-building, you can see that Yelp is surreptitiously tricking businesses to link "up" to Yelp.com. The small business webmaster who posts a link to his Yelp listing, saying, "Check us out on Yelp," is sending link juice "from" his website "to" Yelp. Yelp, in summary, uses a **link-bait strateg**y to manipulate Google.

Consider being the "Yelp" of your industry via badges. Here's a screenshot giving an inside look at how Yelp promotes its link juice via badges:

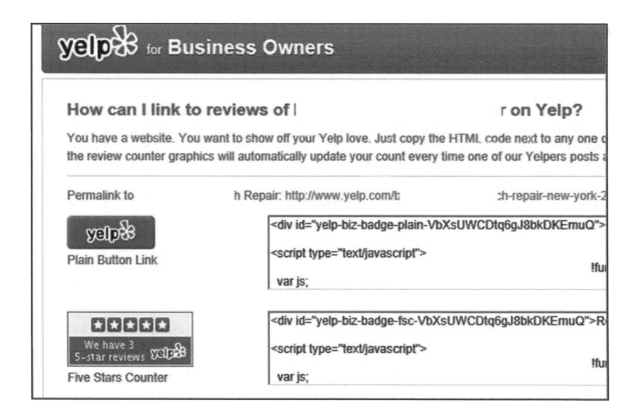

You can view the Yelp badge system at **http://jmlinks.com/7f**. Note: if you use "badge bait," be Penguin-aware. Make sure to **vary the inbound link text** and structure across your badges so as to not trigger a Penguin penalty. For example, the ALT image attribute for some badges would have keyword No. 1, others keyword No. 1, others just your company name, etc.

Widget Bait

If you have a programming budget, create **widgets** such as BMI calculator, the real-time price of gold, a reverse mortgage calculator. Any sort of free tool or widget that is relevant to your industry can be link bait to bring in links in a spontaneous way. Monex, a company that sells gold, silver, and platinum bullion, for example, has an example of "widget bait" at **http://jmlinks.com/7c**. **Infographics** are another way to get links: create an informative, humorous, outrageous or shocking infographic and let the links roll in!

Your fourth **TO-DO** is to have a company meeting and brainstorm possibilities for link bait. If you see opportunities, create a step-by-step plan to implement your link bait strategy. Notice as well that what constitutes "link bait" is also fabulous for social media sharing.

»» CHECKLIST: LINK-BUILDING ACTION ITEMS

Test your knowledge of link-building! Take the *link-building quiz* at **http://jmlinks.com/qzln**. Next, here are your link-building **Action Items**:

> ❑ **Understand** the **basics** of links and link-building, specifically - *quantity*, *quality* (optimized links), and *authority* (PageRank or Domain Authority).

>> ❑ Be **link-aware** as a company or organization, constantly asking people to "link to you," as for example when a journalist or blogger writes an article, you participate in a trade show, or you join an industry association, etc.

❑ Be also **Penguin-aware** and seek for a "natural footprint" of many links - *naked* (http), *branded* (your company name), and *optimized* (your keywords).

❑ Create a **link-building system**, going from easy to most difficult -

❑ **Ecosystem partners** - solicit links from suppliers, friends, colleagues, etc.

❑ **Social media profiles** - set up, claim, and link from your social media profiles as on Facebook, Twitter, YouTube, etc.

❑ **Industry associations and directories** - inventory and get listed in the "best" industry directories that provide outbound links. Don't forget industry trade associations and other organizations key employees may be members of (e.g., "National Association of Women Small Business Owners," etc.)

❑ Solicit links from **bloggers** - identify and solicit links from relevant bloggers in your industry; consider *guest blogging*.

❑ **Non-profits** - identify and sponsor relevant nonprofits with link-backs to your website.

❑ **Link-bait** - if possible, generate a "widget" or "badge" or even a long-form blog post as "content bait." Perhaps a scholarship program. Create content that is "so good" bloggers and others will spontaneously link to it.

Check out the **free tools**! Go to my *SEO Dashboard > Link-building* section for my favorite free tools for link-building. Just visit **http://jmlinks.com/seodash**.

»» DELIVERABLE: A COMPLETED LINK-BUILDING WORKSHEET

The **DELIVERABLE** for this Chapter is a completed link-building worksheet. For the worksheet, go to **https://www.jm-seo.org/workbook** (reenter the passcode "seo19tz"), and click on the link to the "link-building worksheet."

5.2

SOCIAL MEDIA

A topic unto itself, Social Media has many SEO implications. **Social mentions** - that is the sharing of your website links on sites like Twitter, LinkedIn, Facebook and more - is a new kind of **link building**. Having robust **social profiles** (like an active *Twitter feed* or active *Facebook Business Page*) signals Google and its search algorithm that your company is active and important. This is called **social authority**. Indeed, *Google My Business* (Google's platform for local businesses) presents unique SEO opportunities, particularly in the area of having a robust corporate profile with many local reviews, as we shall discuss in the next Chapter. In addition, Google's partnership with Twitter is a clear sign that having a robust Twitter profile and having your links "tweeted" is now a must-do.

SEO is going social, so in this Chapter, we explore the brave new world of **Social Media SEO**.

Let's get started!

TO-DO LIST:

> » Understand Social Media SEO

> » Get Social Mentions!

> » Set up Robust Social Profiles

> »» Checklist: Social Media Action Items

> »» Deliverable: A Completed Social Media SEO Worksheet

» UNDERSTAND SOCIAL MEDIA SEO

Links, as we have seen, count as **votes** in SEO. Google clearly rewards sites that have many keyword-relevant links (especially those from high authority websites), with higher positions on Google search results. Social Media in a sense builds on this network of link authority. How so? While Google has not publicly clarified how it uses what are called *social signals* in SEO, we can postulate some logical patterns of how Google might interpret social signals.

If Website A has its URL "Tweeted" and Website B does not, then Website A must be more important.

If blog post A on trending topic #1 has 12 tweets of its URL, and blog post B on trending topic #1 has 35 tweets of its URL, then blog post B must be more relevant for the corresponding Google search query.

If Website A has 20,000 followers on Twitter, and Website B has only 100, then Website A must be more important.

In a nutshell, having your URL's tweeted, shared on LinkedIn or Facebook, or mentioned on other social networks is a form of link-building.

Evidence that this occurs is visible in how Google quickly figures out trending news. It's common knowledge that the first place people go to for breaking news is Twitter, and accordingly, a quick Google search of a trending topic (try searching Google, for example, for "The Kardashians," or "Donald Trump," or "iPhone Games") and you'll often find new and fresh content that is being shared heavily on Twitter.

For instance, here's a screenshot of the search for "wildfire," showing recent news and tweets about California Wildfires:

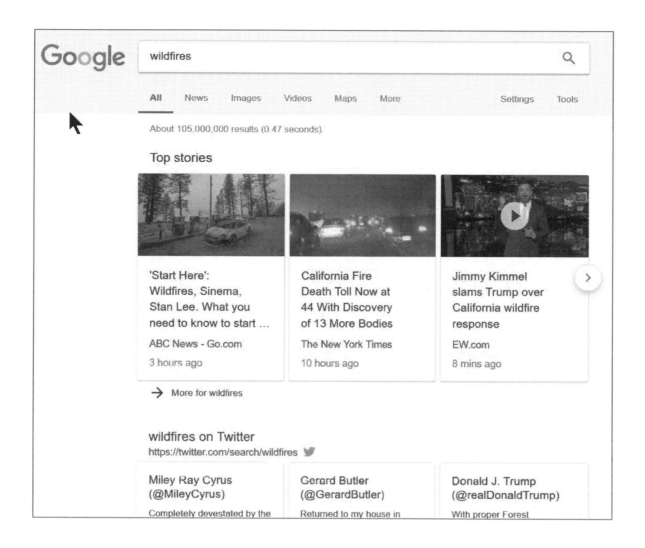

Compare that with a search for "wolverine:"

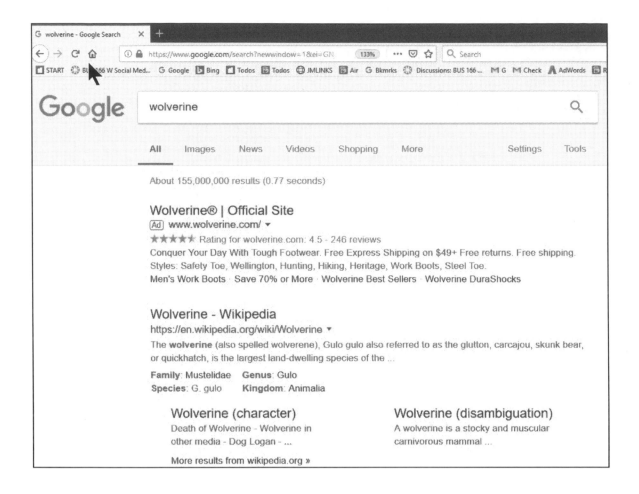

What these two searches tell us is that – by monitoring social media – Google figures out that the former search is for news and news events, while the latter is a stable search that is definitional in character. Behind the scenes, Google is using social networks like Twitter, Facebook, and YouTube to "figure out" which searches are time-sensitive and which ones are not. Now, take that a step further, and you'll realize that many searches are mixed. A search for "iPhone," for example, is a mixture of stable and news-oriented information. Social media is the intervening factor; the takeaway is that we can influence Google by influencing our social media profiles and buzz.

Another clue is Google's relationship with Twitter. Google has a formal partnership of Twitter in which Google gets first crack at the Twitter "firehose" of breaking news. It stands to reason, therefore, that having your URLs shared on Twitter might help them for SEO purposes.

How does social media impact SEO?

First and foremost, sites that enjoy **inbound links via social mentions of URLs** from social sites like Twitter, LinkedIn, or even Facebook are clearly topical and relevant to Google. A simple *site:twitter.com* search on Google reveals over 382 million indexed Tweets, and a simple *site:facebook.com* search on Google reveals over 714 million indexed Facebook posts.

Google clearly pays attention to the social sharing of links!

SOCIAL SHARES ARE THE NEW LINK-BUILDING!

Second, robust and active **social profiles** are another obvious clue to Google of your website's relevance. Many sites link out to their Yelp account, Twitter account, Facebook page, LinkedIn page, etc., and those social sites can be indexed by Google. Google can clearly "see" how active your company is on social media, how many "followers" you have, and whether those followers, in turn are active and/or important. Most importantly, Google can "count" your "reviews" on Google My Business, Yelp, YellowPages and other local review sites.

(**Note**: we discuss the impact of reviews in the next Chapter, 5.3 on "Local SEO").

It stands to reason that having an active social media footprint, with active posts, many engaged followers, and many reviews is a new signal to Google about your website's relevance. Indeed, much of this is keyword centric, another reason why knowing your keywords is paramount to SEO success!

Third, social search has made the Web more **human**. Whereas in the past, the creators of Web content were relatively invisible, new ways of communicating "microdata" can tell Google how many reviews your site has, who the content author is, and whether this author has an active, engaged follower community or not. Realizing that SEO is now a **social game** positions your company for not just the present but the future of SEO success on Google.

Note: this Chapter focuses on using social media for SEO purposes. For social media marketing in its own right, please see my *Social Media Marketing Workbook* available on Amazon at **http://jmlinks.com/smm**.

To be clear, remember that "traditional links" remain far, far more important than social shares to this day: so if you have to choose between a "traditional link" (e.g., from a blog post) and a "social share" (e.g., the Tweeting of your URL), choose the former. **Links still remain the dominant currency of SEO, worth far more than social media shares.**

» GET SOCIAL MENTIONS!

Getting **social mentions** of your URLs is a lot like traditional link building. First, look for easy social mention targets. Ask customers, suppliers, and ecosystem partners to tweet your URLs, share your company's blog posts on Facebook, and to "like" them on Facebook. Second, "reverse engineer" competitors or use common Google and social media searches to find social media sharers who might be interested in your content.

Get Tweeted

In this regard, Twitter is the most important network for SEO purposes. You want to not only set up your business Twitter account and tweet out your own URLs (e.g., a new blog post or new press release). You also want to get real people on Twitter to tweet those URL's, too.

To find people Tweeting on your keywords, go to Twitter advanced search at **http://jmlinks.com/14w**, type in your competitor names or your keywords and look for Tweeters who have a) many followers, and b) tweet on your keyword themes. Then reach out to them and encourage them to tweet your latest blog post, press release, or informative new widget. Here's a screenshot showing a search for tweets on "organic food":

Second, you can use Buzzsumo (**http://www.buzzsumo.com**) to identify social shares of your keywords. Here's a screenshot:

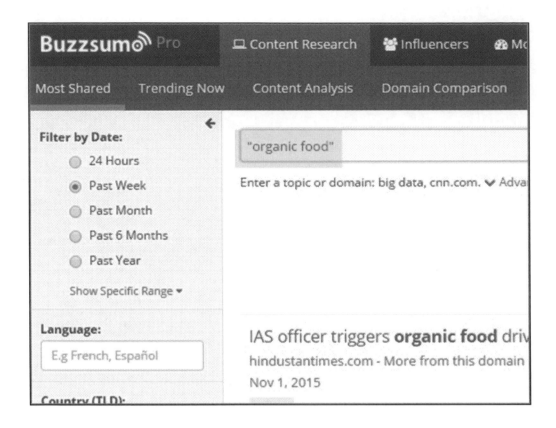

Inside of Buzzsumo, you can click on "View sharers" to find the Twitter accounts of people who shared a piece of news. Here's a screenshot:

Buzzsumo, unfortunately, is a paid tool with only limited functionality for free.

So, third, an alternative is to use the website *Hashtagify.me* and look for *#hashtags* that are similar to your keywords. (Note do not use spaces when researching hashtags, so its *#organicfood* not *#organic food*). You can then also look for the top Twitter accounts for those hashtags. Here's a screenshot of **http://hashtagify.me** for *#organicfood*:

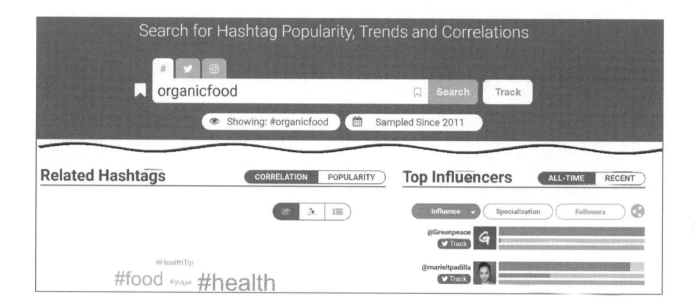

Finally, if you've written a blog post on a trending topic, consider advertising on Twitter, Facebook and/or LinkedIn to get it "picked up" while still timely, thereby encouraging more "free" shares of your URL.

> **VIDEO.** Watch a video tutorial on how to get "social mentions" at **http://jmlinks.com/17v**.

Don't forget that Google is another great way to search other social media sites for heavy sharers. Try Google searches like *site:facebook.com {your keywords}*, *site:linkedin.com {your keywords}*, *site:pinterest.com {your keywords}*, etc. to identify site-specific individuals who are good targets to share your own content. You can try a sample search at **http://jmlinks.com/7h**.

VIDEO. Watch a video tutorial on how to use the site: command to identify social sharers at **http://jmlinks.com/16g**.

Reach out to Bloggers

Don't forget blogs and bloggers! Go to Google, type in your keywords plus the word "blog" and look for relevant blogs. For example, type into Google: "blog proteomics" to find blogs that cover the fun-filled world of *proteomics*. Here's a screenshot:

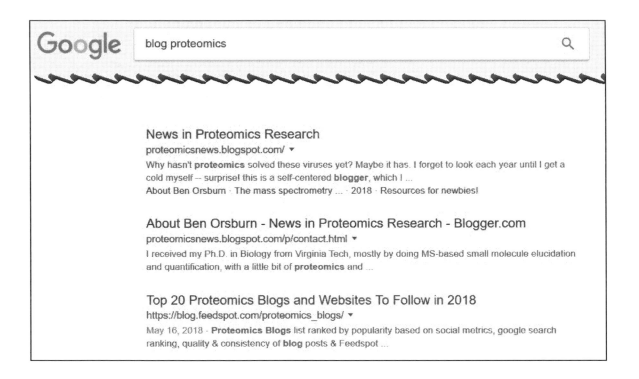

Social Mention (**http://www.socialmention.com**) is another search engine that focuses specifically on social media content. Bloggers are great targets because a link in a blog post is a real, traditional, SEO-friendly link, blog updates signal to Google new, fresh, content, and bloggers are often quite active on Twitter and other social media networks. Blogs are the gold standard, in other words, of social mentions.

As you reach out for links and social mentions, focus on win-win opportunities. For example, if you sell products send out product samples to key bloggers, Tweeters, and Facebookers and ask them for honest product reviews, "tweets" of your URLs, and "shares" of your links on Facebook or Twitter, in exchange for samples.

(Remember, however, that – technically speaking – any type of link-building outreach is a violation of Google terms of service so be judicious, and act at your own risk, and be aware that sending out product samples requires FTC notice to be placed on any blog posts.)

Your first **TO-DO** is to open the "Social Media SEO worksheet," and complete the section entitled "social sharers." For the worksheet, go to **http://jmlinks.com/seo19tz/** (reenter the passcode "seo19tz"), and click on the link to the "Social Media SEO worksheet."

» SET UP ROBUST SOCIAL PROFILES

In addition to trying to get people to tweet or share out your URLs, it's a no-brainer that Google looks for companies with robust social pages. Given two companies competing for a top position on Google, one with thousands of people following its Twitter feed, and another without a Twitter account at all, which company do you think is going to win top placement on Google? This same fact probably goes for other social networks as well, especially ones like Instagram, Facebook, LinkedIn, YouTube, or Pinterest that are open to the Google crawler at least at the account level. (Facebook is closed to Google at the so-called "registration wall.")

For each social media network, be sure to fill out your company pages with relevant keywords and cross-link from each social profile to your website. Here are the most important for most companies with links to their business help guides (if available):

Facebook (https://www.facebook.com/business)

Instagram (https://business.instagram.com/)

Twitter (https://business.twitter.com/)

LinkedIn (http://jmlinks.com/14x)

YouTube (http://jmlinks.com/7j)

Pinterest (http://business.pinterest.com/)

Once you set up a business page, be sure to populate your company description with your relevant keywords and cross-link it back to your website. Be sure to also link from your homepage to your social network pages to make it easy for Google to see which website corresponds to which social network. All of the networks have easy to use badges that enable these important **cross-links**; just look for badges in the relevant business help center as listed above. Be sure to be consistent about your physical address, telephone number, and website address.

Next, start **posting** and **sharing content**. Obviously, it's better if you get real social engagement, but for SEO purposes, you want to at least post something. A simple model is to take your monthly blog posts and tweet out the blog post URLs to your Twitter account, Facebook Page, LinkedIn company page, etc. You can use a scheduling program like Hootsuite (**https://hootsuite.com**) to schedule these in advance. Your objective is to get your URL's out into social media at least on your own account, if not on the "real" accounts of influencers on social media.

You also want to build **followers**. The more followers you have on Facebook, Twitter, Instagram, YouTube, etc., the more important you appear to Google. Ask customers, friends, family, business colleagues, neighbors, random street people, and anyone else to "follow" you on Twitter, Facebook, etc., so as to build up the numeric quantity of followers. Yes, it would be awesome if you were really engaged on social media, but for all intents and purposes on SEO, it's just about raw followers and raw shares of your Web content. Google isn't a person and it isn't so much interested in the quality as in the quantity of your presence on social media.

Posting SEO-friendly Content

Finally, as you post content to a social network, keep your keywords in mind, grow your fan base, and encourage interactivity between you and your fans. Social media is a two-for-one benefit: first, the *direct* benefit from the social media platform itself as you engage with users, and second, the *indirect* benefit as Google "observes" how popular you are and feeds that data into its SEO algorithm.

Your second **TO-DO** is to open up the "Social Media SEO worksheet" and complete the section "Social Media Profiles." For the worksheet, go to **http://jmlinks.com/seo19tz** (reenter the passcode "seo19tz"), and click on the link to the "Social Media SEO worksheet."

»» CHECKLIST: SOCIAL MEDIA ACTION ITEMS

Test your knowledge of social media for SEO! Take the *social media for SEO quiz* at **http://jmlinks.com/qzss**. Next, here are your social media **Action Items**:

❏ Identify **influencers** who can "share" your content, especially on Twitter. Create a list of "key influencers" such as bloggers, persons on Twitter, Facebook, LinkedIn, etc., and have an outreach strategy to alert them to key content.

> ❏ Use "Advanced Search" on Twitter, Buzzsumo.com, and/or Hashtagify.me to build out your influencer list.

> ❏ Use Google search for "blog" plus your keywords to identify influential bloggers.

❏ Set up robust **Social Profiles** on Twitter, Facebook, Instagram, YouTube, etc., and populate with links back to your website. (If you're a local business, see the next Chapter on Google My Business and local SEO.)

❏ Set up Hootsuite.com to manage your social shares, and begin populating them - at a minimum - with content from your blog.

Check out the **free tools**! Go to my *Social Media Dashboard* for my favorite free tools on social media marketing. Just visit **http://jmlinks.com/smmdash**.

»» DELIVERABLE: A COMPLETED SOCIAL MEDIA SEO WORKSHEET

The **DELIVERABLE** for this Chapter is a completed "Social Media SEO worksheet." For the worksheet, go to **http://jmlinks.com/seo19tz/** (enter the code 'fitness' to register if you have not already done so), and click on the link to the "Social Media SEO worksheet."

5.3

LOCAL SEO & REVIEW MARKETING

Let's suppose you have a restaurant, or you're a local plumber, dentist, CPA, or divorce attorney or any of the thousands of local businesses that service customers in their day-to-day life. Before the advent of social media sites like Yelp, Google, YP.com, Airbnb, TripAdvisor and their kind, consumers might have gone to the physical yellow pages or perhaps visited your website after a Google search. You were in charge of your marketing message; *your customers couldn't really "talk back."*

The "Review Revolution" led by Yelp and since followed by Google, YP.com, Airbnb, TripAdvisor, Angie's list, Amazon, Facebook, and other sites, dramatically changed the local landscape. A happy customer can leave a **positive** review about your business, and a not-so-happy customer can leave a scathingly **negative** review.

Reviews, in short, allow consumers to talk back: the good, the bad, and the ugly. And the just plain crazy.

Moreover, it's not just that customers leave reviews. It's that customers read reviews, indeed that they rely on reviews when making judgments about which businesses to patronize. If they see five star or four-star reviews on Google or Yelp, they may reach out to your business with a phone call or email inquiry, or visit your restaurant, bar, or coffee shop. If they see two-star or negative reviews on Yelp, Google, or other local review sites, they may skip over you and go to competitors who have better online reviews.

Online reviews, in short, can make, or break, your local business.

Using Yelp and Google as models, this Chapter explores the "Review Revolution." While the focus will be primarily on *local* businesses, it's a fact that the "review revolution" impacts any business in which customers Google the business name plus "reviews" prior to making a purchase, which is pretty much all businesses.

Let's get started!

To-do List:

» Explore How Review Sites Work

» Inventory Companies on Yelp, Google, or Other Relevant Sites

» Claim and Optimize Your Listings

» SEO Your Local Website

» Cultivate Positive Reviews

» Monitor and Improve Your Online Reputation

» Measure your Results

»» Checklist: Review Action Items

»» Deliverable: A Local SEO Marketing Plan

» Explore How Review Sites Work

Imagine it's 1994, ten years prior to Yelp's founding, and you have a local Italian restaurant in Los Angeles, California. One day you are lucky enough to be visited by the review critic for the *Los Angeles Times*. You recognize her from her picture in the paper, and you realize that she can make – or break – your new Italian eatery. You do your best not to let her know you recognize who she is, and you do your utmost to ensure that she has a positive experience at your restaurant. One week later your hopes and prayers are answered: a positive restaurant review in the local newspaper. Business booms.

Alternatively, if she had written a critical review of your restaurant, business would not have *boomed*. It would have *busted*. **The restaurant critic, in short, had an immense amount of power over local restaurants.** However, if a) you were a small restaurant you had minimal chance of ever getting reviewed, and b) if you were a divorce attorney, plumber, massage therapist, CPA or many other types of local businesses, there were essentially no reviewers available. For those types of businesses, there were essentially no reviews at all.

Enter the **Review Revolution**. In October 2004, Yelp (**http://www.yelp.com**) was founded. Consumers could now review not just local restaurants but plumbers, dentists, massage therapists and thousands of other types of local businesses. The Review Revolution was like any other mass revolution: the masses burst open the doors of the castle, turned over the table and chairs, and even executed the "ruling class." *It was a bit bloody. It was a bit noisy. And it was a bit unpleasant.* If, for example, you were the *Los Angeles Times* restaurant critic, your absolute power over restaurants was broken. The Review Revolution brought democracy to local reviews. Now anyone could review anything. Say "bye bye" to the review aristocracy, and hello to review by the masses. And this didn't just happen on Yelp. It happened to books on Amazon, to apps on the Apple App Store and Google Play, to music on those digital platforms, to movies on the IMDB archive, and on and on.

But here's the rub. Like the French Revolution, the Review Revolution brought the masses into the ecosystem. It has not been very organized or coherent; online reviews run the gamut from informative to ridiculous, from true to faked. Whereas the big reviewers of the *Los Angeles Times, San Francisco Chronicle*, and *New York Times* were educated and civilized (though they could be brutal in their reviews), the new review class can be rough and tumble. Anyone – and I do mean anyone – can write a review: good, bad, or ugly. And let's not forget: *just plain crazy*. To be frank, we are still living in this unsettled Review Revolution, and like the French Revolution, there is no going back: the old system is dead.

UNDERSTAND THE REVIEW REVOLUTION

If you're reading this Chapter, you've probably already grasped that online reviews can make or break your local business performance. Many, if not all, potential customers consult online review sites like TripAdvisor, Airbnb, Yelp, or Google before engaging with local businesses. If they see *positive* reviews, they are primed for a *positive* experience. If they see *negative* reviews, they are so *negatively* primed that they may avoid any contact whatsoever with your business. Reviews now impact all types of local businesses; nearly every local business is being reviewed online 24/7 365. And products are being reviewed on Amazon, employers are being reviewed on Glassdoor.com, and nearly every business (even B2B businesses) are being reviewed via Google "reputational searches," that is, when prospects simply Google your company name plus the word "reviews," as for example, "Geico reviews" or "Zoho reviews" on Google.

The Review Ecosystem

Reviews are a fact of life, but how do reviews work? Let's step back for a moment and ponder the **review ecosystem**. With Yelp as the most important independent local review site, we will use Yelp as our model and recognize that what's true for Yelp is generally true for all review sites because they all follow the same social media rules of engagement. (Most of this also applies to reviews on Google, which is far and away the #1 site for consumer reviews online.)

Here's how review sites work:

1. **Businesses have listings**. Business listings are created *without the permission or participation of the business owner* and exist whether or not the business owner has claimed, optimized, or participated in the review ecosystem. *You as the business owner do not have the right to "delete" your listing on a review site!* It's like a business Page on Facebook, to the extent that your business has an online "Page" on Yelp, Tripadvisor, Healthgrades, etc. But unlike on Facebook, you are not in control!

2. **Customers write reviews**. Registered Yelp users (or Google users, or Airbnb users, or Glassdoor users, etc.) are able to write reviews about any business they choose. *If your business is not listed, users can even create a listing for your business and then review it.* These reviews may be good or bad, extremely positive or so negatively

scathing as to infuriate you as the business owner. The Yelpers are basically in control, not the businesses.

3. **Customer reviewers also establish reputations**. The more reviews a customer writes, the older his or her profile as a reviewer on Yelp, the more friends on Yelp, the more thumbs up or thumbs down to their reviews, the stronger their profile gets. Yelp has filters to filter out "fake" or "weak" reviews from showing entirely. The stronger the customer profile, the higher their reviews rise on the pages of those businesses that they have reviewed. Your business and the Yelpers are both simultaneously establishing a reputation, and that reputation impacts whether your information (your listing, their review) shows prominently on Yelp. (Remember: the same is true for Google, TripAdvisor, Airbnb, and even Amazon).

4. **Businesses establish a reputation**. As your business is reviewed on Yelp, the more positive reviews it has, the more customers see it prominently in the search results, and the more come to visit it (especially first-time customers). But the more negative reviews you have, the less you're seen in search, and the fewer customers you get. This is called a "virtuous circle" and a "vicious circle."

5. **Prospective customers read reviews**. Potential customers visit sites like Yelp, CitySearch, TripAdvisor, Google, and search for businesses via keywords. They find businesses of interest and read the reviews. Generally speaking, people believe reviews especially if there are a lot of them, and even if they do not know the reviewer personally (which they generally don't). This is called "stranger marketing." Reviews thus function as a "trust indicator":

   a. **Positive reviews** incrementally help your business to get new customers;

   b. **Negative reviews**, however, can have a disproportionately devastating impact on your business.

6. **Businesses claim their local listings**. Businesses have the right to claim and optimize their listings. By claiming its listing on a site like Yelp, a business can "optimize" it by improving the business description with accurate keywords, uploading photos, responding to reviews, and in some cases as on Google posting social updates. While businesses cannot delete their listings nor their negative reviews, they can participate in the new social media ecosystem of reviews.

Another major point to grasp is the "**virtuous circles**" and "**vicious circles**" of review marketing: the *more* positive reviews you have, the *more* likely you are to rank at the top of new customer searches (and thus get *more* customers and *more* positive reviews), while the *fewer* reviews you have and/or the *more negative* reviews you have, the *less* likely you are to rank at the top of new customer searches (and thus get more customers). And yet still another key point: the official policy of all the review sites is that you, as a business, should just passively do nothing and not even so much as ask for reviews.

For an overview to Yelp by Yelp, visit **http://www.yelp-support.com/**. For your first **TO-DO**, sign up for a Yelp account (as a consumer, not a business) if you do not already have one. Next, go to Yelp (**http://www.yelp.com/**) to explore some of the following categories in your local city by typing these keywords into the Yelp search box:

Sushi Restaurants

Jazz

Plumbers

Divorce Attorneys

DUI Attorneys

Bail Bonds

Let's take Bail Bonds, for example. Here's a screenshot of a search for "bail bonds" near San Francisco, CA:

Use the clickable links below to do the search:

- Here's a search for "Bail Bonds" near San Francisco, CA at **http://jmlinks.com/4i**.

- And here's one of the top search results: *Le Bail Bonds* at **http://jmlinks.com/32k**. (There's something so classy about being bailed out of jail by the French).

Here are some things to notice about the *Le Bail Bonds* listing.

First, scroll down about half way and look for "From the business" in red. It starts with "We have multiple offices." This is the **business listing**, as edited and submitted by the business. This indicates that this business has claimed their listing. (You'll also see a blue "Claimed" check mark next to the business name). Note the inclusion of relevant keywords, the types of search queries users might type into Yelp. Here's a screenshot:

Second, notice the **photos** at the top of the listing at **http://jmlinks.com/32m**. Click on the photos, and notice how they are "keyword heavy" including the phrase "bail bonds" and the location "San Francisco." These can be submitted either by the business or by users. So, if you don't submit photos, your users might (and they might be favorable, or unfavorable, to your business).

Third, read some of the **reviews**. Notice that for any individual reviewer, Yelp indicates how many friends they have on Yelp and how many reviews they have written. For example, here is a screenshot of a review by Leslie L of San Jose, California:

Fourth, click on a **reviewer photo**, and you'll go up to their **Yelp profile**. For example, click on "Leslie L" and that will get you up to her profile at **http://jmlinks.com/46s**. You can see that Leslie has 2 friends, has written 16 reviews, and uploaded 5 photos:

Read her reviews and make a guess as to how "real" and how "unsolicited" her reviews are. Some reviews and the reviewers who wrote them will look very legitimate, and others might look solicited, paid, or even faked. You'll soon realize that Yelp, like all the review-based sites, is a hodgepodge of unsolicited and solicited reviews, real and fake reviews, and so on and so forth. To the untrained eye, it can be hard to tell which reviews are truly real and which ones are fake; all the review systems are plagued by fake or paid reviews, even if the average customer is not that aware of this problem.

For example, here's a screenshot of a suspicious review:

Notice how Chloe D, has *zero* friends, has written only *one* review, lives in *Manhattan* and yet reviewed a *San Francisco* Bail Bonds. Is this a real review? A solicited review? Or a faked review?

Fifth, return to Le Bail Bond's company page on Yelp, and scroll to the very bottom and click on "reviews that are not currently recommended." Yelp has a filter that attempts to filter out "fake" reviews and filter in "real reviews." Here's a screenshot:

You can see that Yelp has filtered out 22 reviews which its algorithm feels are fake and/or solicited. For example, here's a filtered review by David A who has 0 friends and only 1 review:

Read some of the other "non-recommended" reviews and attempt to guess which ones are truly real and which ones might be fake. Do you think Yelp is doing a good, or bad job, with its filter? How do the reviews shown prominently compare or contrast with the reviews at the bottom, or the reviews that are hidden?

You should quickly realize that the reviews that "stick" tend to be from people with robust profiles, extensive reviews, and a relatively long history on the review site. Their reviews also tend to be beefy and specific, with a lot of content that describes a real experience. The reviews that get filtered out tend to be from people with sparse profiles, few or just one review, and a short history on the review site. The content of the reviews tends to be generic or sparse as well. This isn't always the case, but this is the general pattern. The artificial intelligence inherent in these review algorithms, in short, is getting better and better at giving top billing to real reviews and filtering out fake reviews. Far from perfect, yes, but that's the trend.

Now, before you go crazy and start soliciting reviews, keep reading. It's more complicated than this, but you should begin to see that review marketing – like all of marketing – is a **game** of being pro-active and not passive.

Compare Yelp to Other Review Sites

Reviews do not exist only on Yelp, however. Take any review site (Google, Airbnb, Avvo, Healthgrades, Amazon) and do the same exercise.

For instance, check out some reviews on Amazon, as a contrast to Yelp, by clicking on **http://jmlinks.com/4m** and **http://jmlinks.com/4n**. For example, here's a screenshot of the #1 ranking *garage door remote* on Amazon showing it has 868 customer reviews:

And here's a screenshot of one of the "customer profiles" of a reviewer of the product:

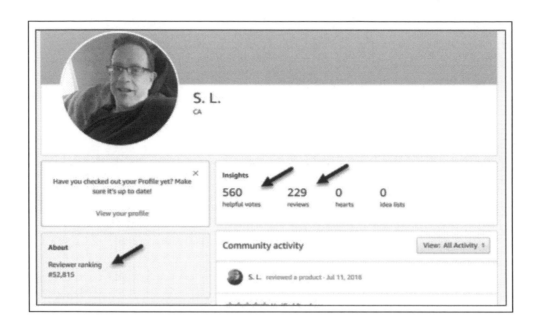

Notice some facts:

- The #1 organic result for "garage door remote" on Amazon has 868 reviews, and 270 answered questions.

- The #1 organic result for "garage door clicker" is titled, "Chamberlain Group KLIK3U-BK Clicker Universal 2-Button Garage Door Opener Remote with Visor Clip, Black" – lots of keywords "stuffed" into the product title.

- The customers who are reviewing it are being scored by how robust their profiles are, how many reviews they have written, the age of their profiles, helpful votes by others, etc., and probably (in terms of Amazon) whether they have purchased a lot or not many products on Amazon.

What's unique about Amazon is that – unlike Yelp or Google – Amazon has data on purchases, that is, Amazon knows whether or not the reviewer actually purchased the product. These are called "verified purchase" reviews on Amazon. This type of data on purchases is available on review sites like Airbnb as well, and is something that distinguishes that class from sites such as Google or Yelp that do not really have purchase behavior.

So as you audit and identify the review sites that matter to you look for differences and similarities to the general patterns. This can impact how you play the game as for example on Amazon where you need to encourage people who actually purchased your product to write reviews as compared with non-purchasers.

Is the new review system fair? Is it a better opportunity for your business than in 1994 when there were no online reviews? Whether it's fair or not, good or not, is a different issue than how you as a business can (and should) play the game of reviews to win. You do not make the review world; you simply live in it.

LIFE IS NOT FAIR. NEITHER ARE REVIEWS. GET OVER IT.

None of this is perfect, and I am not singling out Yelp, Amazon, or Google. I am drawing your attention to the Review Revolution and the fact that it is not just real people spontaneously reviewing businesses but rather a mix of people writing real spontaneous reviews, people writing solicited (yet real) reviews, and even fake people writing fake reviews.

Users Believe Reviews

Users believe online reviews! According to a BrightLocal study, fully 92% of consumers now read online reviews (vs. 88% in 2014), and 68% say positive reviews make them trust a local business more (vs. 72% in 2014). You can read the full study at **http://jmlinks.com/5b**. Another excellent book on the social aspects of the Review Revolution is Bill Tancer's, *Everyone's a Critic*, at **http://jmlinks.com/37b**.

Unhappy Small Business Owners

In my face-to-face classes on social media, review sites are among the most controversial. Yelp, in particular, is literally hated by many small businesspeople because

a) they have received what they think are unfair negative reviews on Yelp, and b) Yelp has a reputation for strong-arming businesses into paid advertising. (Yelp disputes this charge, though rumors have dogged the company for years – see **http://jmlinks.com/37c**).

Here's why local businesses often get quite emotional about sites like Yelp:

1. Often times, the only reviews they have about their business are negative reviews, which they feel are inaccurate or unfair.

2. They do not understand how to claim or optimize their listings, nor how to respond to reviews.

3. They do not realize that generally, if they do nothing, they are going to get negative reviews disproportionately.

4. They do not realize that there is a small yet very vocal minority of "haters" on reviews sites that troll businesses and write scathing and bitter negative reviews.

5. They do not understand how reviews work, and how to influence reviews in their favor.

Moreover, many small business owners do not step back and compare 2019 with 1994. Then, only the rich, famous, connected, or lucky got reviews in the local papers. Getting reviewed was like winning the lottery: great if it happened in a positive way, but not something upon which you could build a marketing strategy. Today, however, any business can get reviews, and consumers can read those reviews online. The reality is that the Review Revolution created an enormous **positive marketing opportunity** for your business.

Let me repeat that:

The Review Revolution created an enormous positive marketing opportunity for your business!

You can either be bitter and angry that your business has negative reviews, or you can be positive, learn the game, and start to leverage the unbelievable fact that – today – even "boring" businesses like plumbers, divorce lawyers, or CPAs can get reviews and use review marketing to market their businesses.

Who Writes Reviews?

Let's talk about who writes reviews. Let's get real. Let's assume you are a local plumber. I have a clogged toilet. I go online and find your business. You come out, you fix my toilet, and you give me a bill for $300. You did a good job, and I am happy with the service.

Will I go online to Yelp and write a review? It's doubtful. Unlike my relationship with a local French restaurant, I am not "proud" that I have a leaky toilet, and I got it fixed. While I will likely go on Facebook and share a selfie of me and my wife at the local French restaurant, and likely go on Yelp and write a positive review to "showcase" how wealthy I am, and what a great husband I am, I am not "excited" that you provided me with excellent service with respect to my waste removal system in my bathroom, otherwise known as my toilet. No selfies to Facebook, hopefully, no Snapchat of me on my newly fixed toilet, no positive review to Yelp.

My toilet has been fixed. I'm happy. Done. Over. End. Writing a review is the last thing on my mind.

Now, let's say you come out for my toilet repair, and you do NOT do what I consider a good job. Perhaps you crack my tile floor, or perhaps you get dirty water on my rug, or perhaps I just don't like you, or perhaps I find your fee of $300 unreasonable.

I'm mad. I hate you. I pay the bill. I'm angry, and I want revenge.

I think to myself, "I'll show you." I go online and vent my anger in a Yelp review. I explain to fellow Yelpers (and the world) how terrible you are, how they should never use your business, etc. etc. I do this to "let off steam" as well as to "feel good about myself" that I am "doing the world a favor" by righting the wrong of your terrible business. I want you to go out of business. I want you to fail. That's justice to me, the unhappy customer.

(Don't believe this happens? To read reviews of the "worst food of my life" on Yelp, visit **http://jmlinks.com/4z**). You'll see a lot of unhappy, bitter, nasty people on Yelp, and that's just for food.

Here are the **dirty little secrets** of the review ecosystem (with the possible exception of entertainment venues like restaurants, bars, museums, etc.):

- Consumers **believe** online reviews when making a purchase decision.

- However, outside of "fun" industries like restaurants and entertainment, the **most likely customer to leave an unsolicited review is the unhappy customer.** The very unhappy customer is very likely spontaneously to write a nasty review about your business!

- Outside of "fun" industries, **happy customers are NOT likely to write reviews**. They are not pre-motivated to share their experience with your plumbing company, your CPA firm, your DUI attorney services on Yelp without a nudge from you. Outside of "fun" industries, you must solicit reviews from happy customers to succeed.

Two other customer segments are likely to leave reviews.

- **Review geeks / extreme Yelpers** – which would be people like myself, digitally connected and participatory in the Yelp (or Google, TripAdvisor) ecosystems. Review geeks are not necessarily primed to leave positive, or negative reviews. They just tend to review frequently. As Yelp has evolved, more and more people ARE leaving reviews spontaneously about local services, which is a good thing.

- The **hostile minority** - these are unhappy campers who, because of sites like Yelp, now have a way to vent their rage at nearly everything. These "unhappy campers" tend to leave unhappy review after unhappy review: bitter and negative, they tend to hate everything and leave a destructive trail of negative reviews in their wake. Unfortunately, without any fault on its part, Yelp enabled the very unhappy, bitter people of the world to spread their negativity by venting against businesses. Don't believe me? Try some Yelp searches, look for negative reviews, and click "up" to the profiles of the reviewers. In just a few minutes, I guarantee that you will find some very negative, pathetic sad little people.

UNHAPPY CUSTOMERS OFTEN WRITE REVIEWS

Contrast what you see with "non fun" businesses, with what you see around "fun" businesses like restaurants, bars, or coffee shops. Here, Yelp (and other review sites) leverages the *social media narcissism* so present in our society. Similar to what you see on Facebook, people like to "showcase" their positive achievements. *Look at me! I went to fancy restaurant X, I went out to dinner, I went to this amazing museum, ate at this exclusive diner, drank at this cool bar, smoked cigars as this cool cigar bar, etc.*

For businesses outside of restaurants and the like, the takeaway here is to realize the following:

If you do nothing, the most likely reviews you will get will be negative reviews.

And another truth. In more and more industries, your competitors are pro-actively soliciting reviews and pretty much getting away with it. So if you are passive, you might have ten positive reviews and a couple negative ones, but you'll be competing against a pro-active business that has forty positive reviews and just a couple negatives. It's an arms race to get positive reviews.

Don't Shoot the Messenger

Now, don't shoot the messenger. Every business will get at least a few negative reviews, sooner or later. If you have just a couple, that's OK and normal (compare yourself to other, similar businesses to establish a baseline). But if you're getting negative review after negative review after negative review, you don't have a Yelp or online review problem, you have a business problem. Don't shoot the messenger; the Review Revolution gives you a new window on how actual customers feel about your product, service, or front-line, customer-facing employees.

Official Policy

Now, let's return to the Review Revolution, and look at the problem from the perspective of a business owner in some "non-fun" line of business such as plumbers, CPAs or accountants, divorce attorneys, or roofing companies. You're unlikely to get positive reviews unless you do something pro-active. But what's the official policy on reviews?

The official policies of Yelp, Google, TripAdvisor and the like is that you – as the business owner – are not allowed to solicit reviews in any way, shape, or fashion. Yelp, for example, advises business owners:

> *Don't ask customers, mailing list subscribers, friends, family, or anyone else to review your business.* (Source: **http://jmlinks.com/4g**).

TripAdvisor's explanation is one of the most detailed, and you should read it at **http://jmlinks.com/4h**. It's informative and contradictory in that, like all the review platforms, it ignores the fact that the most likely reviews come from unhappy customers and/or the bitter minority of weirdos on the Internet.

Even Amazon has changed its once more lenient policy to one in which it is now taboo to give away free products yet require a review (**http://jmlinks.com/37d**). Amazon states, "In order to preserve the integrity of Community content, content and activities consisting of advertising, promotion, or solicitation (whether direct or indirect) is not allowed, including… Offering compensation or requesting compensation (including free or discounted products) in exchange for creating, modifying, or posting content."

The Review Dilemma

So here's the **review dilemma**:

- *On the one hand,* if you do nothing, you are very likely to receive negative reviews from unhappy customers and not so likely to receive positive reviews from happy customers (true in all cases, except perhaps entertainment-type industries), but

- *On the other hand,* the official terms of service forbid you from soliciting reviews from customers.

Damned if you do, damned if you don't.

The reality of the Review Revolution is that in most cases and certainly in competitive industries like divorce law, DUI cases, plumbers, roofers, etc., most successful companies are pro-actively soliciting reviews. This does not mean that they are faking or buying reviews; it only means that they are nudging, cajoling, begging, emotionally incentivizing, and otherwise motivating happy customers to go online and take the time to write positive reviews around their business.

Is this fair? No.

Is this in accord with the terms of service? No.

Is it the reality? Yes.

Is it the public reality? No. Yelp, Google, TripAdvisor, Amazon, and all the other companies do their best to police reviews, but the reality is that the fact that reviews are heavily manipulated by vendors is an open secret.

But wait a second.

> *Is life fair? No.*
>
> *Was it likely that your plumbing company would have been reviewed in the paper in 1995? No. Your small restaurant? No.*
>
> *Even though the posted speed limit on the highway is 60 mph, do most cars actually go 60 mph? No.*

The Review Revolution has given you an enormous, positive opportunity to reach new customers, just like the Interstate Highway System gives you the opportunity to travel cross-country at 65 to 80 mph even though the posted speed limit may be 75 mph (in the West) and 60 mph (in the East).

> *Don't be the fastest car on the road. Don't be the red Mazda Miata going 95 mph in front of the cop. Just be in the fast car group, just not the fastest, most egregious car.*

For now, just understand that **positive reviews are the key to success**, that soliciting reviews is technically against the terms of service, and begin to realize that you are going to have to create a strategy to solicit positive reviews, despite the posted terms of service.

Let's turn, first, to identifying companies to emulate on the various review sites. I'll return after that to dealing with the problem of soliciting reviews without getting into trouble.

» INVENTORY COMPANIES ON YELP, GOOGLE, OR OTHER RELEVANT SITES

If you are a local business, it will be pretty obvious that reviews matter. Even if you are a national business, however, you should realize that online reviews still matter. (This is because many people will Google your company name plus "reviews" to check out your reputation before completing an important purchase).

Your first step, therefore, is to identify which review sites matter to your business. Your second step is to browse similar businesses on those sites and conduct an inventory of what you like and dislike about their listings, realizing that unlike on Facebook, listings on review sites generally occur with or without the permission of the business. Actual control is much more limited. Your third step is to claim and optimize your listings, and your final step is to create a pro-active system to solicit positive reviews in such a way that you don't get in trouble with the review platforms.

Among the most important review sites are:

Yelp (**http://www.yelp.com/**) – the largest local review site with great strength in restaurants, more popular in "Blue" states like New York or California than in "Red" states like Florida or Texas.

Google (**http://www.google.com/**). Accessibly by doing Google searches on relevant keywords. In some cases, you'll need to first find a company, and then Google its name to find its Google page (more below).

Facebook (**https://www.facebook.com**). Rather new to the review ecosystem, Facebook is beefing up its reviews of local businesses. See **http://jmlinks.com/37e** for Facebook's help file on business reviews.

TripAdvisor (**http://www.tripadvisor.com/**). The leading travel review site.

YP (**http://www.yp.com/**). The traditional yellow pages gone digital.

VRBO (**http://www.vrbo.com/**) – a site for identifying short-term vacation rentals.

Airbnb (**http://www.airbnb.com/**) – the leading site for vacation rentals.

Amazon (**http://www.amazon.com/**) – earth's largest retailer, with reviews on billions of products.

Glassdoor (**http://www.glassdoor.com/**) – reviews about businesses from the perspective of employees.

Facebook is a special, and growing case of reviews. Consumers don't pro-actively search Facebook (yet) for reviews, but they are beginning to leave them. So Facebook reviews generally function only as "trust" indicators, and/or encourage eWOM (electronic word of mouth). To enable Facebook reviews for your business, see **http://jmlinks.com/32p**.

IDENTIFY COMPANIES WHO DO REVIEW MARKETING WELL, AND REVERSE ENGINEER THEM

The easiest way to find logical review sites for your company is as follows:

1. Identify the **keywords** by which prospective customers might search for you. For example, if you are a Sushi restaurant in San Francisco, those keywords might be words such as "Sushi," "Sushi Bar," "Japanese Restaurant," "Japanese Caterers," etc.

2. **Google** those keywords and note which review sites come up.

   a. Also try Google searches by keyword plus words like "directory" or "reviews" as for example, "family law attorney directory" or "family law attorney reviews."

3. Click over to the review sites, and **make a list** of them.

4. Go over to each review site, re-input your search query keywords, and begin to browse company listings on the review sites you have identified.

For example, take "vacation rentals Lake Tahoe" and search it on Google (**http://jmlinks.com/4p**). Also try "directory of vacation rentals." Then, browse the search results, and you'll see sites such as:

https://www.flipkey.com/

http://www.homeaway.com/

http://www.vrbo.com/

http://www.tripadvisor.com/

https://www.tahoeaccommodations.com/

http://www.vacationrentals.com/

https://www.airbnb.com/

In this case, you then find out if you already have a listing on each site, if so claim it, and if not create one, and then optimize it. You then begin to solicit positive reviews on each of the most important sites.

You can also check out Bright Local's list of best citations by category at **http://jmlinks.com/46t** as well as Moz's at **http://jmlinks.com/46u**. These capture the most common places to be listed, but I recommend that you also pro-actively search Google for "directories" by keyword, as well as browse your competitors to identify industry-relevant sites.

By using this techniques, you can quickly make a list of the key review sites that are most relevant to your company.

Google is the Most Important Review Site

Among listing and review sites, "Google My Business" (GMB) (**https://www.google.com/business**) is the most important by far. First and foremost, it's owned and operated by Google and has clear priority on Google search. Having a strong presence via your listing on GMB is the No. 1 way for your business to show on local-related Google searches. It doesn't take much to look forward and realize that if local matters to you, and your customers use Google, you'll need to optimize your Google My Business listing! Even if local does not matter to you, try searching for your company name plus "reviews" and your Google My Business listing and reviews will often show up in position #1, but take note of what does show up and begin to claim and optimize other listings as well.

Return to Google, let's just be honest up front. Google has done a **terrible** job of managing the Google My Business program. They are constantly changing the format, rules, structure, set up – enough to drive a social media marketer insane!

As of September 2018, here's the current set up:

Consumers simply browse Google. Consumers simply go to Google, type in keywords such as "Pizza," "Italian restaurants," or "Family Law Attorneys" and see companies show up in the "snack pack," which is the three listings showing (usually but not always with stars). Here's a screenshot:

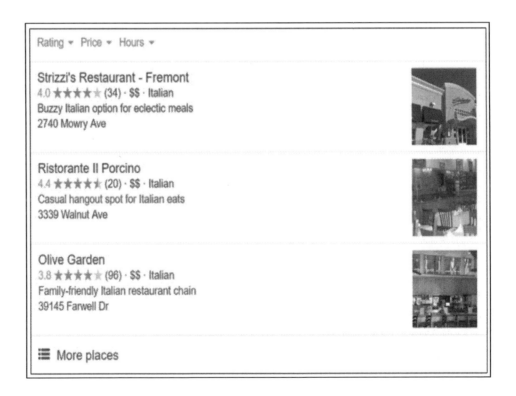

Consumers need a Google account to post reviews. Consumers can post reviews to Google with either a Google+ account or just a Google account. Anyone, however, can read a review.

Consumers rate businesses. Consumers rate businesses on a five-star system and can leave detailed reviews (good, bad, ugly) on the system, whether or not the business likes it.

Businesses can "claim" their Google listings at Google My Businesses. To "claim" their listings, businesses go to Google My Business at **https://www.google.com/business** and they can add a description (now invisible to consumers), photos (visible on Google), and respond to reviews.

Businesses can post announcements to their Google My Business Listing. Google now allows a local business to make a post to its business which will show up when someone Google's the business name as well as often (but not always) when someone does a relevant search on Google, and your business wins a placement on Google Maps. See **http://jmlinks.com/37f** for information on this new opportunity.

Google reviews are critical to success at local SEO. Here's why:

1. **Reviews drive your company to the top of Google**. The *more* reviews you have on the Google system, the *higher* you show on Google searches for local keywords.

2. **Consumers read and rely on Google reviews**, even if they don't understand where they came from or how to write them. The reality is that while *few* consumers *write* reviews, *many* if not most people *believe* them.

Inventory Companies and Their Local Listings

As you browse local review sites, identify relevant companies and make a list of their listings on Yelp, Google, or other sites that are relevant. Make a note of:

- Does their **listing** appear **claimed**?

- **Photos**: cover photos and profile pictures. Do you like what you see? Why or why not?

- **Reviews**. How many reviews do they have? Are they mostly positive or mostly negative? Click on the reviewers. Do they seem "real"? Unsolicited? Solicited? Faked? Are vendors responding to reviews? Try to reverse engineer how they might be soliciting or encouraging reviews.

- **Questions and Answers**. Google now allows customers to ask questions and vendors to give answers. Do you see this feature in use in your industry?

- **About Tab**. Check out their about tab, or listing. Read it. Do you like how it's written? Does it include relevant keywords?

For your second **TO-DO**, download the **Review Research Worksheet**. For the worksheet, go to **http://jmlinks.com/seo19tz** (reenter the passcode "seo19tz" , and click on the link to the "Reviews Research Worksheet." You'll answer questions as to whether your potential customers are using reviews, which review sites are important, and inventory what you like and dislike about their review marketing set up and marketing strategy.

» CLAIM AND OPTIMIZE YOUR LISTINGS

Now that you've identified which local review sites matter, it's time to claim and optimize your listings. All of the sites work in essentially the same way, although there are differences in the details. The basic steps are:

1. Identify the local review site for which you want to "claim" your company listing.

2. Find your listing on the site.

3. Follow the instructions to "claim" it, usually by phone or postcard verification.

4. Optimize your listing description by writing keyword-heavy text, uploading photographs, and populating your listing with your hours of operation and other details.

5. Make sure that your website links back to your listing, and your listing links to your website.

6. Make sure that the business name, address, and phone number are the same on both the listing site and your website (be consistent).

To do this for Yelp:

1. Go to **http://biz.yelp.com/**

2. Enter your business name, and address and hit **Get Started** in red.

3. Follow the instructions to claim your business, usually by phone verification.

4. Once you have claimed your listing:

   a. Click on Business Information on the left; re-write your description to contain logical keywords that potential customers might search for, including synonyms (*pizza*, *Italian restaurant*, *catering*, for example).

   b. Choose relevant categories from the list provided.

   c. Enter your basic information, hours, specialties (business information), history, and "meet the business owner" with an eye to logical keywords.

   d. Click on photos on the left, and upload nice photos.

5. Make sure that the address and phone on Yelp are the SAME as the address and phone on your website.

6. Make sure that your website links to your Yelp listing (usually in the footer), and that your Yelp listing links to your website.

VIDEO. Watch a video tutorial on how to claim and optimize your business on Yelp at **http://jmlinks.com/16x**.

To do this for Google:

1. Sign in to your Google account or Gmail (if you use Gmail).

2. Go to **https://www.google.com/business**

3. Click on the green "Start Now" link on the top right. Or, if you don't see that, click on the blue "Add location" button at the top right.

4. Follow the instructions to claim your business, usually by postcard verification, and sometimes (if you're lucky) by phone verification.

   a. When you get the postcard, enter the PIN as indicated in the instructions.

   b. This will verify your listing and give you control.

   c. DO NOT LOSE THE LOGIN EMAIL AND PASSWORD as it is very hard to reclaim a listing!

5. Optimize your business description by clicking on "info" on the left column. Using the "pencil" icon then edit each option.

   a. **Business name**

   b. **Address**. Enter your correct local address, and make sure it matches the address on your website exactly.

   c. **Categories**. This is very important – choose highly relevant categories, and fewer are better than more, so be as specific as possible though you must use Google's pre-set categories.

   d. **Hours of operation**.

   e. **Phone number**. Do not use an 800 number – use a local number, one that also exists on your website.

   f. **Website**.

   g. **Description**. Write a short, keyword-heavy description of your business.

6. Click on "photos" on the left to change your profile picture, and cover photos, as well as add interior and/or exterior photos.

VIDEO. Watch a video tutorial on how to claim and optimize your business on Google at **http://jmlinks.com/17d**.

VIDEO. Watch a video tutorial on why Yelp matters for both SEO and social media marketing at **http://jmlinks.com/17e**. Note that Yelp drives reviews on the Bing

Search Engine. For example, check out this Bing search for *Pizza* at **http://jmlinks.com/37h**.

Other local listings like YP.com or Citysearch follow similar procedures. To find all of your "second tier" listings, you can go to Yext (**http://www.yext.com/**) and enter your business name and phone number in the box in about the middle of the page. Then click on the "scan now" blue button on the right. Here's a screenshot:

For free, Yext will identify all your local listings. You can then click over to each and claim and optimize each. Or, if you have budget, you can subscribe to Yext, and they will do this for all local listings including Yelp but **excluding** Google. A competitive service to Yext is MOZ Local at **http://jmlinks.com/37g**. Whitespark at **https://whitespark.ca** is yet another one. Yext is the most expensive, and fastest. The other two are slower and less expensive. My preference would be Whitespark as it seems to be the cheapest and they do the most meticulous job, "by hand," while the other two are automated.

Citation Consistency and Google Local Searches

To show up on Google search, it is important that ALL review sites and your website have the SAME company name, the SAME phone number, and SAME physical address. Make sure that your company name, phone number, and physical address appear on your website, usually in the footer. (This is called *NAP* (*Name, Address, Phone*) consistency).

"Citations" refer to the external listings on review websites that confirm (to Google and Bing) that your business has a certain phone number and physical address. This is used by the search engines to filter local search results by their proximity to the searcher or the geographic terms used in the search query.

Using a service like Yext, MOZ, or Whitespark allows you to claim, optimize, and make consistent this information across hundreds of review sites. This consistency is a big help to showing at the top of local searches on Google or Bing / Yahoo. Regardless of how you do it, try to get NAP consistency between your website, the two most important local review sites (Google and Yelp), and then the 2nd tier sites using a service like Yext, MOZ, or Whitespark (or doing that manually if you're a glutton for punishment).

Organize and Claim Your Local Listings

For your third TO-DO, make a spreadsheet of ALL relevant local review sites. Go to each, and claim / optimize your local listings. Be sure to note your login and password!

- CLAIM YOUR GOOGLE AND YELP WITH A PERMANENT CORPORATE EMAIL (NOT AN EMPLOYEE EMAIL) such as **local@yourcompany.com** or **marketing@yourcompany.com**. If not that, create a Gmail to use for all your local listings.

- **DO NOT LOSE YOUR GOOGLE AND YELP LOGIN AND PASSWORDS!**

Lost password retrieval on Yelp and Google is a **disaster**! Neither system has a good password retrieval function; on Yelp in particular, if your password is lost, God help you. Do not lose your passwords! Write them down somewhere where you will be able to find them in a few years.

》SEO YOUR LOCAL WEBSITE

SEO or *Search Engine Optimization,* of course, is the art and science of structuring your website so that it ranks well on Google searches. *Local* is an area that crosses both SEO and social media marketing. While you are working on your review marketing efforts, let's review the SEO of your website to make sure that your website SEO and your local review efforts are in harmony:

- **Optimize Your Home Page**. Make sure that your Home Page, especially the TITLE tag contains your keywords and your city. If you are a Miami plumber, make sure that both the word "Miami" and the word "plumber" appears in the visible text of your homepage. Make sure that there is visible content on your homepage that includes your target keywords and every city in which you have an office. If you have multiple locations, create landing pages for each one and link each landing page to the local listings for that city. A few vendors that do a good job of this are PetFood Express (**http://petfoodexpress.com/**) and Home Depot (**https://www.homedepot.com/**). Notice how each has a "store finder" section of the website, and each local store has a local landing page on the primary website.

- **Create a Consistent NAP**. Include a consistent NAP (Name / Address / Phone Number) on your website that matches the NAP on your Yelp, Google, and other local review sites.

- **Cross-link** from your website to your Google and Yelp listings.

- Make sure that all your listings, especially Google and Yelp, **link back** directly to your website.

Optimize Your Contact Us Page

Even if you have only one location, be sure to have an "about us" or "contact us" page on your website as an optimized page for that city and target keywords. Optimize that page for your target home city by including the city name and keywords in your TITLE tag, plus visible content. Also, on that page, include an embedded Google map, which you can generate by searching for your company on Google, clicking up to the maps tab, and then click the share tab. Next, click on "embed map" to get the HTML code to embed a Google map on your website. Here's a screenshot:

Finally, use the microdata / schema.org system to embed the appropriate JSON-LD schema markup on your website. You can also use the Google "Structured Data Markup Helper" at **http://jmlinks.com/46v** for this function. J.D. Flynn has also created an online tool that will guide you through creating JSON-LD data for you at **http://jmlinks.com/32q**.

VIDEO. Watch a video tutorial on local SEO at **http://jmlinks.com/46w**.

» CULTIVATE POSITIVE REVIEWS

Returning to the social media and review aspects of local, we'll assume you've claimed and optimized the relevant listing services for your local business. Most often this will be at least Google and Yelp, and in specific industries, it might include TripAdvisor, VRBO, or Airbnb. If you sell products, it might be your product listings and uploads on Amazon. Or it might be on Glassdoor.com.

At this point, you have two options:

1. Wait **passively** for positive customer reviews, and hope that the positive reviews will outpace the negative reviews (according to the official policy of Yelp, Google, etc.).

2. Be **pro-active** and try to encourage your happy customers to post reviews.

Which do you think the winners in local search and social media are doing?

Legal Disclaimer

You are responsible for everything you do in terms of your Internet marketing. Nothing I am writing here should be construed as required or recommended advice. Legally, I am recommending that you do nothing (option #1).

Take responsibility for your own actions as a marketer, and act on your own risk!

Soliciting Reviews

That said, here is the reality. If you wait passively for reviews (unless you are in the a very fun industry like restaurants, coffee shops, or bars), the most likely scenarios will be a) no reviews, or b) bad reviews, or at least a preponderance of bad reviews. You the business owner or marketer can, however, fight back against this dynamic. Here are some strategies to solicit positive reviews about your business:

Face to Face. This is the most powerful way to get positive reviews. The employee who is "face to face" with the customer builds rapport with the customer. A scenario might be:

Technician: "OK, I've fixed your toilet. Let's run through it together, and verify it's in working order.

Client: Yes, it's great. Thank you so much!

Technician: You're welcome. Hey, if you have a moment, could you do us a HUGE FAVOR and write a review on Google or Yelp about your experience?

Client: Yes.

- If the client knows how to do this, just give him or her a card with a direct link to the review site location.

- If the client does not know how to do this, give him or her a card with step-by-step instructions.

Phone Reminders. Either at the time of service or shortly thereafter, call the customer to see "how it went," and if they're happy, ask them to write a review online.

Paper Reminders. Either at the time of service, or shortly thereafter, mail a physical postcard thanking the client for their business, and asking them to write a review on Yelp, Google, etc.

Email Reminders. Either at the time of service, or shortly thereafter, send an email thanking the client for their business, and asking them to write a review online.

The reality is that face-to-face is, by far, the strongest way to motivate customers to write reviews, phone contact the next strongest, and so on and so forth.

Help Customers Write Reviews

Many customers may not understand how to write a review, so a step-by-step instruction sheet would be helpful. Use a URL shortener like **http://bit.ly**, or **http://tinyurl.com** to shorten the link to your local review listing page.

Google: Generate a REVIEW US URL on Google

Google, as I have explained earlier, is really a mess. To find a short, easy link to your customer reviews on Google follow these steps.

1. Go to the GradeUS Google review generator tool at **http://jmlinks.com/13j**.

2. Enter your business name and city or postal code, and press the blue "Get Google Review Links."

3. Select your company from the list it provides, and hit "Continue."

4. Click on the link for "Open in Search Results" and highlight the huge URL string it gives you from Google.

5. Copy this URL string.

6. Go to **http://tinyurl.com/** and paste this URL into the box "Enter a long URL to make it tiny."

   a. If you like "customize" your URL to make it easy to remember / or just cool.

   b. Here's an example: **http://tinyurl.com/revjasonseo**.

Alternatively –

1. Go to Google at **https://www.google.com/** and enter your company name plus a keyword and/or your city.

2. Click on the "blue" Google reviews link (you MUST have at least ONE Google Review to use this method!).

3. Highlight the huge URL Google gives you in the top of the browser.

4. Copy this URL string.

5. Go to **http://tinyurl.com/** and paste this URL into the box "Enter a long URL to make it tiny."

   a. If you like "customize" your URL to make it easy to remember / or just cool.

   b. Here's an example: **http://tinyurl.com/revjasonseo**.

You can write this in an email or on a printed sheet of paper. Here's an example of an email I might send to my clients.

Greetings!

Thank you so much for the opportunity to serve your Internet marketing and consulting needs. As the owner of the *Jason McDonald SEO Consulting Agency*, I truly appreciate your business!

If you have a moment, I would REALLY appreciate an honest review on one of the local listing sites. Here are the instructions:

Google.

1. Sign into your Google and/or Gmail account at **https://www.google.com/**.

2. Go to **http://tinyurl.com/revjasonseo**.

3. Click on the white "Write a review."

4. Write your review

Yelp:

1. Sign into your Yelp account at **http://www.yelp.com/**.

2. Go to **http://bit.ly/jason-yelp**.

3. Click on the red "write a review" button

4. Write your review

Thank you,

Jason McDonald

TO GET POSITIVE REVIEWS, ASK HAPPY CUSTOMERS TO REVIEW YOU

WhiteSpark, which is a leading local review tool company, offers a free tool to help you create nice-looking Web pages and handouts to encourage reviews at **http://jmlinks.com/4t**. In addition, a few paid services are emerging that "pre-survey" your customers. Essentially, they first ask your customer if they liked your company and its product or service. If yes, then that customer is prompted to write a review. If no, then the customer is given a longer detailed survey and that survey is sent to you the business owner; the customer is NOT prompted to write a review. One such service is ReviewBuzz (**http://www.reviewbuzz.com**). Others are GatherUp (**https://gatherup.com/**) and ReviewInc (**http://www.reviewinc.com**).

Note, however, that recently Yelp in particular began to crack down on these services, blocking reviews that originate via their pre-surveys. The "nerd word" for this is called, "review gating." Even Google has now clarified that they are against review gating (See **http://jmlinks.com/47w**). All of this gets you back to the "damned if you do, damned if you don't" conundrums of review marketing, and it reinforces the importance of you, as a small business owner or marketers, taking matters into your own hands and doing your utmost to ask happy campers, and only happy campers, to "do you a favor" and write you a review online. Automating this process is more likely to trigger penalties as opposed to doing it customer-by-customer, face-to-face.

Be Judicious. Understand "Plausible Deniability"

Understand that according to the official policy, even a mild handout asking for an "honest review" is a violation of the terms of service of most of the review providers! Therefore, I do NOT recommend that you post these publicly on your website. Be judicious: give them out in printed or email format, and only to those happy customers who have been pre-selected by your staff.

Obviously, if a client is unhappy and you cannot fix it to make them happy: DO NOT ASK THEM FOR A REVIEW.

In fact, a common strategy is to manually use "review gating" as follows:

- **Conduct a survey** of customers after they use your service asking them a) if they are happy, b) if they would write a review, and c) if they know how. This could be done formally (an email survey on a site like SurveyMonkey (**http://www.surveymonkey.com**)) or informally just be pre-asking the customer face-to-face, over the phone, or via email. You can also use Jotform and "conditional logic" to set up this type of pre-survey on your website (See **http://jmlinks.com/37j**).

- **If they ARE happy**, then ask them nicely to **write a review**.

- **If they are NOT happy**, either a) make them happy, or b) do **NOT** ask them for a review.

In this way, you avoid motivating unhappy customers to review you online. Indeed, if you are in a sensitive industry (e.g., Bail Bonds, apartment rentals) in which many customers are not happy, I do not recommend you even publicize to your clients face-to-face or in the real world that you are on the review sites. If many of your customers will be negative, then do not make it "easy" for them to give you a negative review!

Paying for Reviews

Let's face it. Review marketing is the "contact sport" of social media marketing. In certain industries (e.g., DUI attorneys, private detectives, breast augmentation services), many reviews are solicited if not faked and sometimes incentivized with monetary payments.

Should you pay for reviews? Generally speaking, I would not pay for reviews. (I am talking about real clients not completely faked reviews). Some companies do incentivize by giving $25 Starbucks or Amazon gift cards once a review is published; however, if this becomes known to a Yelp or a Google you wrong a very strong risk of being severely penalized.

Offering monetary incentives to get reviews is a dangerous strategy, so be forewarned.

Yelp will even mark your listing with an aggressive naughty notice if you are busted paying for reviews. You can browse real examples of this on Yelp at **http://jmlinks.com/4u**. First and foremost, therefore, if you choose to "go to the dark side" and offer payments, I would not publicize it! And: **I AM NOT RECOMMENDING THAT YOU DO THIS**. I am just pointing out that it is done.

Also, note that not only is "paying for reviews" likely to bring down the wrath of Yelp, you can also bring down the wrath of Yelp by offering to pay a negative reviewer to take down their review. Yelp even now explicitly forbids spiffing employees when they successfully get a review. Anytime you are offering money in exchange for a Yelp behavior then you run that risk – so be forewarned about just how uptight Yelp is about reviews and payments! (Google and other sites have similar policies).

Incentivize Employees

A better way to increase your positive review count is to offer your employees an incentive, rather than the customer, for reviews published online. Assume for example you are a local pizza joint. Offer your employees a $25.00 bonus EACH after each positive review on Yelp. Or if you are a roofing company, give the technician a handout explaining how to write a review online, and give him a $25.00 bonus EACH TIME a customer posts a review. In that way, you motivate your front-line employees to be customer-friendly, and when there is a positive customer experience, to politely ask the customer to write an honest review on Yelp, Google, etc.

Motivate your employees to ask for reviews!

I would not put any pro-active review solicitation strategy in writing on the Internet, just as I would not call the California Highway Patrol and inform them that, in general, I go five miles faster than the posted speed limit while driving the highways and byways of the Golden State.

Let sleeping dogs lie.

But just as going 65 mph in a 60 mph zone is unlikely to cause a police action, polite nudges to encourage real reviews from real customers are unlikely to be a big problem. If you do it, just keep it private, and <u>do so at your own risk</u>.

Don't Overthink It. Just Ask for Reviews from Real Customers

In my experience, if most businesses would simply *ask* a few clients for reviews, they would get them. Yes, you'll ask ten clients to get one review. But you'll get that one review. The real problem is to motivate employees to ask and ask and ask and ask to get that one review to go live on Yelp, Google, or other review sites.

Recognize, understand, and accept that you will ask ten people to get just one review. That's just how it is: customers are self-centered and lazy (but we love them).

Getting positive reviews is hard work. It's not done in a day. Slow and steady will win the race. Just create a culture at your business of great customer service and an awareness of that "special moment" when a customer is happy to ask for a positive, honest review.

JUST ASK. IT'S SO SIMPLE. JUST ASK.

Do anything and everything honestly and ethically possible to encourage your best customers to "spread the word" by writing reviews about your business online. After just a few positive reviews, you will be amazed at what they do for your business.

Responding to Negative Reviews

Negative reviews will happen. As the business owner, you may feel as if someone walked up to your newborn baby sleeping calmly in her stroller and said to you:

Your baby is ugly. Your baby stinks. I hate your baby. I had a bad experience with your baby, and I am going to tell the world how much the baby that you are working for blood, sweat, and tears is terrible.

Here's an example:

You're human. You're close to your business. It is like your baby. Your first reaction will be **ANGER.**

Resist the temptation to respond in kind. Do not go online and argue with the negative consumer. Do not insult them. Do not use unprofessional language. *When you wrestle with a pig, the pig gets dirty, and the pig likes it.*

Instead:

- **Calm down**. Wait at least 24 hours before doing anything. Sleep on it.

- **Have someone else deal with negative reviews**: an outside consultant or employee who is not emotionally involved. Let a calm head prevail, and it probably will not be the head of the business owner.

- **Try to fix the problem**. If at all possible, reason with the person (you can usually contact them via Yelp, Google, etc.), and see if you can fix the problem. In some cases, you can, and then you can politely ask them to change the review.

- **Respond**. State your side of the situation in a positive, professional manner while acknowledging the right of the reviewer to her own opinion.

Remember: every business will get a few negative reviews, but if your business has more than the average… you may have a "business" problem and not a "review" problem.

Don't shoot the (review) messenger.

Do Not Validate the Bad Review

Please note that if you have a negative review on a site like Yelp, Google, Amazon, etc., and the reviewer has a **weak profile** (e.g., *this is their first review, few friends, etc.*), if you respond to it, you are *validating* that review and making it *more likely* to appear high in your profile. Generally speaking, therefore, I recommend waiting at least a month before responding to a negative review by someone with a weak profile. There is a strong chance it will be filtered out as fake (especially on Yelp). But if after a month, it is still there, then consider a response.

Responding to Reviews

To **respond to a negative review**, do as follows. First and foremost, take the high ground. You can log into your business account / profile and respond to negative reviews. This is one of the benefits of claiming your business profile. But be positive and professional. Acknowledge their right to their opinion, but be firm as to your right to state your opinion as well. Second, state your side of the situation but realize you are NOT talking to the unhappy customer. You are talking to the person reading your reviews and deciding whether to reach out to you for a possible business engagement. Explain your side of the story. Often times, negative reviews come from nasty, unhappy people (which you can politely point out as for example, by asking the reader to click on the reviewer's name and see all their other negative reviews to realize that this is just a negative person). Or, the person wasn't a good fit for your business (so explain why). Or the person is being plain crazy. For example, I have had plastic surgeons condemned on Yelp because their waiting room was too hot, or other clients condemned because they didn't respond to an email. Finally, if the review is fake (i.e., by a competitor) or obscene or racist, you can complain to Yelp, Google, etc., and in some cases, they will remove the reviews. (To do this, log in to a personal account on Yelp, and right-click on the offensive review. You can then flag it and complain).

To read Yelp's official guide to responding to reviews, visit **http://jmlinks.com/5e**. To read Google's, visit **http://jmlinks.com/5f**. To read TripAdvisor's, visit **http://jmlinks.com/5g**. For whatever review site that matters to your business, you can usually search their help files for advice on how to respond to reviews. However, remember that the official policies are often very naive about how the game is truly played.

SWAMP NEGATIVE REVIEWS WITH POSITIVE REVIEWS

A better strategy is to ignore the bad reviews and focus on soliciting positive reviews to "swamp" the negative reviews in an ocean of positivity. Again, in no way shape or form, am I advising you to be dishonest or solicit fake reviews. I am simply advising you to ask happy customers to just take a few minutes and tell their happy stories. If you proactively solicit positive, real reviews, you can drown out or swamp the negative reviews with a preponderance of positive reviews. In short, getting positive real reviews is the best way to respond to negative reviews.

You don't ask; you don't get.

For your fourth **TO-DO**, download the **Review Solicitation Worksheet**. For the worksheet, go to **http://jmlinks.com/seo19tz** (reenter the passcode "seo19tz" , and click on the link to the "Reviews Solicitation Worksheet." You'll create a strategy to encourage positive reviews about your company.

» MONITOR AND IMPROVE YOUR ONLINE REPUTATION

Reputation management is a new buzzword about protecting one's online reputation, whether for an individual or a business. To understand reputation management, first back up and consider the sales funnel, often explained as *AIDA: Awareness, Interest, Desire, and Action*. Prospective customers go through distinct phases as they consider solutions for their problems, needs, or desires:

> **Awareness.** An **awareness** of the problem and the beginning of Internet searches and social media outreach to friends, family, and colleagues about the problem, need, or desire and possible solutions. In this phase, searches are often "educational" in nature as in "how to cater a wedding" or "wedding ideas."

> **Interest.** As a customer becomes aware of available market solutions, they develop an **interest** in vendor offerings and even may make a shortlist. At this stage, and the next, they move closer to an "action," i.e., a purchase or engagement with a vendor solution. Searches at this point become "best wedding caterers" or "Boston catering companies," etc.

Desire. Interest shifts towards **desire** and the customer begins to narrow down his or her shortlist. At this point, searches become *reputational* in nature. They may search a business name PLUS words like *reviews* or *complaints*. If your business were named Gina's Italian Kitchen, for example, they might search Google for "Gina's Italian Kitchen Reviews" or "Complaints against Gina's Italian Kitchen," or "Gina's Italian Kitchen Wedding Catering Reviews." **Reviews** is the operative word; if he or she finds *positive* reviews, that confirms your business is a good choice, whereas if he or she finds *negative* reviews, they may take you out of the consideration set entirely.

Action. A choice is made to purchase the service or engage with your business. Upon completion, the customer may decide to leave her own review about your business for others.

Reputation management, in short, is monitoring and protecting your online **branded** and **reputational** searches. To be frank, it is also about attempting to upgrade positive reviews and positive brand mentions so that your online brand image shines.

To understand the search patterns, you can use the example of my company, The JM Internet Group. For example –

      a "branded" search is: "JM Internet Group"

      a "reputational" search is "JM Internet Group Reviews"

Review sites such as Yelp, CitySearch, Google, etc., as well as ones specific to your industry, can have an extremely positive – or extremely negative – impact on your online reputation. Indeed, branded searches on Google (searches for your company name, or your company name plus 'reviews') often return Google profiles and reviews directly on the right side of the page. For example, here's a screenshot of the search "Mecca Coffee Company" on Google:

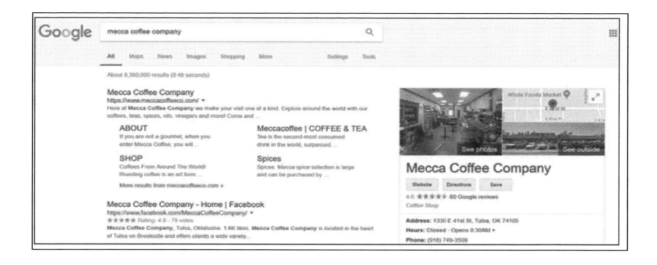

You can try the search at **http://jmlinks.com/32n**. Notice the primacy of reviews and the highlighted Google listing information plus review count on the far right. Scroll down the page and notice how Google identifies reviews on sites like Facebook, Yelp, and even Beeradvocate. Someone interested in going to the Mecca Coffee Company in Tulsa is likely to search for the company by name or perhaps for "Mecca Coffee Company Reviews." This is even more true for high-value searches like probate attorneys, roofing companies, or kitchen remodeling contractors.

GOOGLE YOUR COMPANY NAME PLUS REVIEWS AND MONITOR YOUR ONLINE REPUTATION

In addition to identifying, claiming, and optimizing your business listings on relevant review sites, you should also monitor your business on these sites. Usually, the act of claiming your listing in and of itself will generate an email anytime someone reviews your company. Paid services such as ReviewPush (**https://www.reviewpush.com/**), Free Review Monitoring (**https://freereviewmonitoring.com/**), and ReviewTrackers (**http://www.reviewtrackers.com/**) are sophisticated alert systems so that you always know whenever a new review is published about your business.

The reality is that you need to monitor your business reputation at least monthly, if not even more frequently. This means:

1. Doing Google searches for your company name as well as your company name plus "reviews;" and

2. Identifying the key customer review sites that matter for your business, such as Google, Yelp, YP.com, Avvo, etc. (this will vary by industry); and

3. Monitoring your review count, average star score, and whether you are getting more positive reviews each week or month;

4. Responding to negative reviews as needed; and, of course –

5. Pro-actively soliciting positive reviews on the key review sites to bolster your reputation.

For your fifth **TO-DO**, at a minimum set up a monthly checkup of your listings on the major review sites, you have identified. Note in a spreadsheet how many reviews you have, how many are 5, 4, 3, 2, or 1 stars. If you have budget, consider using a paid monitoring service.

» MEASURE YOUR RESULTS

Let's sum up the bottom line. Reviews impact your business in two important ways:

- as a positive (or negative) "trust indicator" that you are a trustworthy business partner; and

- as a signal to search engines and review sites that you should rank high on searches for relevant keywords.

MONITOR YOUR REVIEWS

Measurement of reviews, therefore, is focused on these two variables. On your keyword worksheet, I recommend that you create a tab called "local." Then every month, create a line item (for example, March 2019), and note down for your business:

The review site, number of reviews you have, and cumulative star rating.

Secondly, try searches for your strategic keywords on Yelp, Google and/or on other relevant review sites (e.g., Airbnb, TripAdvisor, etc.), create a line item for each month, and indicate your position on those searches. For example, Andolino's Pizzeria was measured as No. 2 for the Google Search "pizza Tulsa" as seen in this screenshot on September 26, 2018:

This would be recorded as Andolini's ranking #1 in the Google local pack, and having 959 reviews with a 4.5 star score. In other words, the restaurant is in good shape on both review sites. If it had dipped to a lower position on Yelp, for instance, then a to-do would be to encourage more Yelp reviews.

The two major aspects of monitoring your reviews, therefore are 1) your review count on each review site, and 2) your position on keyword searches on those sites. To the extent possible, you can then accelerate your efforts for a lagging site and relax a bit for a site for which you rank well and have positive reviews. (Note to monitor your rank, you can use the Fat Rank plugin for Chrome to monitor your rank on Google searches at **http://jmlinks.com/25w** or graduate to a paid rank measurement service such as AHREFS.com, MOZ.com, or SERPS.com. A good free tool to vary your location on Google search can be found at **http://jmlinks.com/26z**.)

»» CHECKLIST: REVIEW ACTION ITEMS

Test your knowledge of the Review Revolution! Take the *Review marketing quiz* at **http://jmlinks.com/qzrv**. Next, here are your review **Action Items**:

❑ **Research** whether your customers (and competitors) utilize reviews. Which sites seem to matter for reviews, and why?

> ❑ Identify a few *customer profiles* that match your *buyer personas*, and determine how active they are as reviewers.

> ❑ Identify **companies** or **products** to "reverse engineer" who is doing a good job on various review sites both in terms of their search rank and their review volume and aggregate star ratings.

❑ Set up or claim **business listings** (e.g., claim your Google My Business account, Yelp account, Airbnb listings, etc.). Be sure to write down the passwords and keep them safe!

❑ **Optimize** your **business listings** by writing keyword-heavy copy into the business or product description, and uploading relevant photos.

❑ **SEO** your website for local search by including city names and keywords on your homepage, plus launch city-specific landing pages especially for those cities in which you have a physical location. Be sure to include your physical address and phone number so that it's easy for Google to see where you are located in the physical world. Include JSON-LD markup language / Schema markup language using the Google Webmaster's Structured Data Mark up Helper at **http://jmlinks.com/46x.**

❑ **Optimize** your **NAP consistency** by having a consistent name, address, and phone on your website and on all relevant listing sites. Consider using a service like Moz Local, Yext, or Whitespark to claim and optimize your secondary listings.

❑ Create a **review solicitation strategy** that you are comfortable with. This may be as simple as simply requiring employees to "ask" for a review after each job, or as complex as a pre-survey that has a review follow up.

❑ Pay attention to your company's branded searches on Google and whether review sites are showing up as part of a **reputation management** strategy.

❑ **Respond** to **negative reviews**, but be polite and take the high ground.

❑ Measure your **KPIs** (Key Performance Indicators) such as total reviews and aggregate star ratings each month.

Check out the **free tools**! Go to my *SEO Dashboard > Local SEO / SMM* for my favorite free tools on local and review marketing. Just visit **http://jmlinks.com/seodash.**

»» DELIVERABLE: LOCAL SEO MARKETING PLAN

Now that we've come to the end of our Chapter on local reviews, your **DELIVERABLE** has arrived. For your final **TO-DO**, download the **Yelp / Local Marketing Plan Worksheet**. For the worksheet, go to **http://jmlinks.com/seo19tz** (re-enter the passcode "seo19tz"), and click on the link to the "Yelp / Local Review Marketing Worksheet." By filling out this plan, you and your team will establish a vision of what you want to achieve via local reviews.

6.1

METRICS

Google Analytics is the best free Web metrics tool available today. It is, however, only a tool. It doesn't tell you what to measure, nor what to do with the information you acquire. Before you even start with Analytics, your first step is to think through *what* you want to measure, and *why* you want to measure it. Common metrics are your *rank* on Google for target keyword queries, *traffic sources* or how people find your website, your top *landing pages*, your *bounce rate*, and whether landings on your website convert into *goals*, such as registrations or sales. Second, after you've identified what you want to measure, you need to turn to not just Google Analytics but other metrics tools and understand how to use them. Third, there are even more advanced techniques that can "slice and dice" your data so that you truly know what's going on with your website. Finally, there's no point in getting all this data unless you do something with it, so you need to take the knowledge gained from Analytics and turn it into actionable to-dos.

Let's get started!

TO-DO LIST:

» Define What to Measure

» Measure Your SERP Rank

» Measure Your Domain Authority and Social Metrics

» Use Google Search Console (Webmaster Tools)

» Use Google Analytics Basic Features

» Use Advanced Features in Google Analytics

»» Checklist: Metrics Action Items

»» Deliverable: Google Analytics Worksheet

» DEFINE WHAT TO MEASURE

Metrics, especially as seen through the prism of Google Analytics, can seem overwhelming. Most marketers and small business owners want to measure whether they are ranking on Google, whether they're getting traffic, and whether that traffic is converting (or not) into sales or sales leads as indicated by feedback forms. In terms of more specific items, here is a breakdown of things you should commonly measure or record every month on the 1st of the month:

1. **Your Rank on Google Searches.** SEO starts with whether your website is in position 1, 2, or 3 on Google or at least page one. Using your keywords as identified on your keyword worksheet, you want to measure your rank on Google and its improvement over time. By knowing which keywords you rank well for, and which you rank poorly for, you'll know where you need to concentrate your efforts.

2. **Your Domain Authority and Links.** Off Page SEO is all about links, so you want to use a tool like MOZ.com or AHREFS.com and measure the domain authority of your website, and the number of inbound links. With your link-building efforts, this should improve over time.

3. **Social Media & Reviews.** Social media is increasingly important for Off Page SEO, so you want to measure your "followers" on Twitter, your "likes" on Facebook, and your "followers" on LinkedIn for your company page. In addition, if local matters to you, you want to keep track of your **review count** on at least Google and Yelp. Through your promotion efforts, you want to see an increase in **followers** and **reviews** over time.

4. **Traffic Sources.** Turning to Google Search Console and Google Analytics, you want to measure your "traffic sources" to learn how people *find* your website, especially your best performing keywords and referrer websites.

5. **User Behavior.** Once they land on your website, do they convert to a sale or sales lead, or do they just browse around and leave? Learn what people *do* once they land on your website, especially marketing goals such as registrations or completed sales. Understand *successes* and *failures* and investigate ways to improve your conversion rate.

For your first **TO-DO**, call a marketing meeting, sit down with a blank piece of paper or a Word / Google doc, and brainstorm what metrics are most important to you as a marketer. How do people find you? What do they do once they land on your website? Many marketers speak also of **KPIs** (**Key Performance Indicators**), which can be something as specific as inbound calls from customers or something as conceptual as your brand equity. In terms of SEO, what background metrics, such as rank on Google and reviews on Google or Yelp, turbocharge your success on Google? Identify these and other KPIs that can be translated into something concrete to measure.

It's also important to keep the general "flow" of the "sales ladder" or "sales funnel" in mind:

Awareness / need > keyword search query > your website ranking on Google > click from Google > landing on your website > user behavior > sales lead or sale

Your KPIs should take measurements at any point along this process, with an eye to what can go "right" or what can go "wrong" at any step. For example, you might not rank on Google at all. Or you might rank, but not get the click because your TITLE and META DESCRIPTION are not enticing. Or you might get the click, but not the sale or conversion because your landing page experience isn't very compelling, etc.

» MEASURE YOUR SERP RANK

Your **SERP rank** (Search Engine Results Page) measures your website's position versus a target search query. Once you know your keywords, then the first KPI is whether you rank or not for various related search queries on Google. (You may read on the blogosphere that rank doesn't matter, but that's just silly. Measuring rank is indeed getting harder to measure because of localization and personalization, but this doesn't mean you shouldn't pay attention to your rank on Google vis-à-vis your keyword targets! *No rank, no click, no click, no sale.*)

Let's review some of the ways to measure where your website ranks on Google vis-à-vis your target keywords.

#1 Measure Your Rank Manually

Simply go to Google and use "incognito" mode in your browser. In Chrome, that's hidden in the top right under the "three dots." You can also login to your Google account (top right when you are on Google.com) under your picture. Alternatively, you can go to Google.com (**https://www.google.com/**) and make sure you are "signed in." Then, go to **https://www.google.com/preferences** and find "Private results." Click "Do not use private results." Here's a screenshot:

Private results

Private results help find more relevant content for you, see.

◯ Use private results

◉ Do not use private results

Next, while browsing in "incognito mode" or with "private results" off, do your searches by entering your various keyword phrases into Google. Then find your domain on the Google results page and count your position from the top, being careful to only count the organic results (i.e., ignoring ads and ignoring the "local pack"). Record them as 1,2,3, etc. up to 10 on an Excel spreadsheet or on a tab on your keyword worksheet.

#1b Measure Your Rank Manually for Local Search Queries

As we discussed in the previous Chapter, Google varies the results for certain "local" searches based on your user location. For example, a searcher in Tulsa, Oklahoma, sees different search results for "Pizza" than a searcher in Portland, Maine. You can check your localized search results via the AdWords Preview Tool at **http://jmlinks.com/15g** or via the SERPS.com location tool at **http://jmlinks.com/26z**. Record your rank on Google for location searches in the "local pack" as A, B, or C, or if there are variations in organic, then track those as well location by location. Here's a screenshot of the AdWords Preview tool for "pizza" with location set to Tulsa, OK:

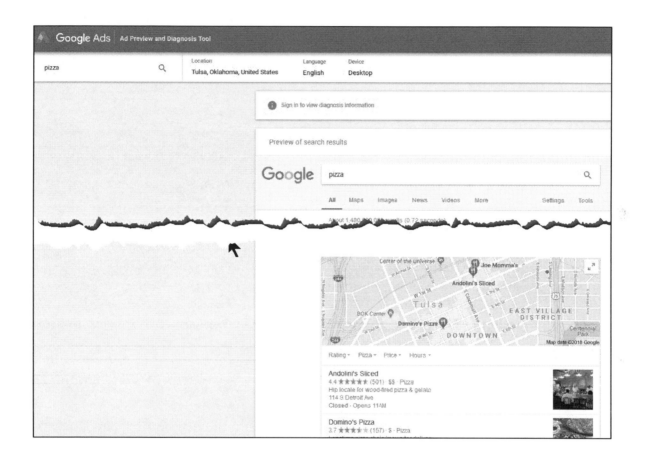

And here's a screenshot of the "local snack pack:"

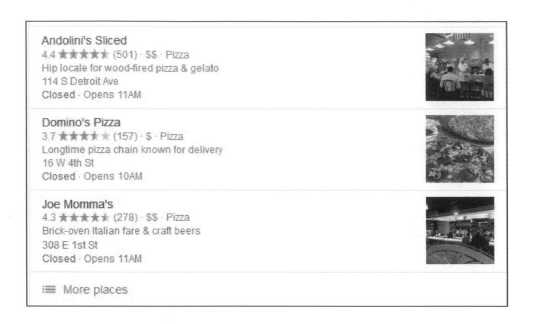

Andolini's would thus be position "A," Domino's position "B," and Joe Momma's position "C." Note that it is industry practice to record positions in the Local Pack as "A, B, C," not "1, 2, 3" to distinguish them from your rank in the organic results.

At any rate, you can see that you need to manually:

- Check your rank on Google vs. your target keywords in the organic positions; and, if necessary,
- Check your rank on Google in the "local pack" vs. your target keyword city-by-city; and, if necessary,
- Check / recheck your rank on Google in organic positions if those also vary by city in addition to the "local pack."

VIDEO. Watch a video tutorial on how to check local rank at **http://jmlinks.com/17s**.

It's time-consuming to do this, so if at all possible, I recommend paying for a paid tool such as WhiteSpark.ca, which will automatically record your rank by keyword, ignore personalization, and allow for localization city-by-city. Moz.com, AHREFS.com, SEMRush, and other vendors also offer paid rank-checking tools. Time is money so I recommend a paid tool for this measurement.

» MEASURE YOUR DOMAIN AUTHORITY AND SOCIAL METRICS

Your **PageRank** or **Domain Authority** is a measurement of your authority on the Web. It is not really publicly released, so use third-party tools such as MOZ.com or AHREFS.com that will give you your **domain authority**. As we learned in link building, think of your **Web Authority** as a measurement of how important your site is on the Web.

I recommend you measure your **domain authority** as a surrogate for Google PageRank on a monthly basis. Go to MOZ Link Explorer at **http://jmlinks.com/7y**, input your website homepage URL, and note the two metrics at the top of the page: domain authority and linking domains. Record each of these on your keyword worksheet each month. Here's a screenshot for jm-seo.org:

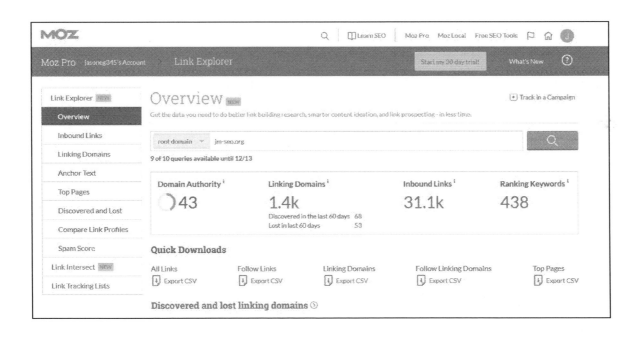

Domain authority is a surrogate for Google PageRank, or a metric that measures how important Google thinks your website is. A site like *nytimes.com* might be 100, whereas *jm-seo.org* is a 43, and a tiny, unimportant site might be a 7. What's important is your domain authority relative to competitors, and whether this improves over time. **Linking domains** is the number of websites that link to you; again, you want this to grow over time. You can see here it's a 1.4 thousand, meaning 1400 websites link to the domain. **Total links** at 31.1k indicates the total number of links to the site. The **Spam score** (located on the far left column) is an attempt, after Google's Penguin update, to measure whether your site is on the "naughty list" or not.

Another good site to use for this purpose is AHREFS.com. Here's a screenshot from their tool:

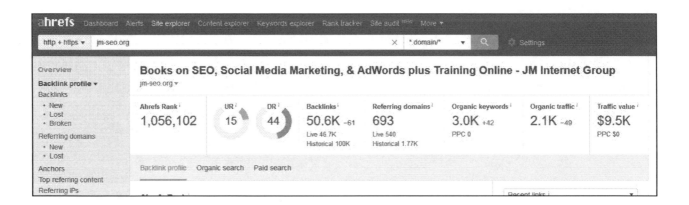

The nomenclature is a bit different, but both tools essentially give you a score for your domain, a number of other domains linking to you, and a raw number of inbound links.

Choose a tool you like, be consistent, and record at least your domain authority, and linking root domains each month. This gives you an indication as to whether your link-building is working or not.

Social Media Metrics

Next, measure your followers on Twitter, Facebook, LinkedIn, etc., your page views, and your review count on Yelp and Google. You want these all to move in a positive direction, over time. Increasingly, SEO is "going social," so it's a good time to be aware of how your social authority is improving over time.

Record your follower count on Twitter, Facebook, LinkedIn, etc. each month by logging into each account and recording the number. That's easy enough. To track your review count as a local business on Google, simply Google your company name and record the review number. Here is a screenshot of Tulsa's Mecca Coffee Company showing thirty reviews on Google:

Yelp is the No. 2 review site, so I also recommend tracking your Yelp reviews as those feed Yelp as well as Bing. Just go to **https://www.yelp.com** and search for your company by name and city. Here's a screenshot for Mecca Coffee Company showing six reviews on Yelp:

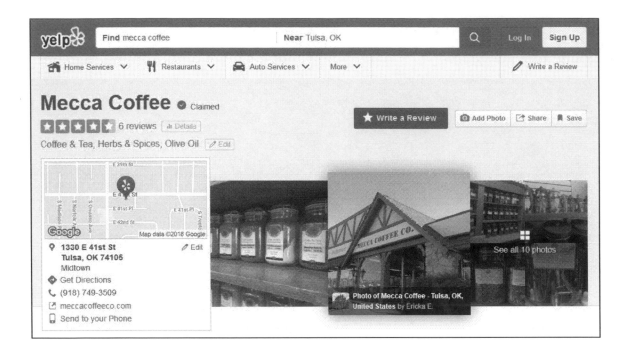

You'd also want to track the third most important review site, **Facebook**. Mecca Coffee has 89 reviews on Facebook with a 4.8 star score. You can see it at **http://jmlinks.com/47u**.

If you are a local business, **reviews** are incredibly important. So on your keyword worksheet, create a tab called "social" and add in your social media sites such as Google or Yelp that have customer reviews. Chart the number and the average star score each month. Mecca Coffee would thus record 66 Google reviews with a 4.5 star average, 6 Yelp reviews with a 4.5 star average, and 89 reviews on Facebook with a 4.8 star average. Do this each month.

» USE GOOGLE SEARCH CONSOLE (WEBMASTER TOOLS)

I'll assume you've claimed your **Google Search Console** (Webmaster Tools) account as well as the corresponding **Webmaster Tools** account on Bing. These give you some unique items that are not available in Google Analytics. First and foremost, Google Search Console will give you a rough idea of your **inbound keyword queries**. On the left hand menu, click *Performance*. Next, drill into queries, where Google will give you a rough idea of those queries for which you performed well. On the far right, you can click the arrow to download your query data. You can also see data for pages, countries, and devices. Take this data with a grain of salt, as it's not clear that it's entirely accurate but it gives you some data on the keywords people are entering, for which you rank on Google, and the clicks from Google to your website.

Next, again on the far left, click on **Links**. Google will give you a dashboard of your top linked pages and top linking sites. Click into *Top Linking Sites > More* to see a complete output of all the sites linking to you. Here's a screenshot:

Record that raw number each month; in this example, it's 39,451. Over time you should see this number grow as you build more and more links to your website.

You can also link Google Search Console into Google Analytics, so you can see this data in one place. For information on how to link them, visit **http://jmlinks.com/15b**.

As for Bing Webmaster Tools, similar data is available.

> **VIDEO.** Watch a video tutorial on how to use Google Webmaster Tools (Search Console) at **http://jmlinks.com/17u**.

» USE GOOGLE ANALYTICS BASIC FEATURES

Now that you have these measurements, it's time to dive into Google Analytics (**https://analytics.google.com/**). If you haven't already, install the required tracking code on all pages of your website. If you're using WordPress you can use Google Analytics for WordPress by MonsterInsights at **http://jmlinks.com/8e**. Alternatively, the latest and greatest way to install Google Analytics is to install Google Tag Manager (**https://tagmanager.google.com/**) and then follow the instructions to install Google Analytics "on top of" tag manager. Learn more at **http://jmlinks.com/15c**.

Once you have installed the Javascript code on your site and allowed enough time to elapse for data to accumulate, it's time for some basic Analytics. Log in to Analytics, and scroll down the left-hand menu. Here's a run-down:

- Click on **Audience**, to see basic data about how many visitors are coming to your website daily, where they are coming from, and basic traffic sources such as search engines vs. referring sites.
  - o Click on **Geo** to see where your website visitors come from by country, state, and even city.
  - o Click on **Technology** to see browsers that they use (e.g., Chrome, Firefox, Edge, Safari).
  - o Click on **Mobile** to see your web traffic: desktop vs. tablet vs. phones, and even phone types.
  - o Click on **Users Flow** for a nice, pictorial map of how people "flow" through your website.
- Click on **Acquisition** and browse "referring" sites such as blogs, portals, news releases, etc., that are sending users from their website to yours via clicks.
  - o Click on **All Traffic > Channels** to see how people get to your website, by *Direct* (URLs and bookmarks), *Organic Search* (Search Engines), *Referral* (links from other sites) and *Social* (social media sites like Facebook or Twitter).
  - o Click on **Source / Medium** and **Referrals** for another view of the above data with an easy-to-read breakdown by name.

- o Click on **Google Ads** (formerly AdWords) if you are running advertisements on Google; here, you can get data down to the keyword level.
- o Click on **Search Console, Queries** to see which keywords and key phrases are performing well for you in generating incoming web traffic. (Link your Google Analytics to your Google Search Console for this feature).
- o Click on **Social** for detail on social media networks; click on Users Flow here for a pictorial representation.
- o Click on **Campaigns** to see activity you have "tagged" as a campaign or UTM string. (To "tag" inbound links as from a Bing advertising campaign, a Facebook or Twitter campaign, etc., see **http://jmlinks.com/15d.**)

- Click on **Behavior** to see what people do on your website.
  - o Click on **Behavior Flow** for a nice, pictorial map of how people "flow" through your website.
  - o Click on **Site Content** and then drill down to **All Pages** (your most trafficked pages), **Landing Pages** (first page they touch), and **Exit Pages** (last page they touch).
  - o Click on **Site Speed** for information on how fast your website is, including **Speed Suggestions**.

- Click on **Conversions** to see whether traffic is "converting," usually buying stuff on eCommerce and/or filling out feedback forms as sales leads.
  - o Click on **Goals** (if you have defined goals, see below) to see what goals exist and whether they are converting.
    - You can also drill down into *Reverse Goal Path*, *Funnel Visualization*, and *Goal Flow* for some visuals about how people get to your goals and whether or not they convert.
  - o Click on **Overview, Reverse Goal Path,** and **Funnel Visualization** (if you have defined these elements to see the paths taken to/from a goal).
  - o Click on **eCommerce** (if you are running an eCommerce site) for information on purchases.

VIDEO. Watch a video tutorial on basic Google Analytics at **http://jmlinks.com/17y.**

Basic Google Analytics provides you a lot of key information on incoming web traffic such as geographic location, mobile platform, and browser version. Finally, you can click on the date field at the top far right of Analytics to change the date filter for data or to compare two time periods.

» USE ADVANCED FEATURES IN GOOGLE ANALYTICS

Beyond Basic Analytics, there are advanced features in Google Analytics that you do not want to miss. One feature is called **Page Analytics**. To activate it, first install the Install the Page Analytics Plugin for Chrome (**http://jmlinks.com/18z**). Next, make sure your are logged into Google Analytics and then visit your website. On the top right of the Chrome browser, you'll see a little orange icon with a squiggly line in it. Make sure this says enabled. Here's a screenshot:

It's very easy to miss! It's very small and in the top right of the Chrome browser. With that turned on, then visit your website. If the Force is with you, Google Analytics will populate your website with little orange percentage icons that tell you what percent of people are clicking where on any page on your website. Here's a screenshot from JasonMcDonald.org:

This tells you that on my homepage 9.5% of the people click on the link for "SEO Consultant" and 5.1% click on "Social Media Expert." I highly recommend that you enable this add-on to Chrome and browse your site to see how users flow through your website. It's amazing!

Segments in Google Analytics

Next, return to Google Analytics proper and let's explore **segments**. Segments allow you to "slice" and "dice" your data based on criteria such as "new visitors" vs. "repeat visitors" or the geographic locations from which visitors come. Imagine that you want to see how people from Oklahoma behave on your website vs. people from Texas, or whether people who come from Facebook convert better than people from Twitter. That's what Segments allow.

Unfortunately, however, Google hides this feature behind the "Add Segment" area when you first log in. Simply click on that to bring forth Segments:

Segments offers "pre-built segments," available on the left-hand side under *View Segments > System*. Here you'll find segments such as "Mobile and Tablet Traffic." Click this to "filter" your data to see ONLY people coming from mobile phones and tablets, for example. Others of note are:

Organic Traffic. Click here to filter and see ONLY traffic from search engines.

Paid Traffic. Click here to filter and see ONLY traffic from AdWords and other forms of paid advertising as on Bing or Yahoo.

Referral Traffic. Click here to filter and see ONLY traffic from links on other websites.

Sessions with Conversions. Click here to filter and see ONLY traffic that actually converted (completed a goal or made a purchase). (Note: this requires that you first establish at least one goal in Analytics or connect Google Analytics to your e-commerce platform).

Tablet and Desktop Traffic. Click here to filter and see ONLY traffic from tablets or desktops.

The concept is to *first* click on a Segment, and *then* click the blue **Apply** button. *Next*, with these Segments on, browse other data in Google Analytics on the right menu such as the Geo information, or landing page information to see what's going on with respect to ONLY that Segment. You can enable up to four segments to compare at any given time. (For help with Google Segments, visit **http://jmlinks.com/15e**).

VIDEO. Watch a video tutorial on Google Analytics segments at **http://jmlinks.com/18a**.

For example, here's a screenshot comparing "Organic Traffic" and "Referral Traffic" by looking at landing pages:

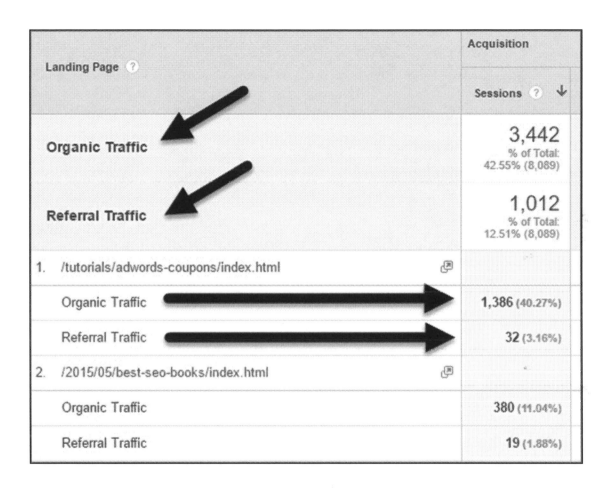

This shows that organic traffic was responsible for 1,386 visits to the AdWords Coupon page vs. only 32 for referral traffic. In this way, you can compare / contrast traffic sources or other elements as you scroll through AdWords data. It's marketing "slicing and dicing" at its best!

Custom Segments

You don't have to be content with the pre-built segments in Google Analytics. Simply click on the red "New Segment" button and follow the step-by-step wizard to create a custom segment. Scroll down the left-hand menu to filter your data by parameter; "conditions" is probably the most useful feature here. Remember to use the "Help" file (available top right, under the three dots) if you don't understand what a term means. You can read the Google help file on how to create a custom segment at **http://jmlinks.com/19b**.

You can use a custom segment, for example, to track user behavior that originates in a newsletter, a Facebook ad campaign, or even to compare the behavior of people from Texas vs. people from Oklahoma.

Creating and Emailing Reports

Throughout Google Analytics, you can take any "view" that you set up an "export it" by clicking on "export" in the top right. Here's a screenshot:

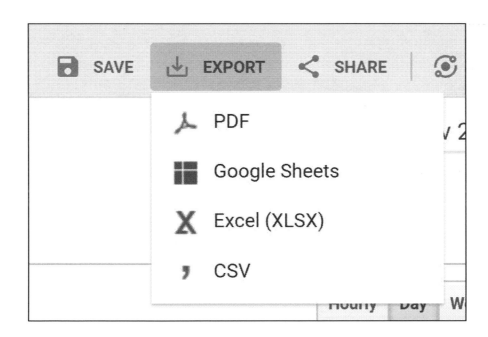

If you click on "Share" (again as indicated in the top right, above), you can email any report you create. For example, you could set up a custom segment to look only at your Oklahoma traffic, and then have Google automatically download and email this "report" every 1st of the month. Here's a screenshot:

Email Report: *Audience Overview* ✕

From jasoneg3@gmail.com

To

Subject Google Analytics: Audience Overview

Attachments 📄 PDF ▾ AUDIENCE OVERVIEW

       📄 PDF

Frequency ✕ Excel (XLSX)

▶ ADVANCED OPTIO ⟩ CSV

Send Cancel Add to an existing email

Goals and Conversions

Having played around with segments, next set up "Goals" for Analytics by registering your "Thank you" page after a registration or purchase. A goal is something you want people to do on your website. Common goals are:

1. Fill out an inquiry form.
2. Sign up for an email newsletter.
3. Make an e-commerce purchase.

In each case, find the URL for the "thank you" page, and record that. You'll use this "Thank You" URL as your goal in Analytics. For example, if you send a web inquiry via JM-SEO.org, you'll end up at **https://www.jm-seo.org/thanks/** which becomes the URL / goal for web inquiries.

To set up a goal, go to the primary login page on Analytics by clicking on "gear icon" at the **bottom left corner** inside of Google Analytics. Here's a screenshot:

Next, click on your profile name (usually your website URL). Then click on "goals" in the middle of the page. Here is where you define a "goal" and a "funnel," which is the steps taken to reach the goal. Once you've defined a goal, Google Analytics will happily record the complete goals under the "Conversions" tab on the left in Analytics. Here's a screenshot showing that JM-SEO.org received 89 email inquiries or goal #2's in October, 2018:

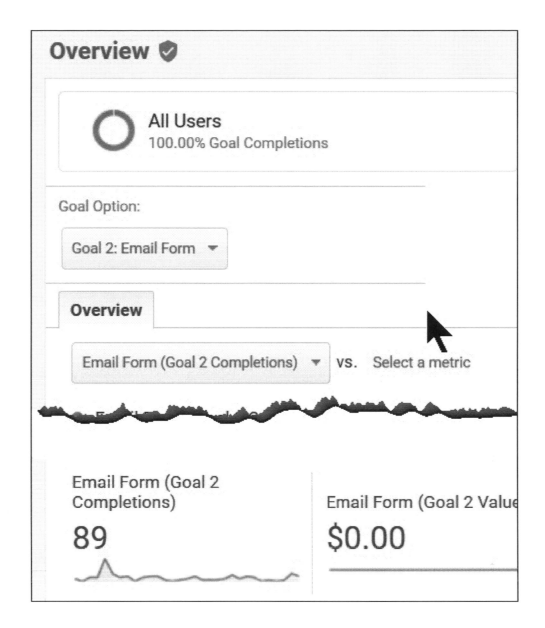

Note that if you enable one or more segments such as All Traffic, Mobile Traffic, and Tablet / Desktop Traffic, you can compare segments against goals. For example, here's the same goal comparing All, Mobile, and Tablet / Desktop traffic, showing I received 89 total inquiries, with 32 coming from Mobile and 57 from Tablet / Desktop:

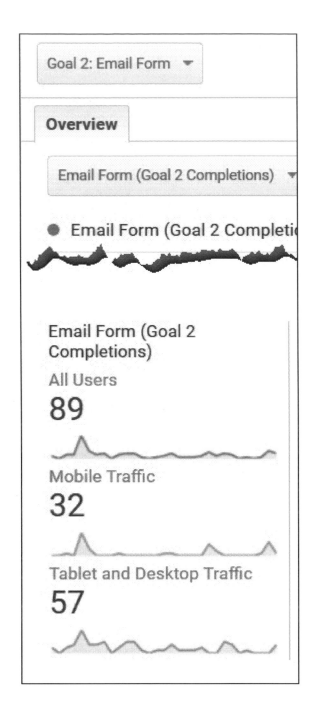

You can also change your time horizon, express this information graphically, and export it into a PDF or automated email. In Advanced Analytics, you can therefore see not only how people get to your website but the steps that take as they click through your website up to a goal, and you can use Segments to slice and dice which people are more or less likely to complete a goal.

VIDEO. Watch a video on how to set up goals in Google Analytics at http://jmlinks.com/17z.

For detailed help with goals, visit the official explanation at **http://jmlinks.com/19a**. Note: if you connect your e-commerce platform to Google Analytics, it will automatically take completed sales as "goals," which is pretty nifty as you can "slice and dice" your customers via segments to figure out who converts and who doesn't.

Sessions with Conversions

Finally, once you've enabled at least one goal or connected to e-commerce, Google Analytics turns on a very important segment: Sessions with Conversions. Turn that on by accessing the Segments Menu and then System. Here's a screenshot:

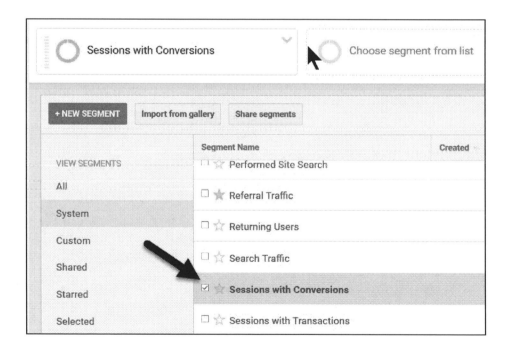

With "Sessions with Conversions" turned on, you can then browse through Google Analytics looking at only those people who completed a goal / conversion. This is as if Macy's could analyze the store behavior of only those people who actually bought something, vs. everyone else who was "just looking." The "Session with Conversions" segment is a fantastic way to cut out the noise and discover how you're getting your most valuable web traffic, the traffic that converts.

Help in Google Analytics

Help is available at the **top right** corner under the "Question Mark" icon on the top right inside of Google Analytics. Here's a screenshot:

Another way to find "Help" is to visit **https://support.google.com/analytics/**. Once there, type in your query, such as "What is a Bounce Rate?" and you'll find pretty good answers.

Google Analytics Learning Resources

Finally, don't miss some of the free official Google videos available for learning more about Analytics. These are located at the **Google Analytics Academy** at **http://jmlinks.com/8a**. Ironically, these Analytics IQ Lessons are hard to find inside of Analytics. (They're hiding under the "Discover" tab at the far left). Click on "Discover" and you'll see not only the Analytics Academy but also links to the Help Center, Analytics Blog, and other tools that work with Google Analytics. Be sure to check out Google Data Studio (**https://datastudio.google.com/**) and Google Optimize (**https://optimize.google.com/**), which are Google's latest and greatest reporting and analysis tools built on top of Analytics.

»» CHECKLIST: METRICS ACTION ITEMS

Test your knowledge of metrics! Take the *metrics and Google Analytics quiz* at **http://jmlinks.com/qzme**. Next, here are your keyword **Action Items**:

❑ **Define** what you want to measure including your **KPIs**, ranging from your rank on Google to completed actions like feedback forms.

    ❑ Systematically measure your **rank** on Google each month. If possible, subscribe to a paid tool as they are easier-to-use than manual rank checking.

    ❑ If appropriate, measure your **rank vs. local keywords** into the "local pack" on Google.

    ❑ Measure your **review count** on Google and Yelp, as well as your aggregate review stars.

    ❑ Measure your **domain authority** to gain knowledge on your link-building efforts.

❑ Use **Google Analytics** basic features to learn about what happens once people land on your website.

    ❑ Use **segments** to slice and dice your data by customer type, origin, or other parameters.

    ❑ Define **goals** such as feedback forms or eCommerce sales to measure what's converting, what's not, and why.

❑ Take the **knowledge** obtained from your metrics effort, make **changes** to your website strategy and content, and continually **improve** the ROI from your SEO efforts!

Check out the **free tools**! Go to my *SEO Dashboard > Metrics* for my favorite free tools for Google Analytics and metrics. Just visit **http://jmlinks.com/seodash**.

»» DELIVERABLE: GOOGLE ANALYTICS WORKSHEET

The **DELIVERABLE** for this Chapter is a completed Google Analytics worksheet. For the worksheet, go to **http://jmlinks.com/seo19tz** (reenter the passcode "seo19tz"), and click on the link to the "Google Analytics worksheet."

7.1

LEARNING

SEO is a competitive game that never stops evolving! The Google algorithm changes and adjusts, user behavior evolves, and your competitors also improve their SEO skills. Recently, for example, social media and mobile search have become ever more important to SEO, as have both localization and personalization issues. Google continues to consolidate search results between mobile and desktop, and Panda and Penguin continue to evolve. In 2019, the transition continues to "voice search" and "artificial intelligence," which no real clarity on what that means (especially the "intelligence" in "artificial intelligence.") Google+ is (finally) dead, and Google is cozying up to Twitter up to even a possible acquisition. New algorithm changes are no doubt in the works over at the Googleplex!

All require the successful practitioner of SEO to adapt.

"Never stop learning" must be your motto! In this Chapter, I point to resources to help you be a life-long learner.

Let's get started!

TO-DO LIST:

» Download the Free Companion *SEO Toolbook*

» Use the Worksheets

» Bookmark and Read SEO Media Resources

» A Final Request: Please Review me on Amazon

» Download the Free Companion Toolbook

The *SEO Toolbook* is a companion to this *SEO Workbook* and contains hundreds of free tools, organized by the Seven Steps. Register for **free** materials, including my SEO Toolbook, SEO Dashboard, and companion worksheets to this book at **http://jmlinks.com/seo19tz/**. Re-enter the password **seo19tz** when prompted.

You can also access my dashboard directly at **http://jmlinks.com/seodash**. That has links to the Toolbook, plus my favorite tools are easy to click and organized by topics / Chapters.

If you know of any other free tools, please email me as I am always on the lookout!

» Use the Worksheets, Resources, Videos, and Quizzes

Throughout this *SEO Workbook*, I have referenced helpful worksheets, videos, and resources. Don't miss the fun-filled quizzes. These follow the Seven Steps methodology and can be accessed at the book landing page after you have registered.

VIDEO. Browse available YouTube videos at **http://jmlinks.com/19c**.

Subscribe to my YouTube channel as well as free alerts on free toolbooks at **http://jmlinks.com/free**.

» Bookmark and Read SEO Media Resources

SEO changes frequently, so I urge you to pay attention to Google directly as well as the many wonderful blogs that cover search engine optimization. Those are available in the *SEO Toolbook*.

Stay Informed: Blogs, Conferences, and Books

Among the best blogs, I recommend *Search Engine Land* (http://searchengineland.com/) and *Search Engine Journal* (https://www.searchenginejournal.com/) in particular as well as the SMX conference (http://searchmarketingexpo.com/). I also recommend checking Amazon for new books on SEO; don't take my word for it – pay attention to what other experts and gurus say about search engine optimization. In terms of books, here's a direct link to Amazon's SEO bestseller list: **http://jmlinks.com/15h**. If you're looking for a "deep dive" book in terms of technical SEO, I highly recommend Eric Enge, Stephan Spencer, and Jessie Stricchiola's *The Art of SEO: Mastering Search Engine Optimization* at **http://jmlinks.com/15j**. It assumes you know the basics as taught in my book, and then leads you deep into the jungle of technical search engine optimization.

NEVER STOP LEARNING

If you have any problems, questions, comments, or just want to talk about life and SEO, please email me at **j.mcdonald@jm-seo.net**, via **http://jmlinks.com/contact**, or call 800-298-4065 for help. Good luck!

» A FINAL REQUEST: PLEASE WRITE A REVIEW ON AMAZON

If you've read this far, I want to extend my profound thanks. It's a true labor of love to write any book, and this book has been no exception. If you have a spare moment and the spirit moves you, I would really appreciate an honest review about the *SEO Fitness Workbook* on Amazon.

- Here's a link directly to the book on Amazon: **http://jmlinks.com/seo**. Just visit that link and write your short, honest review of the book.

When you've done so, please send me a quick email. Thanks in advance for your support.

Never stop learning!

Made in the USA
San Bernardino, CA
20 July 2019